INSIDE
CUBA

Books by John Miller and Aaron Kenedi

Inside Islam

Inside Israel

Inside Iraq

Where Inspiration Lives

God's Breath: Sacred Scriptures of the World

Muhammad Ali: Ringside

Revolution: Faces of Change

San Francisco Stories

Legends: Women Who Have Changed the World

Praise for the *Inside* Series

Inside Islam

"*Inside Islam* . . . reminds us how vital it is for Americans to have a greater understanding of the international environment. The collection is a good introduction not just to the variety of religious experience in the Muslim world, but also to the political dynamics that help fuel fundamentalist hatred of the West in general and of the United States above all."

—The *Los Angeles Times*

"This compilation of essays and book excerpts . . . offers a timely and valuable introduction to the multifaceted world of Islam."

—*Publisher's Weekly* (starred review)

"Standout essays in this essential book."

—*O, The Oprah Magazine*

"A timely gathering of articles and essays on a rapidly expanding influential faith."

—*Kirkus Reviews*

"Deeper introductions to Islam exist, but none has the quality of writing collected here. . . . Readers interested in Islam will treasure this accessible collection."

—*Booklist* (featured review)

"Islam will continue to have a profound effect on Americans, and every thinking person should have a fundamental understanding of Muslim views. *Inside Islam* is a suitable place to begin. . . . The book provides a solid foundation for understanding this complex society."

—*Rocky Mountain News*

"This book provides valuable reading to those who seriously seek to understand current world events."

— The *Tampa Tribune*

"*Inside Islam* is full of valuable and provocative perspectives. . . . This book is one way to get started learning about the many sides of Islam."

—*Body & Soul*

Inside Israel

"[An] eminently readable collection."

—The *Jerusalem Post*

Inside Iraq

"The eloquent voices of experts such as Tony Horwitz, David Rose, and Michael Kelly describe a strange land torn by tribal conflicts, held together through terror and oppression visited on it by a brutal tyrant."

— The *Richmond Times-Dispatch*

"Do you find yourself wishing you had more facts at hand as you talk with friends and family about the potential war with Iraq? This compilation of book excerpts, magazine articles and essays will supply plenty of them."

— The *Boston Herald*

INSIDE
CUBA

THE HISTORY, CULTURE, AND POLITICS

OF AN OUTLAW NATION

Edited by John Miller and Aaron Kenedi

Introduction by Andrei Codrescu

MARLOWE & COMPANY
NEW YORK

Compilation copyright © 2003 by John Miller and Aaron Kenedi
Introduction copyright © 2003 by Andrei Codrescu

Published by Marlowe & Company
An Imprint of Avalon Publishing Group Incorporated
161 William Street, 16th Floor
New York, NY 10038

Editor's note: Changes for consistency have been made to the essays in this book.

Cover and interior design: Miller Media
Cover photograph: Beth Wald
Permissions research: Shawneric Hachey
Proofreading and copyediting: Mimi Kusch

ISBN 1-56924-484-7
Library of Congress Control Number: 2003107391

9 8 7 6 5 4 3 2 1

Printed in the United States of America
Distributed by Publishers Group West

SPECIAL THANKS TO
AMY RENNERT
AND MATTHEW LORE

Contents

ANDREI CODRESCU

Introduction

NORTH AMERICAN THIRST for Cuba is unquenchable. We've been involved with her history, her charms, and her moods since the adolescence of the United States republic. In the nineteenth century we helped her break up with Spain and encouraged her independence, and, ever since, we have resented this proud independence because we wanted her all to ourselves. The passage of time has done little to lessen either our fascination or our irritation. At one time, we saw our idealistic self reflected in her revolution, only to be quickly disappointed by her ideological promiscuity. At other times, we tried force to make her yield to our vastly superior strength, and failed, amazingly. Our love has been, for the most part, unrequited, and our anger only made it worse. In other words, we don't understand her. The reason for this perennial incomprehension is that we mostly see Cuba from the outside. Cuba has many faces, public and private. Cuba is Persephone: young in the spring of our outsider's gaze, worried and haggard in the winter of her dailiness. And she has, literally, been split in two by history.

Inside Cuba takes yet another look at this tormented affair, paying particular attention to the current predicaments and their roots in history. When Columbus discovered the island, thinking that it was a continent, his first act was to lie about her to his queen. He swore he had found the fabulous Indies with its treasures, a fiction he maintained until he could put a positive spin on other profitable and acceptable features, such as her climate, landscape, and harbor. No self-respecting fortune seeker could admit that he had landed among peaceful Tainos who smoked tobacco and welcomed everybody. Columbus reveled among the sensual Tainos without knowing that this dalliance would lead to the total slaughter of his hosts by the fiercely independent Caribs living in the interior. In one way or another, this first contact became paradigmatic. A history of easy conquests and fierce aftermaths followed.

The products of the island—slaves, sugar, and tobacco—tied her firmly to North America's greatest vices. After the abolition of slavery in North America, Southern planters fled to Cuba where slavery was still legal. By the time those products failed to bring profit, it was too late to maintain any sort of distance. We were hooked on Cuba, and her sugar, tobacco, and slaves were transformed into psychological products. In this late age of tourism, North Americans are still avid consumers of the sugar of her sensuality, her fiction-inspiring cigars, and the apparent submission of her beauties to the almighty dollar.

Inside Cuba is a relatively sober book, concerned for the most part with Cuba today, beginning with Castro's revolution, the most dramatic episode of its modern history. The well-known facts do nothing to dispel the mystery of that event. A few seasick men on a leaky boat sail from Mexico for Cuba, land in the wrong place, have terrible mishaps, blunder through bad omens, and end up ruling the island in less than a year. The tourists and the Mafia flee, and their client government falls, giving way to the dictatorship of a charismatic *caudillo* who's been giving us nightmares for nearly half a century. Castro's hold on power is as mysterious as his seizing it: the mistakes and miracles that made this seizure possible were repeated in reverse by Cuba's powerful North American suitor, paradoxically reinforcing Castro's hold in the attempt to overthrow him.

Some of the writers of these essays are pop historians, others are unabashedly subjective travellers. Louis A. Pérez Jr.'s examination of "the rhythm of Havana" is a thorough survey of the island's engagement with the North American imagination through its music and culture. The transformations of Cuba's images is a growing and reciprocal process. Cuban rhythms are exported, changed, re-imported, and re-exported, as are Cuban and Cuban-flavored styles and simulacra. The Cuba inside Cuba and the Cuba inside Miami eventually merge in the enduring mix of Ricky Ricardo and Lucy Arnaz, a mestizo-Anglo union with the strength of an archetype. Almost immediately, this stormy archetype is in predictable trouble. The story of Desi and Lucy's symbolic child, Elián González, as told here by Ann

Louise Bardach, is a symbolic tale of the two quarreling but inseparable Cubas, and the picaresque account of a battle fought in the mirror.

The Gulf of Mexico is a tragic mirror full of sunken treasure ships and rafts of people desperate to escape Castro's dystopia. Inside Cuba today, there is a further split between the dwindling and pessimistic supporters of the regime and the new entrepreneurs working for dollars in total disregard of ideological hubris. The facts of this bizarre new Cuban economy are reviewed here mostly through the depressing lens of their effects on Cuban society, though there is at least one essay in which Castro's accomplishment in educating Cubans receives its due.

I went to Cuba in 1999, just before the pope's historic visit to the island. This great propaganda coup for Castro was ironically unsuccessful when the thousands of American reporters gathered on the island for the occasion had to leave in a hurry when the Monica Lewinsky story broke, monopolizing the airwaves. (Oh, happy days!) This kind of irony is constant throughout our relationship: Castro's macho victory undermined by Clinton's penis, another battle over the body of a tempestuous mistress. The Bay of Pigs, that failed attempt by CIA-backed Cuban exiles to take back the island, was the same kind of macho showdown (though, grantedly, more serious). In that conflict Kennedy blinked and nearly destroyed the world, to the ever-persistent chagrin of his generation, men whose youth was romantically imprinted by jaunts from Harvard to Havana whorehouses. I best recognized my own journey in Christopher Hitchens's admirably jaunty report of his own trip, where the fading splendor and factual squalor of Cuba are masterfully shown in every encounter.

The question that this book, as well as everybody ever touched by Cuba fever, asks is this: After Castro, what? It's the million-dollar question, and the answers are numerous and contradictory. The aging Cuban leadership may yet achieve a Chinese-style entrepreneurial socialism (watch Che Guevara turn over in his grave!) or collapse entirely, giving way to chaos and war. If the United States will end the embargo that, ironically again, keeps Castro in power, this process may be less than compulsive. If Castro dies and the embargo is still in place, the prospects are grim. One thing, though, is for sure: our romance with Cuba is far from over; there will never be a divorce because there was never a formal marriage; the struggle goes on. The Special Period, as the Cuban regime calls these times, is also named *la lucha,* or "the struggle." That word carries every meaning it can bear.

—ANDREI CODRESCU
BATON ROUGE
MARCH, 2003

THE
HISTORY

WENDY GIMBEL

Havana, Before and After

O N THE MORNING OF JULY 10, 1555—as the sun rose over the entrance to a narrow harbor—the honorable Juan de Lobera, mayor of Havana, was a very worried man. The French corsair Jacques de Sores had landed on the island of Cuba, just outside de Lobera's small settlement. With his band of marauders, de Sores approached the village on foot. (Chroniclers claim that they violated some poor, frightened priests they'd met along the way, and then rode them around as though they were horses.) In no time at all—it took just thirty minutes, according to historians—the governor fled the island and the pirates took the town.

Jacques de Sores, an ambitious

WENDY GIMBEL *has written for the* New York Times, Vogue, Mirabella, *and* The Nation. Havana Dreams, *published in 1998 (from which this piece was excerpted), is a semi-autobiographical story of four generations of Cuban women. Gimbel lives in New York City.*

9

buccaneer not easily satisfied, craved the precious cargo rescued from the wrecks of Spanish galleons that had sunk in the fierce hurricanes off the island's coast. A cunning pirate, he had no doubt that he would find the riches stored in the Castillo Real de la Fuerza, a bleak fortress overlooking the harbor.

For de Sores, storming the vulnerable castle proved no problem, but absconding with the treasure turned out to be more difficult than he might have dreamed. Arrogant, confident of his strength, the pirate had considered the favorable odds, but he had not counted on the single-minded tenacity of Mayor Juan de Lobera. With a few frightened settlers, the stubborn Spaniard had barricaded himself inside the castle, and there he remained, refusing to surrender.

Furious at his stubborn, intractable foe, an exhausted de Sores had no recourse but to sack the town of Havana and burn it to the ground. One can only imagine, after all that trouble, how frustrating it must have been for the pirate to discover, when he entered La Fuerza, that it contained no treasure at all. Juan de Lobera had resisted, it seems, not because he was guarding a treasure, but because it was his destiny.

Returning to Havana in the early 1990s, I thought the city might be replicating this strange, isolated moment in its history. Fidel Castro, holding out against all odds, was standing fast in his citadel; the Cuban people, caught inside his fortress, had no choice but to go along with him and wait for the future to reveal itself. What was certain was that there was treasure—and it wasn't hard to rescue. Havana's wealth was in the narratives, the individual stories woven through its four-hundred-year history. I couldn't have known then what would happen when I opened the treasure chest, held a single story up to the light.

When Christopher Columbus sailed from Spain in 1492, he believed that the currents would take him as far as the court of the Mongol emperors. It never occurred to him that a huge continent stood in his path. The world was larger than the Italian mariner had thought, and instead of the fabled land of precious stones, of lustrous pearls and fragrant spices, he found himself in the Bahamas. It was there that he first heard of a treasure island, one he thought Marco Polo might have visited. In the belief that he could reach this marvelous Eden, Columbus sailed south, and then west, until he finally landed in Cuba.

For the exuberant explorer, his head swirling with dreams of riches, of Marco Polo's treasure island, or the fabulous empire of Cathay, it was difficult to find himself on an island of tobacco-smoking Tainos living in miserable thatched huts. In fact, Columbus insisted that his men sign an oath—on pain of having their tongues excised—swearing that Cuba was not an island but part of the mainland of China. It took him a while to settle into the position of a clever merchant intent upon exploiting his commercial position: "Where there is such marvelous scenery," he wrote in a letter to his patrons, Ferdinand and Isabella of Spain, "there must be much from which profit can be made."

Other Spaniards intent on profit soon followed. The brutal conquistador Diego Velázquez mined the island for gold, massacred the Indians, and fed himself on parrots.

Hernando de Soto—a man who had climbed mountains in Peru, crossed faltering bridges that stretched across gigantic chasms, and stormed the Inca warriors in the square of Caxamarca—came to the island on another search for the elusive "El Dorado." But in Cuba there was very little of the precious metal; most of it was in the minds of the ruthless explorers.

Sebastían de Ocampo, an ordinary soldier with a practical nature, determined that Cuba could be valuable to Spain, even if nothing the conquistadors touched turned to gold. At the beginning of the sixteenth century, he founded Puerto Carenas—a sheltered natural-harbor town on the western side of the island, where the huge, cumbersome vessels sailing between Spain and the New World could be serviced and secured. In 1519, Puerto Carenas became San Cristóbal de La Habana, absorbing the name and population of the original Havana—an unsuccessful settlement sixty miles farther along the coast. In 1624, the Spanish crown decreed the second Havana to be La Llave del Nuevo Mundo (the key to the new world).

More than a hundred years before the Dutch founded New Amsterdam, Havana was thriving, hosting more than her fair share of dreamers, schemers, and reprobates. Like a palimpsest, this ancient city bears the traces of its earlier, imperfectly erased tales. Weaving together these narratives of greed and ambition, Havana's master tale reveals itself: *Treasure Island*, perhaps, crossed with *The Tempest*.

The tales of treasure hunters give Cuba's history an undulating, wavelike pattern. In all of these stories, Havana stands like a beacon at the edge of the sea, luring adventurers to her shores with the promise of fabulous riches: Spanish conquistadors, French buccaneers, the English Admiralty, American industrialists, and Mafia gangsters. The characters change, the costumes are different—say, the British in scarlet coats, the Las Vegas mobsters sporting pointed shoes and diamond rings—but the narrative remains the same. In Havana, everything that glitters turns to gold.

In the sixteenth century—and for more than a hundred years after that—Havana defended the very entrance to the Caribbean. The historian Antonio Benítez-Rojo, author of *The Repeating Island*, points out that without this "Caribbean machine"—the elaborate system of fleets, garrisons, and ports—the Spanish would have been in the absurd position of the gambler who hits the jackpot but has no hat in which to catch his winnings.

Pirates sailed for Havana because it was the gathering place for the Spanish treasure fleets—the regal, three-masted galleons which caught the tradewinds out of Seville, headed for the Spanish Main, collected the wealth of the Americas, and returned home across the Atlantic. Each year, carried by the great Atlantic currents, these huge "floating cities" sailed back and forth between Seville and the New World, breaking the journey in Havana.

Some of the galleons went to Veracruz and returned to Havana laden with Mexican gold and silver. Others went by way of the northern coasts of Panama, Colombia, and Venezuela. They carried mined gold and silver from Colombia and Peru, bales of cochineal, casks of indigo, chalices encrusted with emeralds and pearls. In Havana Harbor, the pirate-fearing galleons waited for each other—often there were more than a hundred ships in a *flota*—and, in an impressive convoy, caught the westerlies and sailed for Spain.

This storehouse for the fabled treasures of the Indies must have been a thrilling place for Jacques de Sores or any other self-respecting pirate. Imagine the bloodthirsty, arrogant buccaneers, their bravado as they prowled the seas outside the harbor ready to pounce: the Chevalier de Gramont, a Frenchman, feared by the Spanish for his cruelty to prisoners; England's Sir Francis Drake, who threatened to burn Havana to the ground but changed his mind and sailed, instead, for Roanoke, Virginia; Edward Teach, known as Blackbeard, who tied ribbons into his beard and wore lighted tapers protruding from under his hat.

On the high seas, the admiral of the treasure fleet gave formal banquets to which he invited guests from the other ships. While they dined on sweetmeats, everyone watched the more congenial passengers, including a rambunctious friar or two, performing the popular "cloak-and-dagger" comedies. Not that these festive events were without reminders that galleons were not palaces and that the Atlantic Ocean was not the Court of Madrid. Rats as large as rabbits often ate the biscuits and killed the parrots or the chickens long before the crew could hurl the birds from cages into cooking pots.

How amazing to have seen the majestic square-rigged galleons, with their enormous masts and topsails, appearing over the horizon! The people of Havana danced in the streets as though they were celebrating Carnival. The Spanish stocked the town with rare delicacies and imprinted the residents with sophisticated European manners and culture. From Spain to the New World they brought casks of wine, almonds, honey, and pimentos; bolts of velvet cloth, dancing monkeys, and the plays of Lope de Vega.

After the Spanish explorers and the French pirates came the English sailors. In the seventeenth and eighteenth centuries, as Spain's power waned, Havana had every reason to fear a full-scale invasion by this next wave of adventurers. "When the greed of acquisition of territory is once roused in a nation," a contemporary historian has remarked, "it is difficult to appease it."

Though England's mercantile intent was to take any or all of the Spanish colonies, it was the great fortress cities of the Caribbean that had attracted her strategic gaze. Havana, a walled city with an impressive circle of forts, had become the greatest stronghold in the Americas. It would be the key to the New World for Great Britain as it had been for Spain.

In 1762, in a successful siege that lasted eleven months, the British took Havana. The Duke of Cumberland assured Lord Albemarle, the leader of the expedition, that everyone in England wished him to emerge from the action as rich as Croesus. "Health and owned merit are sufficient ingredients for happiness," asserted the practical Duke; "so much the better if you add wealth to it."

As always, Havana was more than accommodating to this intrusion of fortune hunters. Commodore Keppel,

Albemarle's younger brother, demonstrated an enthusiasm for riches which was familiar even if his British mannerisms were not: "The Admiral has given us leave to take yonder town, with all the treasure in it; so we have nothing to do now, but make our fortune as fast as we can, for the place can never hold out against us. We shall all be as rich as Jews. The place is paved with gold."

Having more elaborate commercial fantasies than Jacques de Sores, the British weren't satisfied with the usual spoils of victory. Instead of succumbing to nostalgia for the gold and silver bursting from the holds of Spanish galleons, they set out to make their fortunes in the slave trade. Importing thousands of slaves from Dahomey, Lagos, and the Gold Coast, the British delivered a human cargo whose suffering created undreamed-of wealth. In the agony of this forced labor, the island began its transformation into a vast sugar plantation.

Historian Hugh Thomas, in *Cuba: The Pursuit of Freedom*, calls attention to William Cowper's "Pity for Poor Africans," the fashionable couplets in which an eighteenth-century Englishman justified his position on the slave trade:

I own I am shocked at the purchase of slaves
And fear those who buy them and sell them are knaves;
What I hear of their hardships, their tortures and groans,
Is almost enough to draw pity from stones.
I pity them greatly but I must be mum,
For how could we do without sugar and rum.

In 1763, signing the Peace of Paris, which ended the Seven Years' War between Spain, France, and England, the Spanish gave Florida to the British in exchange for Havana. At the time, most people thought that Spain's Charles III had gotten the better end of the real-estate deal.

There had been a sea change. Once a society of modest ranchers, artisans, and bureaucrats, Cuba had become a sugar-rich plantation society. Before the British siege of Havana, the island had been allowed to trade only with Spain; her surrender to the British had brought her her first experience with unhindered capitalism. Given the enormous number of slaves that Britain made available—and with greater markets—sugar production rose until, as historians point out, Cuba had become the most prosperous sugar colony in the world.

Throughout much of the nineteenth century, the *criollos*—the land-holding descendants of Spaniards who had come to the island during the preceding two hundred years—made great fortunes in sugar and emerged as an authentic island oligarchy. The social and political prominence of the *criollos* would outlive their future economic defeat at the hands of the Americans and the *recién llegados* (the recently arrived Spanish immigrants who succeeded them and became the early-twentieth-century nouveaux riches).

Antagonistic to the *peninsulares* (the native Spaniards), resistant to foreign designs on the island, the *criollos* were the earliest Cubans to harbor nationalist sentiments. Consider the history of *las damas de la Habana*—the *criollos* ladies who sold their precious gems to finance George Washington's victory over the despised English at the Battle of Yorktown. (These patriotic feelings against foreign domination hibernated during the time of the early Cuban republic but would awaken in the 1950s, when Fidel Castro decided to overthrow the American-backed government of General Batista.)

It was the *criollos* who gave Havana a distinctive, sophisticated style. During the sugar harvest, they might visit their plantations. But most of the time, they made their homes within the walled town whose government and culture they dominated. You can feel their presence in the gracious central *plazas*, the fanciful *palacios*, *iglesias*, and *conventos*. Carved into the entrances of their houses are their coats of arms—Pedroso, Montalvo, O'Reilly, Beltrán de Santa Cruz y Aranda, Calvo de la Puerta. . . . With their wealth, the *criollos* built magnificent structures for themselves: palaces with immense grilled windows, stained-glass fanlights (*mediopuntos*), Andalusian tiles, staircases of Italian marble, and patios ringed with frangipani and ginger lily.

To amuse themselves, they gave formal balls, *bailes de etiqueta*, danced the *contradanza habanera*, attended *conciertos* and *zarzuelas*. At the end of the afternoon, they promenaded along the tree-lined Paseo de Tacón. In the evening, they attended the opera and the theatre (the Teatro de Tacón imported artists from abroad), and yielded to the temptations of the gambling casinos. In Havana, wrote a nineteenth-century traveler, "the man of cultivated tastes" may revel in "a paradise of delights."

Slavery ended. With the sugar crisis of the 1880s which brought a plunge in the world market price of sugar, the debt-ridden *criollos* found themselves on the edge of ruin. Vast amounts of capital were needed to transform the slave-based sugar business into a modern industry which relied on machines to run the mills. It would come from the imperial Americans with their fistfuls of cash—the last of the adventurers before the coming of Fidel Castro.

Throughout the early decades of the twentieth century, the Americans not only bought and managed sugar plantations (including those in financial trouble, on which American banks were foreclosing), they also became the major market for Cuban sugar and the ultimate supplier of equipment for most of the plantations and mills, including the railroads that linked the plantations to the mills and the mills to the ports.

Listen, for example, to a story that's a paradigm—the tale of Central Soledad, a sugar plantation outside of Havana. In the beginning of the nineteenth century, Juan Sarría, a Spaniard, had bought Soledad, an enormous tract of fertile land where hundreds of slaves planted and harvested the sugar cane. A savage, brutal ruler, Sarría, thought nothing of murdering his workers and flinging their bodies from the balconies of his hacienda. Domingo, his gentle son, renounced the rustic world of his father's plantations and graced the most decadent salons in Madrid. Juan's grandson, the dynasty's third generation, returned to Cuba to manage the Sarría estates, but he was more accustomed to palaces than to the rough countryside. His thoroughbreds are said to have cantered on silver horseshoes. In the countryside, it was widely believed that Sarría was a visiting prince.

A Bostonian whose father had sent him to Cuba on business, Edwin Atkins, came upon Soledad during the sugar crisis, when the Sarrías, like most planters, needed an infusion of capital. Before abolition, the slave traders had supplied all the cash; now the money for machinery to replace forced human labor would come from Americans, eager to invest in return for the deeds to valuable land.

"I can remember," wrote Atkins in a memoir, "when I first visited Soledad with José Maria Sarría [Juan's grandson], I reined up my horse as we reached the top of the ridge that overlooks the *batey* and expressed admiration at the beautiful view of valley and mountain. 'It is yours,' said José María in the usual Spanish formula. And I felt pretty sure it was, for I believed then that we should have to take possession to protect ourselves." As Atkins foreclosed on the Sarrías' mortgages, the torch was passing to a generation of Americans who believed in their own manifest destiny.

Edwin Atkins and his wife, Kathryn, were greeted at Soledad almost as divine rulers. He wrote: "We, the owners, sat upon a kind of throne constructed by the negroes and surrounded with the Spanish flag and coat-of-arms. . . . As the procession filed in front of us, many of the older African negroes would kneel and kiss our hands and feet, asking our blessing. . . ." In a few years, Edwin Atkins would transform the feudal Soledad into one of the largest modern sugar plantations in the world—twelve thousand acres, twenty-three miles of private railway, five thousand acres of cane.

To meet the beautiful Naty Revuelta was to encounter a Cuban heroine in a state of siege. But I didn't know that yet. We met through a friend, an American woman, who knew I was interested in writing about the bourgeoisie who had remained in Havana. "Naty," she assured me, "knows everyone."

We had coffee at El Patio, a restaurant in Old Havana, once the palace of the Marqués de Aguas Claras. I couldn't have imagined Naty's enthusiasm, couldn't believe how generous she was with her time. I can still see her sitting opposite me, offering names and addresses, checking them against the penciled listings in a small, faded green alligator diary. "Wouldn't the CIA love to get their hands on this notebook," she had said, laughing.

The "everyone" Naty knew, it turned out, went beyond the bourgeoisie. In her youth, she had become enamored of the new Cuba. But unlike most people, she wasn't content to sit on the sidelines, to watch while events unfolded along the parade route. She already had the idea that she could break the rules with impunity—and she wanted to be a player.

Naty's beauty had always provided her with both entrée and absolution. Attracted with an almost magnetic pull to the edge of adventure, and operating within the mode she knew, she formed an intimate alliance with a bold young radical. Sitting in El Patio that afternoon, over many cups of Cuban coffee, Naty Revuelta told me about her romance with Fidel Castro.

After that, I went to her house. Overwhelmed by Naty, I was also intrigued by Doña Natica, Alina, and Mumín. It didn't take long for me to propose to Naty that I write about the Cuban generations of her family. White, middle-class, with forebears from Spain and England, they had arrived long before the revolution but after the age of the *criollos*. Thinking back to the beginnings of this undertaking, remembering my excitement about finding a story and the family's professed delight in being written about, I am surprised at the degree of our communal innocence. But it was true, at least when we started.

From the beginning, we got along well. Carefully guiding me through the streets, lamenting the vanished splendor, Naty seemed to have the same reactions I had to the humbled, crumbling city. Perhaps it wasn't so strange. We were talking about general things. Havana presented to everyone such a sustained image of resigned desperation—a place where everyone seemed to be waiting, but for what no one seemed to know. Juan de Lobera, Jacques de Sores, Fulgencio Batista, and Fidel Castro, locked in their own narratives, had played their historical roles. But what about ordinary Cubans caught inside the fortress, their destinies tied to those arrogant, narcissistic leaders?

Walking with Naty along the Paseo del Prado, where prerevolutionary *habaneros* once promenaded in the late afternoon, I found the silence troubling. It seemed louder than the remembered shouts of children playing, of vendors selling sweet oranges and *helado de zapote*, a sugary ice cream, of festive crowds filing into the Centro Gallego and the Teatro Nacional. The rustle of women's fans, I remember that, too—the rhythm set with the flick of a wrist holding the delicate *abanico*.

Along the streets that crisscross the city, people moved along on Chinese bicycles, in Russian Ladas, in pre-Castro Oldsmobiles and Pontiacs, in pastel Cadillacs with monster fins. Others, wearing stiletto heels or plastic sandals and holding empty shopping bags, waited hours for crowded buses that never came. Clutching their ration books, women waited in front of the government store for a few ounces of coffee, some rice and beans, a piece of fish.

Prowling dogs wandered through the streets, abandoned by their hungry owners. (The Cubans are not like the British; they can live without their dogs.) A friend of Naty's told me in confidence that a man was arrested for eating a neighbor's cat. Things got worse. The owner of the cat gave the thief the evil eye, causing him to have seizures and convulsions. When a man I met went to a dental clinic, the drills were broken and, of course, there was no anesthesia. Naty was waiting to have a doctor examine a tumor in her neck, but her turn hadn't come around. A woman whose hernia operation was not urgent was told to have the surgery while there was still thread to stitch her wound.

At the Hotel Riviera, where I stayed on one of my visits, when you held the telephone receiver in your hand, you heard the strains of "Silent Night" instead of a dial tone. Sitting on a chair in front of the Hotel de Ambos Mundos, where Ernest Hemingway once lived, an old man in worn-out shoes looked through a tattered guide to Bulgaria. A graffiti artist crossed out the "o" from a poster and replaced it with "es." The sign that in Spanish had read "socialism or death" now read "socialism is death." But there is no deliverance.

"What is your fancy?" asked an American guidebook published more than fifty years earlier, in 1941. "Havana is like a woman in love. Eager to give pleasure, she will be anything you want her to be—exciting or peaceful, gay or quiet, brilliant or tranquil." "This isn't the real Havana," Naty reminds me. "You'll have to come back when all this is over."

Refracted through that wide lens, Havana, at the beginning of the nineties, seemed drab, and intolerable. Was the tale of this city a cautionary tale about power or a fable of resilience? How, in this poor, enervated place, did people manage to live? If I changed the lens, focusing more closely on particular individuals, it became clear that, to live in Havana, everyone had invented a strategy for survival. Those who hadn't budged from their homes had fled in their minds instead, and inhabited a more seductive, fantastical Havana.

One Cuban friend of Naty's—an architect in love with each bend and curve of the city—inhabited a splendid, miniature Havana. When we visited him in his studio, he unveiled an intricate plaster model of the city—an ideal construction of perfect structures housed in an air-conditioned room, a Havana as immune to time as a marble statue in a mausoleum. The city in which he walked, the scale model through which he wandered with his wooden pointer, existed entirely out of the historical present.

At the point where his imagination intersected with the tiny buildings, the architect founded his glimmering city, or, rather, restored Havana to its romantic splendor: its stone houses built around patios filled with hibiscus, lemon, and pomegranate trees, its red-tiled roofs which reminded him of Cádiz, its ornate palaces with their arched *portales* and massive, intricately carved wooden doors.

Another of Naty's friends told me that he once watched a fisherman—a man intent on sailing to freedom across the Straits of Florida—as he constructed a boat that was nothing more than a floating oxcart. He made a bow of steel sheets from old washtubs and nailed them to a wooden frame; there was no stern, but there were two sails made of bedsheets. His passengers were to stand inside the boat, for the entire sail across the straits, as though they were sailors at attention, and forever under review. But the fisherman didn't see it as a madman's scheme. He used asphalt—there was no paint available—to paint "El Galeón" on the side of the raft, and then he sailed for the Florida Keys.

In the most ancient part of Havana, on the Calle Amargura (Bitterness Street), Raúl Macheco, a tall, slender black man just over fifty, celebrated his mass in a small room filled with yellow gladiolas. Statues of Santa Bárbara and the Virgen del Cobre hovered over the assembled followers. An *espiritista*—a medium who entered into a trance and became possessed with the spirit of the dead—he attracted attention with his fierce, manic energies. He arranged everyone in a circle, sprinkled them with sweet cologne, looked into a water glass as though it were a crystal ball, and called upon the dead "spirit" guardians to enter him.

Raúl Macheco's Yoruba ancestors, whom slave traders brought in bondage to the island, had folded their sacred gods, the *orisha*, beneath the white man's Catholic saints, and released them again into the world as sacred energies. Macheco assigned salvation to the *babalaos* (high priests) and *santeros* (priests) while he called upon the dead to protect those stranded in Fidel's wasteland.

A man who needed to ransom himself from depression learned that his *muerto* (protective spirit) had predicted that he would come into a great fortune. A woman suffering from cancer heard that, if she made the sign of the cross while carrying a lighted candle, she would be cured: "You must not fear the dark, for the dark is the womb from which all life springs; neither must you fear the Night, for the Night is your friend, the bringer of rest," said the old *babalao*: "Learn to walk with the Night and she will be a good companion."

When Raúl offered his predictions, Naty bridled. "That's not for me," she said, recovering herself as we were leaving. I didn't give the incident a thought until much later, but then I found it in character. Naty hated situations in which she was at the mercy of someone else's narrative. "No," I would tell her more than once. "You can't read a draft of my book and make changes." "But," she would assure me, "I just want to make sure it's right."

It was a matter of temperament. On unfamiliar ground, without control, Naty became uneasy, tense, and self-protective. At her daughter's suggestion, she had brought me to Macheco's *misa*, but she didn't want to participate or be observed by anyone. We both shared a fear of being thought vulnerable—indeed, ridiculous.

Some people were more comfortable with change. Natalia Bolívar Arostegui, a heavy-bosomed, energetic descendant of the *criollos* aristocracy, regarded Raúl as the closest of her friends. She wouldn't think of making a significant decision without consulting him. An anthropologist who writes and lectures on *santería* all over the world, Natalia has survived like some primordial amoeba, ingesting all the changes on the island.

Educated at the fashionable Convent of the Sacred Heart in Havana, and New York's Art Students League, this daughter of the oligarchy had turned from her debutante past and become a member of the student revolutionary movement at the University of Havana. Tortured by General Batista, disillusioned by Fidel, disgusted with the betrayal of the revolution, Natalia was still a vibrant part of her country's present.

The Arosteguis were a distinguished clan. (Because of their services to the Spanish crown, they had the special privilege of being allowed to ride horseback into the Cathedral of Havana.) At the end of the eighteenth century, Louis-Philippe, Duke of Orleans, fleeing the French Revolution, came to Cuba, where Martin Arostegui entertained him and lent him a great deal of money. When Louis-Philippe ascended the throne of France and tried to repay the debt, the gallant Arostegui replied that he had lent money to an exiled duke but not to the King of France. In gratitude, the monarch sent his Cuban friend a miniature painted by Jacques-Louis David, a likeness of the King's own beloved mother.

Nena Arostegui, Natalia's mother, thought nothing of calling the police when *un negro* sauntered along the streets in front of her house in the residential section of

Miramar after dark. In the same house, which Natalia inherited—there are ten barking dogs living on the roof and several ex-husbands in the front parlor—she rules with the presence of an absolute monarch. *"Me quedo en Cuba porque pertenzco aquí. Pase lo que pase, es mi patria."* "I stay in Cuba because I belong here. Whatever happens, it's my homeland."

According to Guillermo Jiménez, an amateur historian who fought with Fidel during the revolution, Natalia remained just because she *is* an old-fashioned aristocrat. A small, pale man with trembling hands, Guillermo had retreated into history in order to make sense of things. "If the wealthy, educated Cubans had remained in place," he says, "if they hadn't put on their jewelry and run to the United States for cover, the country could have gotten rid of Fidel Castro a long time ago." Decadent, self-indulgent, these Cubans were a far cry from the *criollos* of the last century, who had a sense of responsibility to the country, above all to its institutions, and would never have gone away. "Write down what I say for your book," he said. "It doesn't matter if everyone disagrees with me." *"Yo tengo que ser auténtico."* "(I have to be authentic.)"

We got out of Naty's car in front of the decaying white house where the Suárez sisters, Elvira and Lilia, have sat out the revolution. How relieved she must have been that their world was so familiar. With some excitement in her voice, Naty said: "My father wanted to marry Elvira, so she's almost my mother." "These Suárez women," Naty said proudly, "wouldn't know what to make of *santería*. Don't mention Guillermo's attitude toward their friends who fled the country right after the fall of Batista."

Protective of these affectionate dowagers, Naty seemed at her best. For these aristocratic old ladies, immured among their remaining possessions, survival was in pretending that their prerevolutionary Cuba would come back. Since they never stepped out of their house, it was sometimes possible for the sisters to imagine that now was then. Soon they would be shopping at the French salon at El Encanto, packing their Vuitton trunks for their trips to Paris, attending the New Year's Eve party at the Vedado Tennis Club, or the Christmas tea dance at the Havana Yacht Club.

During their afternoon canasta games at the Yacht Club, the two sisters had traded anecdotes about *mulatos* who tried to pretend they were white. General Batista's suspicious racial bloodlines had earned him a blackball from the club's admissions committee, even though its action meant courting the anger of the vengeful chief of state. (The not-so-snobbish Havana Biltmore admitted the general and enjoyed the valuable real estate he gave to the members in gratitude.)

Elvira, who wore moth-eaten mauve silk, had the face of an elderly child—a pleasant girl astonished to find herself grown wrinkled and old. The afternoon canasta games to which she devoted herself began long before General Batista's coup d'état. Throughout the regime of Fidel Castro, her rhythm had remained the same: shuffle, deal, and discard. But with everyone leaving, it had become harder to find partners. Sometimes now, absent friends joined her in hands of imaginary canasta.

Lilia, perhaps the more reflective of the two relics, spent most of her afternoons with a magnifying glass, examining photographs of the family's lost *finca*—the ranch where she and her husband had ridden their thoroughbred horses. The gardens had been famous, but the communists trampled on the orchids, killing the delicate plants. Could she find a photograph of the lovely crystal chandeliers, the most celebrated in Cuba? Or of those polished wooden floors from Barcelona, on which dancers whirled on balmy winter evenings?

Both sisters fretted about their possessions. When the revolution came, friends who were in the diplomatic service agreed to take the sisters' paintings out of the country. These ambassadors were never heard from again. In an effort to protect the valuables still in the house, Lilia had glued her Dresden figurines to the round tables in the entrance hall. She turned the tables upside down to demonstrate her cleverness. It looked, for all the world, as though the porcelain shepherds were dancing on their heads.

The decorative plates that hung on the wood-paneled walls of the dining room bore the coats of arms of *criollos* families. The Suárez family were proud of their descent from the Marqués de la Campiña, who came to Cuba with Christopher Columbus.

Lilia said: "My mother knew all about the noble families of Cuba. She knew which crest belonged to which family: the Montalvos, the Penalvers, the Pedrosos and Herreras. . . . There were so many, and she knew them all. We lost the piece of paper on which she'd written down the history of each title."

Elvira continued: "Some of our friends fled with nothing. They were leaving with one hand covering them in front and the other in back. But we couldn't imagine ourselves going to another country. Who would we have become without position, or without our possessions? We chose to believe, instead, that this would be over very soon." And now: *"Nos pasamos la vida viendo pasar el tiempo."* (We spend our lives just watching time pass.)

For these two women, Fidel Castro's stranglehold on the island—a place from which he should have been banished decades ago—had no reasonable explanation. But nothing could be done about it. Finally, it came down to a matter of social position: "Fidel Castro's treatment of Naty Revuelta was terrible. It's because she lived in our world, one that wouldn't have accepted him." Lilia lowered her voice. *"Pero no pudo acabar con ella."* (But he wasn't able to defeat her.)

JAMES D. RUDOLPH

The Revolution and Its Aftermath

O N SEPTEMBER 4, 1933, at an army base in Havana called Camp Columbia, non-commissioned officers unexpectedly arrested their superiors and took over command of the island's military forces. The "Sergeants' Revolt" had been skillfully organized by Fulgencio Batista y Zaldivar, the son of poor cane cutters from Oriente of mixed racial ancestry, who in time would become the caudillo of all Cuba. He had become acquainted with the civilian opposition during the trials held by the Machado regime. Sergeant Batista was the best stenographer in the army and had transcribed many of these trials. As soon as the students learned of the revolt, leaders of the Student Directorate (a

JAMES D. RUDOLPH
is a professor at the
American University in
Washington, D.C., and
the author of Cuba: A
Country Study *(from*
which this piece is
excerpted), Mexico:
A Country Study,
Nicaragua: A Country
Study, *and* Argentia:
A Country Study.

student-faculty group from the University of Havana that was created to oppose Machado's reelection) joined the sergeants and suggested a broadening of its base of support, thus turning a military revolt into a full-blown revolution. Batista invited the student leaders to nominate what was called a pentarchy, or five-man government, and the following day Céspedes was informed of the rebellion and of his deposition.

Ambassador Welles was surprised by this turn of events. He requested the intervention of United States troops, but to no avail. On September 10 the pentarchy was dissolved, and one of its members, Ramon Grau San Martin, became the revolutionary provisional president. Grau was popular among the students for his political stance while at the university, where he had defended nationalism, socialism, and anti-imperialism as the basic tenets of the revolutionary program. As provisional president, he abrogated the constitution of 1901 and declared that a social revolution had been launched. Grau enacted a number of labor reforms: he instituted an eight-hour workday; declared illegal the importation of workers from the Caribbean; required that all enterprises employ a workforce 50 percent of which were Cuban; requested that all professionals join their professional organizations; and created a Department of Labor. He also denounced the Platt Amendment, purged Machado's followers from the government, dissolved the old political party machine, and gave autonomy to the university. In protest, the United States denied recognition to Grau's government. United States enterprises and their employees in Cuba feared for the future and, though United States warships sent to Cuban waters stayed on alert, they did not intervene. The pentarchy had given Batista the rank of colonel and the position of chief military commander of the Cuban armed forces. As such, he began promoting enlisted men into the officer corps.

Grau's government aroused discontent from several groups for different reasons. The ABC organized strikes, and even the military personnel of Camp Columbia demonstrated against the government. Batista was able to control all factions, and he finally forced Grau out of office on January 15, 1934. The revolution continued under the direct leadership of Batista, who began by nominating Carlos Hevia provisional president. Lacking support, however, Hevia resigned in two days. He was then replaced by another Batista appointee, Mendieta, a respected member of the old National Liberal Party who led the Nationalist Union and was an experienced politician of moderate views. United States recognition of his government was almost immediate.

Mendieta issued a provisional constitution and reorganized the government. However, strikes and other disturbances undermined his administration. In May 1934 Mendieta signed the Treaty of Relations, which modified the terms of the treaty of May 1903 and also abrogated the Platt Amendment, even though it allowed the United States to continue to lease its naval base at Guantánamo Bay. In August of that same year, the two countries signed the commercial Treaty of Reciprocity, which gave preferential treatment to United States exports to Cuba and guaranteed Cuba 22 percent of the

United States sugar market—a figure that would rise to 49
percent by 1949—at a special low duty. The sugar industry
started to recover, which was demonstrated by increased
production and a rise in prices. Economic conditions changed
rapidly, and so did labor expectations, thus leading to a wave of
strikes. In March 1935, seeing that economic recovery was at
stake, Batista crushed the rebellion.

Mendieta resigned in December 1935 and was replaced
by Jose A. Barnet. In January 1936 Miguel M. Gómez (son
of former president Jose Miguel Gómez) won the presidential election, in which women were allowed to vote for the
first time. In a maneuver engineered by Batista, the president was impeached in December 1936 for having vetoed a
bill to create rural schools under army control. Vice President Federico Laredo Bru served the concluding years of
Gómez's term.

Laredo Bru's government enacted a series of reforms.
Under a three-year plan, he pushed through passage of the
Law of Sugar Coordination in 1937, which organized small
farmers into cooperatives and unionized agricultural workers. In 1938 Laredo Bru created a powerful national union,
the Confederation of Cuban Workers (Confederación de
Trabajadores de Cuba—CTC). He also outlawed debt peon-
age and guaranteed tenant farmers a share of their crops and
protection against seizure of their lands. Later on, social
security benefits were extended to rural workers, and state
lands were divided among small growers. Political groups
opposing the United States, from fascist to communist, were
allowed to operate in Cuba. A Constitutional Assembly was

elected in 1939, and it met for the first time in February 1940, under the presidency of Grau. At the end of 1939 Batista resigned his post as commander of the armed forces and ran for the presidency, under a coalition supported by the Communist Party of Cuba (Partido Comunista de Cuba—PCC) and the Revolutionary Union Party (Partido Union Revolucionario—PUR); the two were merged to form the Communist Revolutionary Union (Union Revolucionario Communista—URC). In 1944 the party's name was changed to the Popular Socialist Party (Partido Socialista Popular-PSP). Batista then defeated Grau, who ran as the candidate of the Cuban Revolutionary Party (commonly known as the Auténticos), in the 1940 elections. Batista was a strong president who was able both to neutralize the opposition and to promote social welfare measures, wage increases, and economic growth.

Cuba declared war on the Axis powers soon after the United States entered World War II. The climate of friendly relations with the United States was important for the country's development at the time. Cuban sugar production rose with the war effort, and from 1942 to 1947 the United States purchased all Cuban sugar at a relatively high price (almost U.S. $0.03 per pound) and imposed low duties (U.S. $0.008 per pound). Batista's presidency was marked by the support of sugar interests, and he felt confident enough to court the Cuban left. In 1943 he established diplomatic relations with the Soviet Union. However, Batista's longtime opponent, Grau, won the 1944 presidential elections through a coalition of his own party, the Conservative Republican Party, and the communists. Acknowledging his defeat, Batista went into political retirement in the United States.

Grau, highly regarded in Cuba, won the 1944 election against the Batista candidate, Carlos Saladrigas. He inherited a wartime economic boom and a competent bureaucracy. During his term in office, however, Cuba became a haven for corruption, graft, black marketers, and vice. The country also became fertile ground for political activism, which was carried on mostly by the students and the communists, whose numbers had increased because of a mass exodus from Mexico following the end of Lazaro Cardena's administration in 1940. The opposition had been schooled in the fight against the Machado regime. Their effectiveness had been further increased by the autonomy of the university, which was off-limits to police. Even though the communists had supported Grau's nomination, it was the onset of the Cold War, the shift in Soviet relations with the democratic left, and the spread of anticommunist ideology that led the president to break his ties with them in 1947.

Carlos Prio Socorras won the 1948 elections as Grau's candidate from the Auténticos. A new opposition party, the Ortodoxos, had been created before the elections, however. Sometimes known as the Cuban People's Party, the Ortodoxos had been organized in 1946 by Eduardo (Eddie) Chibás. Like the Auténticos, the Ortodoxos defended the principles of progressive social and economic betterment, but they added an emphasis on administrative decency.

Prio's term in office was directed against violence and the presence of communists in the administration, although excessive labor privileges provoked the flight of business and capital from Cuba. In 1949 United States sailors desecrated a monument in Havana honoring Jose Martí, thus creating a certain amount of friction between the two countries. The two Auténtico presidents had been a disappointment, and corruption became rampant at all levels of government. The Cuban people hoped for a change in the elections of 1952.

The elections of 1952 were centered on the elimination of corruption in Cuba's government, and three factions nominated candidates for the presidency. The Ortodoxos had a very good chance of carrying the electorate on a platform promising decency in government, accompanied by a campaign against corruption. However, they lost their hero in August 1951, when Chibás shot himself at the end of one of his broadcasts. The loss of Chibás created a vacuum in the opposition, but Professor Roberto Agramonte was nominated as the new Ortodoxo candidate. The Auténticos wanted a man above suspicion to run against the Ortodoxos. They chose Carlos Hevia, who had been provisional president in 1934, because he was an honest man, though lacking in charisma. The third candidate was Batista, who had been elected in absentia to the Senate in 1948 and had recently returned to Cuba.

The contest between Hevia and Agramonte was favorable to the Auténtico candidate, and Batista realized he had no chance of changing the odds. On March 10, 1952, three months before the elections, Batista took power in a blood-less coup d'etat with the help of his military friends at Camp Columbia. He suppressed the electoral process and appointed himself provisional ruler. Within a couple of hours, President Prio and his cabinet went into exile. Twenty years of political development in Cuba had suddenly come to a halt, and it was quickly evident that the next phase would be dominated by a military dictatorship. In short order Batista's men occupied the most important military posts, and Batista justified his actions by accusing Prio of having planned to establish a dictatorship in Cuba. Because of Batista's past record with international interest, he quickly gained recognition for his government by noncommunist nations throughout the world. Batista suspended the constitution, dissolved all political parties, and created the Council of State to replace the Cuban Congress. Political dissidents were not immediately harassed, however, and students continued to demonstrate.

Cubans inherently did not trust Batista, however, and they expected to see him piling up more wealth through gambling payoffs. In 1952 sugar production reached 7.2 million tons, and to prevent falling prices, Batista decided to cut production by 2 million tons a year. Public works and small enterprises were favored by the dictator's policies. Overall, his six years in government were characterized by prosperity in exchange for freedom. Resistance kept growing, however, and the dictatorship applied repression even more often and cruelly. By the end of Batista's term, repression had reached unprecedented levels.

Fidel Castro was the son of Spanish sugar planters from the province of Oriente. He studied under the Jesuits and, as a law student at the university, became an Ortodoxo and a follower of Chibás. He was very active in student politics, both at home and abroad, which quite often took violent forms. In 1947 he participated in a failed expedition to assassinate the Dominican dictator Rafael Leónidas Trujillo Molina. As a representative of Cuban students, he attended a preliminary conference for the organization of a Latin American students' union conducted under the auspices of Argentine president Juan Domingo Perón in Bogota in 1948. While in Colombia, Castro allegedly participated in riots known as the "Bogotazo," which followed the assassination of presidential candidate Eliecer Gaitán. Castro graduated from law school in 1950 and was invited to run as an Ortodoxo candidate to the Chamber of Representatives in the elections of 1952, which were preempted by Batista. After the coup the campaign went on for a short time, during which the daring Castro circulated a petition to depose the Batista government on the grounds of its illegitimacy. The court ruled against his motion that revolutions, in contrast, create their own legitimacy. One of the judges, Manuel Urrutia Lleo, did not comply with the majority, and Castro would not forget his independent and revolutionary stance.

On July 26, 1953, Castro led a revolt in which 165 men attacked the Moncada army barracks near Santiago de Cuba. The attack was a failure, but it planted the seed of future revolutionary fervor. Castro was arrested and sentenced to fifteen years in prison. At the end of the trial, on October 16,

1953, the twenty-six-year-old revolutionary delivered a historic statement that ended with the phrase "la historia me absolverá" (history will absolve me).

The Moncada attack prompted Batista to proclaim a ninety-day state of siege to prevent public protests. By early 1954 the economy was booming, everything seemed to be under control, and he decided to hold the scheduled presidential elections in November. Batista nominated himself as the candidate of his newly formed Progressive Action Party to run against his former opponent, Grau. Grau withdrew his candidacy before the elections, however, on the grounds that the elections were likely to be fixed. A high rate of abstention by the opposition gave Batista the opportunity to inaugurate himself as constitutional president on February 1955.

The Moncada incident would have soon been forgotten but for the repressive measures undertaken by Batista against its participants and other Cuban dissidents. Several groups, among them lawyers, priests, lay Catholics, and students, began to defend the victims of Batista's repression. In May, in response to these pressures and as a measure of his self-confidence, Batista declared a general amnesty that allowed the return of exiled members of the opposition and freed most political prisoners, including Castro and his followers from Moncada. On July 7 Castro left Cuba for exile in Mexico.

In spite of opposition organized and funded by Prio and voiced in the press, times were good. Lower sugar production kept prices from falling, and industrial growth and tourism increased both revenues and the country's reserves of foreign currency. The way in which Cuba checked population growth and inflation was an example to the rest of Latin America. However, corruption and nepotism, which enriched some groups while allowing the rest of the population to grow poorer, were important ingredients in the island's prosperity. Several segments of society opposed Batista: the poor, the neglected labor force (whom Batista had favored in the past), the communists, and the old political and intellectual opposition. To the latter Batista was a profit seeker who had halted the development of democratic institutions.

Meanwhile, in Mexico the 26 of July Movement (Movimiento 26 de Julio—M-26-7), named after the date of the Moncada attack, was organizing Cuban exiles. Military training, fundraising activities, study groups, and clandestine politics were growing in numbers and participants. Ernesto (Che) Guevara, an Argentine doctor, joined the group. The conspirators in Mexico began to contact the Cuban opposition back home, and in mid-1956 they issued the Pact of Mexico and later in the year created the Revolutionary Student Directorate (Directorio Estudiantil Revolucionario—DER), whose activities included urban terrorism and sabotage against the government. M-26-7 outfitted an expedition from Mexico, and on board the yacht *Granma* (bought with funds provided by Prio), eighty-one men set sail for Cuba under Castro's leadership and landed in the province of Oriente on December 2, 1956. A combination of factors preordained their initial failure. Poor communications between the expeditionaries and the Cuban underground, bad weather, and government knowledge of their arrival prompted a counterattack by Batista's forces. The revolutionaries dispersed, but the vast majority were killed or captured. The two Castro brothers, Fidel and Raúl, Guevara, and a handful of others fled to the Sierra Maestra with the help of friendly peasants.

Batista's regime began to crumble after the landing of the *Granma*. One factor that contributed to the steady decline of Batista's leadership capability was an interview given by Castro to *New York Times* reporter Herbert Matthews in February 1957, after two months of government claims that the revolutionary leader had been killed. After a five-year period of calm, urban terrorism once again became common. While Batista was being publicly criticized at home and abroad, Castro became a folk hero to the underprivileged masses of Latin America.

In the Sierra Maestra, the revolutionaries were training for their next attack. On March 13, 1957, the DER stormed into the presidential palace in a frustrated attempt to assassinate the president. Batista's forces increased their repression, and censorship became very rigid. But the guerrilla fighters were not losing any ground either, though they were surrounded by Batista's well-armed forces in Oriente. If they could not advance outside the sierra, neither could Batista's men penetrate the island's western mountains. Supplies to the revolutionaries kept arriving, mainly from the United States. The *zafra* (sugarcane harvest) of early 1958 marked a period of great violence and police brutality. In April Castro called for a general strike, but it did not materialize because of opposition by the PSP-controlled CTC labor confederation.

Batista's apparent victory over the strikers was a boost to his regime, and he went ahead with plans for elections in November 1958. Batista's candidate, Andrés Rivero Aguero, was named victor over Grau, an Auténtico, and Carlos Márques Sterling, an Ortodoxo, in the fraudulent elections of November 3. United States support had already been withdrawn from the Cuban government in early 1858, when an arms shipment to Cuba had been cancelled. After the rigged elections, it became even more clear that Cuba was being denied a free democratic process. By the end of the year, the revolutionaries had burst out of the Sierra Maestra. With his army deserting in droves, Batista fled into exile on New Year's Day 1959. The following day Guevara took Havana with the help of six-hundred revolutionaries.

The breakdown of Cuba's authoritarian regime was prompted by a combination of factors, including its political illegitimacy, disrespect for the people's legitimate expectations, and indiscriminate use of repression against political dissidents. Batista's dictatorship had alienated the middle classes. Thus, by the end of the 1950s, the traditional popular forces had been neutralized, and there was no other political group capable of offering the necessary leadership to all Cubans. Coercion was the only path open to the dictatorship in dealing with the revolutionary forces of the opposition, who were able to embody popular aspirations and turn the revolution into a truly popular one. Clientelism had prevented the development of a democratic process in Cuba prior to 1959, and its breakdown created new hopes for change.

The fall of Batista left a political vacuum in Cuba, even though the revolutionary elite represented by Castro and his followers acquired control of the decision-making process. Castro was committed to political democracy and social reforms as defended by Jose Martí. The first revolutionary government was a facade, with Urrutia in the presidency. Urrutia was the judge who had voted in favor of the revolutionaries in the wake of the aborted 1952 elections. On February 16, 1959, Castro became prime minister, but because of conflicts between himself and the president, Castro resigned his post on July 17. The conflict was related to Urrutia's anticommunism, but Castro was initially unable to dismiss him because Urrutia was a patriot and considered an honest man. Castro had provided the Cuban populace with enough reason for withdrawing support from the president, however, and the general clamor reached such proportions that Urrutia had to take refuge in the Venezuelan embassy. Osvaldo Dorticós Torrado, a distinguished lawyer and aristocrat from Cienfuegos who was Castro's choice to replace Urrutia, became president on July 18. A loyal friend of Castro, the brilliant Dorticós announced to a cheering crowd on July 26 that, pressed by popular demand, Castro had agreed to resume his post as prime minister.

The first stage of the Cuban Revolution was characterized by the liquidation of the old power groups (the military,

political parties, labor unions, and agricultural and professional associations) and their replacement by new revolutionary bodies, such as the Rebel Army, the militia, and the
Committees for the Defense of the Revolution (Comites de
Defensa de la Revolución—CDRs). Few political organizations established during the prerevolutionary days were
allowed to continue to operate, except the M-26-7, the DER,
and the PSP. But their effectiveness was limited by the
revolutionary elite, who controlled all aspects of the decision-
making process. In the early days the elite's decisions were
legitimized by popular acclamation at mass rallies. The
confiscation of sugar lands began in mid-1960, and the col-
lectivization of the means of production was coupled with
economic management by the revolutionary elite.

Early revolutionary policies were formulated in
response to the expectations of the middle sectors of Cuban
society, which had backed the struggle against Batista.
These included land reform, improvement of salary and
benefits to workers, diversification of agriculture—less
dependence on sugar-industrialization, regulation of foreign
enterprises, and administrative reform. Wealth and income
were redistributed to the middle and lower sectors of society. Services improved and were extended to the whole
population through social services and lower utility rates,
taxes, and rents. In May 1959 the Law of Agrarian
Reform created the National Institute for Agrarian
Reform (Instituto Nacional de Reforma Agraria—INRA)
to assist rural workers. In order to eliminate the traditional
minifundium (small landholding) and latifundium (large

landholding), it established a minimum size of agricultural properties at twenty-seven hectares for individuals and placed upward limits of four-hundred hectares on holdings by agro-industries. The country was divided into twenty-eight zones under the administration of INRA, which also had the responsibility of providing health and educational services to the population. By 1961 land reform policies had already redistributed over 1 million hectares of land, 167,000 sugar workers had joined cooperatives, and about 50,000 still worked for wages at private farms. That same year saw the creation of the National Association of Small Farmers (Asociación Nacional de Agricultores Pequeños— ANAP). The revolutionary government had kept its promises to the underprivileged masses that rallied behind the new regime, while antagonizing the traditional propertied classes.

Dependence upon a single crop was an obstacle to development, and it made the Cuban economy vulnerable to fluctuations in production and in sugar prices in the international markets (particularly in the United States). To diminish dependence on sugar, the revolutionaries felt that Cuba had to industrialize through import substitution. Industrial development, it was felt, would free Cuba from its internal dependence on sugar, create new jobs, reduce imports, and diversify exports. Agrarian reform gave the government the necessary power to restructure the agricultural sector, making sugar the most important item in the agenda. On July 5, 1960, however, the United States canceled Cuba's quota for sugar exports to the United States. Cuba then nationalized United States enterprises operating in the country, including thirty-six centrales, the Cuban Telegraph and Telephone Company, the Cuban Electric Company, and all oil refineries. Three hundred eighty-two other large enterprises, all Cuban, and most foreign banks were nationalized on October 13. Only the Canadian institutions received compensation from the revolutionary government. Finally, on October 17 the remaining United States banking institutions were nationalized. These steps enabled Cuba to quicken the pace of socialization of the means of production.

As time went on, the revolutionary process grew more radical. The CDRs became the right arm of the revolution, reaching down into the neighborhoods in constant vigilance against possible enemies of the revolution. Lacking a democratic electoral process, the revolution became the sole political arbiter. Dissidents were scorned and linked to United States interests. The main opposition to the regime came from both the People's Revolutionary Movement and the Revolutionary Movement of Redemption, whose objective was to destabilize the consolidation of the leftist government. There was also marked dissension within the M-26-7 and between Castroites, whose loyalty to Castro was unconditional, and the former communists, who felt closer to Guevara and Raúl Castro. The nonradical groups lost, while greater power was shared among the Castroites (also known as fidelistas), guevaristas (followers of Guevara), and raulistas (followers of Raúl Castro). Above all factions stood Fidel Castro, who relied upon his charisma to justify his actions through magnificent oratory.

Relations between Cuba and the United States during

the first period of the Revolution went from mutual uncertainty all the way to the rupture of relations and military action. In 1959 the Cuban communists from the PSP began applying pressure on Moscow in order to secure Soviet assistance and protection. The Kremlin and the White House, however, were in a process of negotiation that had begun with a meeting between President Dwight D. Eisenhower and Premier Nikita Khrushchev in September 1959. At this time Moscow's engagement in Cuba would have hampered these bilateral efforts.

In February 1960, however, First Deputy Premier Anastas Mikoyan of the Soviet Union visited Havana and signed an agreement for credits of U.S. $100 million for the purchase of industrial equipment and technical assistance. The Soviet Union also agreed to purchase almost 400,000 tons of sugar in 1960 and another 4 million tons by 1964. Diplomatic relations between the two countries were established on May 8, 1960, three days after the Soviets announced the shooting down of a United States U2 reconnaissance plane over its airspace. In March, following the Cuban-Soviet economic agreement, the United States had already decided to recruit, train, and outfit a Cuban exile force. This decision would lead to the fateful events of 1961.

The year 1961 was dedicated to upgrading the Cuban educational system, especially the literacy campaign. Education became compulsory and state controlled. In the spring of 1961 all but a few private schools had been taken over by the government. The major setback was the lack of qualified teachers as well as other professionals, such as doctors and scientists, who fled the country beginning in 1959. However, what the revolutionaries lacked in specific skills they compensated for with dedication. Estimates made at the end of the year claimed that 80 percent of all school-age children had been given the opportunity to enroll in the schools and that the rate of illiteracy had dropped to 3.9 percent. Even though the emphasis of the revolutionary educational program was on technical training and ideological indoctrination, the revolutionary leadership also promoted the arts, created the Cuban Film Institute, and began operating all available publishing houses in an effort to generate new values for the Cuban masses.

The Cuban revolutionary government also showed concern for health care, and it started building a network of rural health clinics staffed with at least a doctor, a midwife, a laboratory technician, and a visiting nurse. The clinics were responsible for educating the rural communities on matters of health, and they relied on local cooperation to carry out their program in tropical and social medicine. By 1963 there were 122 rural centers in operation, and medical graduates had to perform a year of rural service. This program was under the umbrella of the INRA, which provided the centers with the necessary facilities and equipment.

In April 1961 Castro stated the socialist character of the Cuban Revolution, and the following December he declared himself a Marxist-Leninist. Analysts claimed that these were clear attempts to gain economic and military support from the Soviet Union and its allies. At that point a new revolutionary phase unfolded for Cuba under the auspices of the Soviet Union. There was a shift from the "trial and error" style of the first two years of the revolution toward an attempt to apply efficiently a Soviet-style system of politico-economic organization and development planning. Centralization was one of the basic tenets of the effort. In July 1961 the revolutionary organizations came together under the umbrella known as Integrated Revolutionary Organizations (Organizaciones Revolucionarias Integradas—ORI), with members of the PSP, the DER, and the M-26-7 under the leadership of Aníbal Escalante of the PSP. On March 26, 1962, Escalante was ousted by Castro on the grounds that he had attempted to exercise excessive control over the ORI by packing it with PSP veterans. Several months later the ORI was dissolved by Castro and replaced by the United Party of the Socialist Revolution (Partido Unido de la Revolución Socialista—PURS), under the control of Castro and his inner group. However, the void left by the withdrawal of United States economic and technical aid was replaced by a centralized system of planning and technical assistance provided by the Soviet Union. Under this new orientation, Cubans were to be prepared to hold managerial positions, and the union movement was to be used as a channel for the central administration. Economic growth and industrialization would be generated through lower consumption and higher rates of investments.

On January 3, 1961, Eisenhower broke diplomatic and consular relations with Cuba in response to Castro's demand that the United States reduce its embassy staff in Havana to fewer than twenty persons. On February 2 recently inaugurated president John F. Kennedy approved previously laid plans for an invasion of Cuba, with April 17 chosen as the date for the invasion. President Kennedy's support was conditioned on there being no direct involvement of United States forces in the invasion itself, even though various United States agencies participated heavily in training and providing support to the exile force. To comply with Kennedy's specifications, the invasion was to be small and covert.

The first air strike by airplanes flying from Nicaragua on April 14 was ineffective, destroying only five of the thirty airplanes in the Cuban air force. The air attack provoked a protest at the United Nations, and a second such attempt was canceled. On April 17 a landing expedition of 1,297 disembarked at Playa Girón, on the Bay of Pigs. The operation was doomed from the start. President Kennedy had reduced the landing's air protection and had forbidden the use of United States aircraft. The exiles were poorly organized and their military support by the Cuban underground opposition elsewhere on the island failed to materialize. Castro, who commanded the forces that met the invasion, knew the area around the Bay of Pigs well and easily suppressed the exile invasion. The invading forces surrendered on April 19. Their casualties were between eighty-five and 150, and the survivors were taken as prisoners in Havana. Castro established a ransom of approximately U.S. $62 million in medical supplies for their release. Even before the arrival of the ransom, however, the prisoners were freed to return to the United States in time for Christmas in 1962.

The victory of Castro's forces at the Bay of Pigs had important consequences for the consolidation of Castro's regime, for the disbanding of opposition groups on the island, and for the fueling of propaganda on "imperialist aggression." Castro doubted that the invasion would be the last attempt to overthrow his government, and he set out to build one of the largest armed forces in Latin America. In the United States, despite the debacle, Kennedy gained popularity for his strong stance against communism.

The Cuban government then turned its attention to the island's economic problems. There had been a sharp decline in sugar production, which hampered the provision of financial resources to developing industries. In spite of innovations in economic planning, the country was still heavily dependent on sugar. Guevara was the architect of a four-year plan designed by the Central Planning Board, which called for agricultural diversification and industrialization. However, by 1962 the results were far from encouraging. Between 1961 and 1963 sugar output dropped first from 6.8 to 4.8 million tons and then to a low of 3.8 million tons. Thus, in three years production was cut almost in half. To compensate for the loss of export earnings, consumption was restricted, and a system of rationing was introduced to Cuba in 1962.

In January 1962 the Organization of American States (OAS) voted to exclude Cuba from participating in the OAS system. The sanctions resulted from Venezuela's well-documented charges against Cuba that its support of Venezuelan insurgents constituted foreign intervention in

Venezuela's internal affairs. Sanctions were fully supported by the United States. It reinforced this decision in 1964 when it recommended that member states abstain from trade and diplomatic relations with Cuba. United States pressure resulted in the withdrawal of all except the Mexican diplomatic corps from Cuba.

Castro's acquiescence to Soviet wishes to install nuclear missiles in Cuba proved near-disastrous, as the Soviet Union and Castro himself brought the whole world to the edge of a nuclear war. The United States government had grown alarmed at the rapid and heavy Soviet military buildup and installation of surface-to-air antiaircraft missile bases in Cuba, and on September 13, 1962, Kennedy requested that Congress give him emergency powers to call up reserve troops. The confrontation between the United States and the Soviet Union began on October 22, 1962, when the United States announced a naval quarantine of Cuba that was to remain in effect until all rockets, Soviet military technicians, and troops for manning the missiles and guarding the sites were removed from Cuban soil.

After six days of nuclear brinkmanship between the superpowers, Khrushchev accepted the conditions imposed by the United States on October 28 without asking for Castro's consent. Nevertheless, the settlement between Kennedy and Khrushchev is thought to have brought about some important assurances for Cuba: the alleged secret agreement prescribed that Cuba would have immunity against military aggression by the United States as long as it did not become a base for Soviet offensive weapons. Cuban-

Soviet relations were seriously strained by the missile crisis, however, because the Soviets had initiated and resolved the situation with little regard for Cuba's interests or its national sovereignty. After the 1962 missile crisis, relations between Cuba and the United States remained frozen. Furthermore, throughout the 1960s—a period when Cuba was committed to exporting revolution—observers recorded a number of covert operations against the Cuban regime, allegedly undertaken by United States intelligence agencies.

JAIME SUCHLICKI

Castro's Revolution

HEN BATISTA and his closest allies escaped to the Dominican Republic in the early hours of January 1, 1959, power lay in the streets. Of the several groups that fought the Batista regime, the 26 of July Movement had an almost undisputed claim to fill the vacuum left by the dictator. Castro's charisma and his revolutionary prestige made him, in the eyes of the Cuban people, the logical occupant of Batista's vacant chair; he was the man of the hour, the new messiah. The other insurrectionary organizations lacked the mystique, the widespread support, and the organized cadres of Castro's movement. The Civic Resistance Movement, formed

JAIME SUCHLICKI *has published articles in* Orbis, Latin American Research Review, *and* Caribbean Studies. *His books include* Cuba: From Columbus to Castro *(1997), from which this piece was excerpted, and* Mexico: From Montezuma to NAFTA *(1996).*

by prominent professional and university professors, was an amorphous thing that followed Castro's orientation. The PSP had accepted Castro's leadership and seemed willing to cooperate with the *"petit bourgeois"* revolutionary. The regular army was harmless and demoralized. Castro's bid for power was unchallenged.

Castro had unquestionable qualities of leadership. Endowed with an extraordinary gift of oratory and an exceptional memory, he would speak extemporaneously for hours. Like Martí had done years earlier, Castro lectured to the Cubans on the evils of their society and the need for profound and rapid changes. The overwhelming majority of the Cubans accepted his leadership enthusiastically. The atmosphere of gloom that prevailed during the Batista era was now converted into euphoria and hope for the future. Even those who had failed to participate in the anti-Batista struggle fervently joined the revolutionary ranks with a guilt feeling for their past behavior.

During the first few weeks in power, Castro assumed no official position except commander of the armed forces. His hand-picked president, former judge Manuel Urrutia, organized a government, appointing a civilian cabinet composed mainly of prominent anti-Batista political figures. Urrutia then proceeded to tear down Batista's governmental structure. In a series of decrees he dissolved Congress; removed from office all congressmen, provincial governors, mayors, and municipal councilmen; abolished all of Batista's censorship and martial law restrictions; and began a clean sweep of Batista supporters in the bureaucracy.

It soon became clear, however, that real power rested with Fidel and his youthful rebel army officers. In public addresses Castro announced major public policies without consultation with the Urrutia cabinet and complained of the slowness of reforms. In mid-February Prime Minister Miró-Cardona resigned in favor of Castro, and by October Castro forced Urrutia to resign and appointed Oswaldo Dorticós, an obscure lawyer and former PSP member, as Cuba's president.

Castro's formal assumption of power initiated a period of increased radicalization. Some of Batista's more prominent military and civilian leaders were publicly brought to trial before revolutionary tribunals and the proceedings were televised; hundreds were executed summarily. Faced with mounting criticism, the regime ended these public trials but continued them in private, while also confiscating property of Batista supporters or collaborators.

On May 17, 1959, the first Agrarian Reform Law was passed. It established a National Institute for Agrarian Reform (INRA), and called for a maximum limit on landholdings with the remaining land being expropriated by the government. Large and medium agricultural estates were taken over, but little land was distributed among the peasantry; most of these lands were eventually converted into state farms with peasants living and working on them and receiving a salary and a small share of the profits.

The Agrarian Reform Law, together with a sharp reduction in urban rents, marked the beginning of the rapid confiscatory and redistributive phase of the revolution, which lasted until the formal establishment of the socialist economy in April 1961 when Castro proclaimed that the revolution was socialist. In order to destroy the structural imbalances that had plagued the Cuban economy, the revolutionary leadership aimed at agricultural diversification and industrialization, thus hoping to lessen dependence upon sugar. They also sought to weaken U.S. economic presence and influence in Cuba and to reduce the glaring inequalities between urban and rural standards. This was to be accomplished partially by nationalizing foreign and domestic enterprises. Natural resources, utility companies, the credit system, and most large and medium industries fell into the hands of the government. A gradual takeover of the mass communication media and the educational system also took place, and both became powerful tools of the state apparatus. The government initiated a program of low-income housing and a massive literacy campaign which, according to official claims, has wiped out the 30 percent illiteracy rate that existed prior to the revolution. Unemployment receded and unskilled urban workers received increases in real income through higher salaries, although skilled workers suffered substantial losses. The upper classes were wiped out, and middle-class families lost most of their income-producing property. Many migrated, particularly to the United States, or were absorbed into the larger proletariat created by the revolution.

Meanwhile, Castro insisted on a high standard of morality for the Cuban population, and for the government bureaucracy in particular. Immortality, as existed in the old Cuba, was associated with capitalism, and capitalism, with all its evil consequences, had to be destroyed. The pressures for economic survival, furthermore, made it necessary to end idleness, laziness, and other vices. The Castro regime thus assumed and continues to assume a puritanical attitude, prohibiting prostitution, gambling, and even such traditional and popular Cuban' institutions as the lottery and cockfighting.

The most important moral reform occurred in connection with the administration of public funds. Stealing from the government was made a capital offense, and the system of sinecures was ended. Although political integrity has not been achieved completely and new forms of privilege and sinecure have appeared, the widespread administrative corruption of the past has been eradicated.

The regime has made an all-out effort to provide a new and more militant role for women. Since the revolution, over half a million women have joined the labor force, and a Federation of Cuban Women under the leadership of Vilma Espín, Raúl Castro's wife, has been organized. Women fill a variety of jobs in and out of the government bureaucracy, and many work overnight on armed-guard duty. Although some of this work is voluntary, there is a great amount of direct and indirect coercion. The former takes the form of directives by the party, the Federation, and other organizations to engage women voluntarily in tasks such as cane cutting. The latter is more subtle. The more militant exert a sort of social pressure on the less militant to participate. Also, since political and even economic advancement in Cuba is reserved for those who sacrifice harder for the revolution, voluntary work is a way of showing your devotion and loyalty to the party and the revolutionary cause. There is also a greater interest and participation in politics and sports, and many more women than before the revolution are university educated. Although it is difficult to assess the depth of change in the values and attitudes of women, as well as the reaction of men to these changes, unquestionably, the old feeling that a woman's place was in the home has collapsed completely, and women have found a new, more politicized and involved role in Castro's Cuba.

The new opportunities offered to women have also had the effect of undermining the family, one of the most important conservers of the old order. Relations between husband and wife have been undermined, and the family has largely lost control of the children. Large numbers of children attend free boarding schools and see their parents for only short periods of time during the year. There is, therefore, not only frequent separation of husband and wife due to the work demands of the revolution, but also separation of parents from children. The regime has systematically encouraged these developments, perhaps aware that the only way to develop Cuba's new socialist man is through the destruction of the culture-transmitting institutions, such as the family and the church.

In February 1960 the regime created a Central Planning Board to plan and direct the country's economic development. Organizational models of East European countries were usually adopted, and the Ministry of Industry, under Che Guevara, took over and administered major industrial installations. The transformation of Cuba's private enterprise system into a centralized state-controlled economy resulted in growing inflation, disorganization, and bureaucratic chaos and inefficiency. Agricultural production declined sharply, partly as a result of neglect and Castro's plan for industrialization, and by 1961 food rationing was introduced for the first time in the island's history. Cuba is still suffering acutely from many of these problems.

The growing radicalization of the regime was accompanied by the destruction of possible opposition and by the growth in influence of the PSP. Political parties were not permitted to function, with the exception of the PSP, which later merged with Castro's own 26 of July Movement to form the Cuban Communist Party, the country's ruling party. Many older political leaders became alienated from the regime; several went into exile, some joined the revolutionary ranks. Most of the leaders and groups of the anti-Batista struggle were coopted into the revolution and later fused with the Castroites, although an increasing number of former Castro allies became disenchanted with the revolution, feeling that Castro had betrayed the ideals he espoused while in the mountains. Abetted by Castro, communists progressively occupied important positions in the government, gaining in prestige and influence.

Evidently, Castro saw significant advantages in using the PSP. The party provided the trained, disciplined, and organized cadres that Castro's movement lacked. But more important, the party had Moscow's ear and therefore could serve as the bridge for any possible Cuban-Soviet rapprochement. Castro knew well that in any conflict with the United States, only the protective umbrella of the Soviet Union could defend him against possible U.S. pressures or attack. No other power, Castro reasoned, could or would confront the United States over Cuba. The experience of Guatemala in 1954, when a U.S.-sponsored invasion overthrew the communist-leaning regime of Jacobo Arbenz, was a clear warning to Fidel and particularly to his trusted adviser, Che Guevara, who had been a minor official in the Guatemalan government at the time of Arbenz's overthrow, that a profound revolution that would affect U.S. interests in Cuba would be a difficult task.

Ideologically, Castro was far from being a Marxist. He belonged to Cuba's vague populist political tradition, Martí and Chibás had called for an end to political corruption, destruction of Cuba's dependence on monoculture and one foreign buyer, and development of a unique and nationalistic identity. Although strongly influenced by falangist and fascist ideas while a high school student and by Marxist ideas while at the University of Havana, Castro embraced none of these and was instead more a product of the Martí-Chibás tradition, although he broke with it in several fundamental aspects. While Martí and Chibás had envisioned reforms in a democratic framework in a nation politically and economically independent from the United States, they both advocated friendly relations with the "northern colossus." Castro did not. He was anti-U.S. since his student days when he distributed anti-U.S. propaganda in Bogota. As Castro and part of the Cuban revolutionary leadership perceived it, the possibility of a repetition of earlier U.S. interventionist policies in Cuba was a major deterrent to achieving profound socio-economic changes in the island and the consolidation of Castro's personal rule—and Castro was committed to both of these goals. Perhaps because of his anti-Americanism, and particularly his conviction that a major revolution with himself in absolute control could not be undertaken within Cuba's political framework and in harmony with the United States, he broke with the Martí-Chibás tradition and led a totalitarian and anti-American revolution.

In the early months of his revolution, Castro reasserted his independence from the United States but maintained normal relations. During his visit to the United States in April 1959, he turned down tentative offers of aid, but insisted that Cuba stood with the West in the Cold War. He also met with several U.S. government officials, including then-vice president Richard Nixon. Yet, as time went on, Castro increased his inflammatory denunciations of the United States. He accused the northern neighbor of every exile raid perpetrated against his country and blamed it for Cuba's economic and political ills.

Initially, the United States followed a "wait and see" policy. The Eisenhower administration seemed to have been caught by surprise over events in Cuba and failed to grasp the magnitude of the changes going on or the nature of the leader sponsoring those changes. Differences arose between those who, feeling that Castro was a Marxist, advocated a hard line toward Cuba and those who counseled patience with the bearded leader.

Although tensions arose in connection with the public

trials and executions of Batista supporters, serious differences grew after the Agrarian Reform Law was promulgated. The United States protested, to no avail, the expropriations initiated under the law. Agricultural expropriations were followed by further attacks on foreign investments, notably in the mining and petroleum industries. Complicating the relations between the two countries were arrests of U.S. citizens, Castro's refusal to meet with U.S. Ambassador Philip W. Bonsal in late 1959, and the sabotage and raids carried out by Cuban exiles from U.S. territory.

Castro's militant Caribbean activities also increased Washington's apprehension. During the first year of the revolution, Cuban filibusters, joined by exiles from various Caribbean nations, launched a series of abortive expeditions in an attempt to raise the standard of revolt in several neighboring countries. The relationship of Castro to these expeditions has never been clearly defined. Many of these exiles had contributed to Castro's victory and now saw an opportunity to develop an international movement to dislodge dictators from the area. On several occasions Castro openly condemned some of the attempts and halted vessels loaded with weapons and men. Although it seems likely that at this early period Castro was unconnected with these attempts, the fact remains that expeditions were launched from Cuba against Panama, the Dominican Republic, and Haiti.

Whether or not the Cuban regime supported these attempts, Castro, Guevara, and Raúl believed that the political social, and economic conditions which had produced their revolution in Cuba existed in other parts of Latin America and that revolutions would occur throughout the continent. From 1960 onward Cuban agents and diplomatic representatives established contact with revolutionary groups in the area and began distributing propaganda and aid. Several Cuban diplomats were expelled for interfering in the internal affairs of the countries to which they were accredited. As tensions mounted with the United States, Castro's assertion of the international character of his revolution increased, as did his involvement in promoting violence in Latin America. By July 1960 Castro was boasting that he would convert "the Cordillera of the Andes into the Sierra Maestra of Latin America," and money, propaganda, men, and weapons began to flow from Havana in increasing quantities to foment the "anti-imperialist" revolution.

The radicalization of the revolution and the deterioration of relations with the United States grew apace with Cuban-Soviet rapprochement. In February 1960, following the visit to Havana of Soviet Deputy Premier Anastas Mikoyan, Cuba signed a major trade agreement with the Soviet Union. The agreement provided that Cuba would receive, among other products, Soviet oil in exchange for sugar. But in June United States- and English-owned refineries in Cuba refused to process Soviet oil. Also, the U.S. House of Representatives approved a bill granting the president authority to cut foreign sugar quotas at his discretion. Castro retaliated, and on June 28 he nationalized the oil companies. In July the United States deleted the remaining tonnage of that year's Cuban sugar quota. In the following months Castro nationalized the remaining U.S. properties together with most major

Cuban-owned businesses. In October the United States announced an embargo on most exports to Cuba, and when Castro restricted the staff of the U.S. embassy to eleven persons, the United States severed diplomatic relations and withdrew its ambassador with the following statement: "There is a limit to what the U.S. in self-respect can endure. That limit has now been reached."

By then the United States had embarked on a more aggressive policy toward the Castro regime. Groups of Cuban exiles were being trained under the supervision of U.S. officials in Central American camps for an attack on Cuba. The internal situation in the island then seemed propitious for an attempt to overthrow the Cuban regime. Although Castro still counted on significant popular support, that support had progressively decreased. His own 26 of July Movement was badly split on the issue of communism. Also, a substantial urban guerilla movement existed throughout the island, composed of former Castro allies. Batista supporters, Catholic groups, and other elements that had been affected by the revolution and significant unrest was evident within the armed forces.

The urban underground saw the landing of the U.S.-sponsored invasion force as the culminating event to follow a series of uprisings and acts of sabotage they hoped would split Castro's army throughout the island and weaken the regime's hold over the people. This would coincide with Castro's assassination and with a coordinated sabotage plan. In the weeks prior to the invasion, violence increased, bombs exploded, shops were burnt.

Yet the planners in exile were not counting on the forces inside Cuba. They placed an unjustified faith in the invasion's success, and feared that the underground might be infiltrated by the regime. Arms that were to be shipped into Cuba never arrived, and communications between the exiles and underground forces were sporadic and confused. The underground was not alerted to the date of the invasion until April 17, the very day of the landing, when it could only watch the Bay of Pigs disaster in confusion and frustration.

The whole affair was a tragedy of errors. Although the Cuban government did not know the date or the exact place where the exile forces would land, the fact that an invasion was in the offing was known in and out of Cuba. The weapons and ammunitions that were to be used by the invading force were all placed in one ship, which was sunk the first day of the invasion. The site for the invasion was sparsely populated, surrounded by swamps, and offered little access to nearby mountains where guerrilla operations could be carried out if the invasion failed. The invading forces could, therefore, all but discount any help from the nearby population.

Some of the air raids by Cuban exiles that were intended to cripple Castro's air force were cancelled at the last minute by a confused and indecisive President John F. Kennedy, Perhaps trying to reassert his authority over the CIA-sponsored invasion to stymie possible world reaction, or to appease the Soviets, Kennedy ordered no further U.S. involvement. Castro's Sea Furys and T33s could, therefore, shoot down the exiles' B26s and maintain control of the air. While the invasion was in progress, Khrushchev threatened

Kennedy: "The government of the U.S. can still prevent the flames of war from spreading into a conflagration which it will be impossible to cope with. . . . The world political situation now is such that any so-called 'small war' can produce a chain reaction in all parts of the world."

The failure of the invasion and the brutal repression that followed smashed the entire Cuban underground. On the first day of the invasion, the regime arrested thousands of real and suspected oppositionists. The resistance never recovered from that blow. His regime strengthened and consolidated, Castro emerged victorious and boasted of having defeated a "Yankee-sponsored invasion." The disillusionment and frustration caused by the Bay of Pigs fiasco among anti-Castro forces, both inside and out of Cuba, prevented the growth of significant organized opposition. Meanwhile, U.S. prestige in Latin America and throughout the world sank to a low point.

Following the Bay of Pigs fiasco, the United States turned to other methods of dealing with Castro. It pursued a vigorous, although only partially successful, policy to isolate the Cuban regime and strangle it economically. The nation pressured its allies through the world to reduce their commerce with Cuba. In the Organization of American States, the United States forced the suspension of Cuba by a slim majority in January 1962, and several countries broke diplomatic relations with the Castro regime at this time. In 1964, after Castro had increased subversive activities in Latin America and had moved fully into the socialist camp, the OAS voted to suspend trade and diplomatic relations with

Cuba; all countries that had not already done so severed relations, except Mexico, who strongly supported the principle of self-determination and refused to bow to U.S. pressures.

As Cuban-U.S. relations deteriorated, closer ties with the Soviet Union developed. Initially, Moscow maintained a cautious stand toward Castro. The Cuban "petite bourgeois" leader seemed impotent to defy the "northern colossus," and the ability of an anti-U.S. regime to survive so close to the U.S. shores seemed remote, particularly in light of the 1954 Guatemala experience. The Soviets, furthermore, were not greatly interested in far-away, raw-material producing Latin America, an area which they considered the backyard of the United States. Khrushchev's attempts at a detente with the United States and his desire to extract concessions from Washington over Berlin were important considerations in limiting Soviet involvement in Cuba lest they provoke a strain in U.S.-Soviet relations. Also, the Soviets recognized that Castro's attempts to identify with the Soviet camp, such as his April 1, 1961, speech declaring the Cuban revolution to be socialist, or his December 1961 speech in which he declared himself a Marxist-Leninist, were designed to involve the Soviet Union in Cuba's defense against possible hostile actions by the United States.

Other considerations were also limiting Soviet involvement in Cuba. Soviet experience with regimes that gained power without Soviet support had shown that these regimes pursued policy lines independent from the Soviets and were difficult to control. As it turned out, the Castro regime proved difficult and at times impossible to influence. Although Castro endorsed half-heartedly the Soviet doctrine of "peaceful coexistence" and the peaceful road to power, he also insisted that the Cuban model of violent revolution was the only valid one for Latin America, and that Cuba should exercise the leadership of the anti-imperialist movement in the area. Naturally, this brought Castro into conflict with Moscow and with the pro-Soviet popular front-oriented communist parties of Latin America, which were not now about to abandon their comfortable and peaceful position in the Latin American political arena to follow Castro's violent path.

Internal developments in the island also worried the Soviets. During the first two years in power, Castro accepted the principle of "collective leadership" and permitted the PSP to increase its prestige and to gain positions of importance in the ORI (Integrated Revolutionary Organizations), a merger of the PSP, the 26 of July Movement, and other groups which occurred in July 1961. By 1962, however, feeling his position threatened, Castro moved swiftly to curb the power of the "old guard" communists and purged Aníbal Escalante, a PSP leader and ORI secretary, exiling him to the Soviet Union. This was the first of several attacks to be suffered by the PSP, which was effectively destroyed as an organization as it became an instrument of Castro's policies.

In spite of these difficulties and apprehensions, the Soviets gradually came to accept the bearded leader. The growing nationalism of Latin America and the enormous popularity of the Cuban revolution in the area were factors limiting the ability of the United States to carry on hostile actions against Castro during the first two years of his regime and encouraging the Soviets' hopes for the survivability of the revolution. Castro's radicalization and his expanding conflict with the United States also increased Moscow's interest. The Soviets saw in Cuban-U.S. tensions an opportunity to offset their failures to obtain U.S. concessions over Berlin. The embarrassment that the "loss" of Cuba could mean for the United States was an added incentive for the Soviets, who were still suffering from the scars left by the rebellion of its own Eastern European satellites. The growing Sino-Soviet dispute was also an important factor pressuring the Soviets into a more militant policy in support of anti-imperialist revolutions in developing countries.

The single most important event encouraging and accelerating Soviet involvement in Cuba was the Bay of Pigs fiasco. The failure of the United States to act decisively against Castro gave the Soviets some illusions about U.S. determination and interest in the island. The Kremlin leaders now perceived that further economic and even military involvement in Cuba would not entail any danger to the Soviet Union itself and would not seriously jeopardize U.S.-Soviet relations. This view was further reinforced by President Kennedy's apologetic attitude concerning the Bay of Pigs invasion and his generally weak performance during his summit meeting with Khrushchev in Vienna in June 1961.

The Soviets moved swiftly. New trade and cultural agreements were signed and increased economic and technical aid was sent to Cuba. By mid-1962 the Soviets embarked on a dangerous gamble by surreptitiously introducing missiles and bombers into the island. Through these actions Khrushchev and the Kremlin leadership hoped to alter the balance of power and force the United States to accept a settlement of the German issue. A secondary and perhaps less important motivation was to extend to Cuba the Soviet nuclear umbrella and thus protect Castro from any further hostile actions by the United States.

On October 22 President Kennedy publicly reacted to the Soviet challenge, instituting a blockade of the island and demanding the withdrawal of all offensive weapons from Cuba. For the next several days the world teetered on the brink of nuclear holocaust. On October 26 a hysterical Khrushchev wrote to Kennedy:

> I think you will understand me correctly if you are really concerned about the welfare of the world. Everyone needs peace: both capitalists, if they have not lost their reason, and still more, communists. . . . I see, Mr. President, that you too are not devoid of a sense of anxiety for the fate of the world, of understanding, and of what war entails. What would a war give you? You are threatening us with war. But you well know that the very least which you would receive in reply would be that you would experience the same consequences as those which you sent us. . . . We, however, want to live and do not at all want to destroy your country. We want something quite different: to compete with your country on a peaceful basis. We quarrel with you, we have differences on ideological questions. But our view of

the world consists in this, that ideological questions, as well as economic problems, should be solved not by military means, they must be solved on the basis of peaceful competition. . . .

Finally, after an exchange of hectic correspondence, Premier Khrushchev agreed to remove the missiles and bombers, and to allow UN-supervised inspection of the removal in exchange for the United States' pledge not to invade Cuba. Although Castro refused to allow a UN inspection, the missiles and bombers were removed under U.S. aerial surveillance and the crisis ended. The United States has never publicly acknowledged that it pledged not to invade Cuba, but subsequent U.S. policies indicate that a U.S.-Soviet understanding was reached over Cuba which included a U.S. "hands off" policy toward the island.

The missile crisis had a significant impact on the countries involved. While it led to a thaw in U.S.-Soviet relations, it significantly strained Cuban-Soviet relations. Castro was not consulted throughout the Kennedy-Khrushchev negotiations, and the unilateral Soviet withdrawal of the missiles and bombers wounded Castro's pride and prestige. It was a humiliating experience for the Cuban leader, who was relegated throughout the crisis to a mere pawn in the chess board of international politics. Castro defiantly rejected the U.S.-Soviet understanding and publicly questioned the Soviet willingness and determination to defend his revolution.

It is ironic that the crisis, hailed at the time as a U.S. victory, was nothing more than an ephemeral victory. In return for the removal of offensive weapons from the island, the United States was satisfied to accept a communist regime only a few miles from its shores. Even the withdrawal of nuclear weapons proved to be only temporary. As recent events have shown, the Soviets have brought more sophisticated weapons to Cuba, but in a different form, using the island as a strategically important base for its nuclear submarines. The real victor, in spite of the humiliation he suffered, was Castro. His regime consolidated and his survivability guaranteed, he could now embark on an aggressive policy to export his brand of revolution throughout Latin America. The Soviet Union, furthermore, went to considerable lengths to appease their Caribbean ally, increasing aid and welcoming him as a hero during his extended trip to the Soviet Union in April-May 1963.

Despite Soviet attempts to appease Castro, Cuban-Soviet relations were still marred by a number of difficulties. After the missile crisis Castro increased contacts with communist China, exploiting the Sino-Soviet dispute and proclaiming his intention to remain neutral and maintain fraternal relations with all socialist states. Cuba signed various trade and cultural agreements with Peking, and Castro grew increasingly friendly toward the Chinese, praising their more militant revolutionary posture. He also defied the Soviets, as he joined the Chinese in refusing to sign the Nuclear Test Ban Treaty (1963). All of these maneuverings increased somewhat Castro's leverage with the Soviets and gained him more assistance.

The Chinese honeymoon was short-lived, however. In

1966 Castro blasted the Chinese for reducing rice shipments to Cuba below the quantities that Castro alleged had been agreed upon between the two countries. He described Mao's ideological statements as lightweight, called for the creation of a "council of elders" to prevent aged leaders from "putting their whims into effect when senility has taken hold of them," and threatened to handle Chinese diplomats the same way "we handle the American Embassy." By then, Castro had also become disappointed with China's attitude toward Vietnam and by its propaganda efforts to sway Cubans to its side in the Sino-Soviet conflict. Castro's insistence on absolute control of the revolutionary movement in Latin America and his awareness of China's limitations in supplying Cuba's economic need were further key factors in the cooling of the friendship between the two nations. More recently relations have remained cordial, but have not reached the closeness achieved before 1966.

The principal area of Soviet-Cuban conflict was Castro's revolutionary ventures in Latin America. In 1963 Castro embarked on major attempts to subvert and overthrow the Venezuelan government. Cuban personnel, as well as aid and money, went to finance the campaign of urban terrorism that Venezuela suffered in the subsequent years. With its vast coastline and its position as the gateway to South America, Venezuela was, from Cuba's point of view, an ideal target for the continental revolution. Venezuela's vast reserves of petroleum would solve the problems faced by an oil-poor Cuba dependent on the distant and unreliable Soviets for its oil needs. That the Venezuelan oil bonanza would fall into

Communist hands and away from the United States was a pleasing prospect for Castro and perhaps for the Soviets too. The overthrow of the leftist João Goulart regime in Brazil in 1964 and the defeat of Salvador Allende, the Popular Front candidate in the 1964 Chilean elections, weakened the Soviet's "peaceful road" to power policy toward Latin America and reinforced Castro's position that violence was the best tactic.

Despite a short period of harmonious Soviet-Cuban relations following Khrushchev's ouster, differences again arose, this time directly involving the communist parties of Latin America. Castro quarreled bitterly with the leadership of these parties for not supporting guerrilla movements and denounced the Kremlin for seeking to establish diplomatic and commercial relations with "reactionary" regimes hostile to the Cuban revolution. Castro proclaimed that the duty of every revolutionary was to make revolution and rejected the communist doctrine that the Communist Party should play the "leading role" in the national liberation struggle. In a small book entitled *Revolution within the Revolution?* by Regis Debray, the young French Marxist, Castro's new line was elaborated. Not only are communist theory and leadership—which insists on the guiding role of the party and diminishes the possibility of struggle in the countryside—a hindrance to the liberation movement, but parties and ideology are unnecessary in the initial states of the struggle. Debray explains that the decisive contribution of Castroism to the international revolutionary experience is that "under certain conditions the political and the military are not separate but form one organic whole, consisting of the people's army, where the nucleus is the guerrilla army. The vanguard party can exist in the form of the guerrilla *foco* itself. The guerrilla force is the party in embryo." At the Tricontinental Conference in Havana (1966), attended by revolutionary leaders throughout the world, Castro insisted on his independent line, seeking to gain the undisputed leadership of a continent-wide guerrilla struggle and offering to provide the institutional means to promote his line.

His attempts at revolution all ended in disaster, however. The Venezuelan venture proved a real fiasco, with the majority of the Venezuelan people rejecting Cuba's interference in their internal affairs. The other major effort, led by Che Guevara to open a guerrilla front in Bolivia, ended in his capture and death in 1967. Neither another Cuba nor "many Vietnams," as Castro had prophesied earlier, erupted in Latin America.

Castro's failures in the area weakened his leverage with the Soviets, increased Soviet influence within Cuba, and forced Castro to look inward to improve his faltering economy. By the late 1960s the Cuban economy was plagued by low productivity, mismanagement, poor planning, and shortages of almost every item. Structural shortcomings seemed more entrenched than ever. The ills of the past were still there, with renewed vengeance. Long-term trade agreements with the Soviets were perpetuating Cuba's role as sugar producer, forcing her to abandon indefinitely any plans for significant diversification and industrialization. Trade continued with one large industrialized nation whose commercial policies reminded Castro of those pursued by its previous trading partner. Cuba's foreign debt also reached alarming proportions without significant improvements in the island's ability to save foreign exchange. The unemployment of the pre-Castro era gave way to a new type of unemployment in the form of poor labor productivity, absenteeism, and ineffective and overstaffed bureaucracy. The regime resorted to coercive methods to ensure a labor supply for critical agricultural tasks. The living standard deteriorated, perhaps more rapidly in urban areas, as high capital accumulation was given first priority over consumer goods.

PACO IGNACIO TAIBO II

Ernesto "Che" Guevara

THE YACHT SAILED DOWNSTREAM, crossing the river mouth in half an hour, riding well below her waterline, with her stern low and the men huddled, crouching, on the deck.

Fidel Castro, speaking years later:

We had tested the *Granma* in still waters and what's more, with just a few crew members. Nobody knew enough to realize that if eighty-two men got onto the boat, weighing a few tons between them, plus weapons, water, fuel, food . . . then it would slow the boat down considerably. It didn't just slow down, it nearly

PACO IGNACIO TAIBO II *was born in Spain, but lives in Mexico City. This piece was excerpted from his 1999 biography of popular Cuban revolutionary, Che Guevara,* Guevara, Also Known As Che. *Other work includes* The Shadow of the Shadow *and* Leonardo's Bicycle.

sank. . . . It was a nutshell bouncing around in the Gulf of Mexico.

That was not the expedition's only problem. Despite all the safety measures and precautions taken, a mysterious and still unknown stool pigeon in the July 26 Movement network was able to transmit a first report which, although vague, managed to put the dictatorship's troops on alert. The message that arrived at the Cuban army high command said: "Boat sailed today with plenty staff and arms from Mexican port."

The voyage had only just begun, but Dr. Guevara already had work on his hands.

We began a frantic search for antihistamines to treat seasickness, but none were to be found. About five minutes after the Cuban national and July 26 Movement anthems were sung, the boat assumed a ridiculously tragic appearance. Men with anxious faces were grabbing their stomachs. Some stuck their heads in buckets and others flopped down in the strangest positions, immovable and with their clothes vomit-stained. Apart from two or three sailors and four or five others, all eighty-two aboard were seasick.

Near daybreak, the decision was made to leave Mexican territorial waters as soon as possible to avoid the coast guard. The helmsman set an eastward course, which was difficult to hold because of the hurricane that was blowing.

It was cloudy at dawn on November 26, and rainfall had soaked the yacht's crammed decks. The boat was making 7.2

knots instead of the expected ten, As evening fell, hunger was becoming more of a problem than seasickness, and the orange sacks on the poop deck were opened. Guevara urged the sickest to drink some liquids, at least. He himself was in a bad way, suffering from a severe asthma attack. Jesús Montané commented: "The expedition had to set off in a hurry . . . and Che wasn't able to gather the medicine he needed to ward off his asthma attacks. . . . We were all struck by the stoicism and self-sacrifice with which he bore his suffering. No one heard a single complaint from him. It was only because comrade Faustino Pérez had had the foresight to take some adrenaline ampules with him that Che could alleviate some of the violent attacks."

The expeditionaries were uncertain about where they were going. They were skirting the Yucatán Peninsula, some forty miles from the coast, so as to avoid the Mexican authorities. René Rodríguez, who was there as cameraman, "but with neither camera nor film, because we didn't have any money to buy any," thought the closest part of the Cuban coast was at Pinar del Río, and several others seemed to go along with him.

Fidel took advantage of the relatively calm weather to adjust the rifles, telescopic sights and to test the machine guns. "No one would stick their head out on the port side—a target had been placed on that side on the bow, and they were firing at it from the poop deck." In the middle of the test firing, the group leader suggested aiming at some dolphins swimming near the boat. Chaos ensued. Efigenio Ameijeiras, the former Havana taxi driver, who was trying out his

Thompson machine gun, recalled: "I was one of those who argued that they shouldn't fire, because the sailors were saying it was bad luck."

On November 27, the third day of the journey, while *Granma* was north of the Yucatán, Norberto Collado, one of the helmsmen, realized that "there were just a few sacks of oranges in the hold, a few dozen hardboiled eggs that barely stretched to one meal, one half-rotten ham, and two tins of ship's biscuit." Part of the food had been left ashore in the hurry to leave. Fortunately, seasickness had wreaked such havoc with the invaders' stomachs that the lack of food was not noticed for the first few days. Fidel imposed rationing when he discovered how critical the situation was.

To make matters worse, engineer Chuchú Reyes, although very proud of the twin diesel engines, to which he had devoted much time and care, found that the clutch was slipping on one of them and that the engine speed could not be increased. Only by keeping the *Granma* at half speed could they avoid burning the engine out. On top of this, one of the hoses from the fuel injection pumps had split, the boat was mysteriously taking on water, and the bailer was not working properly.

That day, under an overcast sky with shafts of sunlight peeping through the clouds and no bursts of rain, the *Granma*, Fidel's "nutshell," overloaded and with its speed cut by 30 percent, headed on a new course, away from Cape Catoche at the end of the Yucatán Peninsula and much farther south of Cape San Antonio in Cuba. The expedition never managed the hoped-for ten knots, sailing at seven and a half knots an hour at best.

"Requested work sold out. Disclosure Publishers," the first telegram said. "Urgently need send college diploma. Love, Bertha," said the second. We will never know what the third one said, because its recipient, Aldo Santamaría, had to eat it when he was picked tip by the Havana police several days later. The telegrams had been sent from Mexico to alert the July 26 Movement network in Santiago, Havana, and Santa Clara that the expedition was at sea so that, as planned, the urban uprising could coincide with the landing. But just when was the *Granma* going to reach Cuba's Oriente province, given the delays caused by the storms, overloading, and engine failure?

Meanwhile, some expeditionaries, seasick and overcrowded, thought only of survival. Chuchú Reyes, the engineer, recalled: "Some comrades spent three days huddled in a corner without moving."

Guillén Zelaya, a young Mexican who had joined up with the expedition, remembered that the Argentine doctor continued to suffer from asthma attacks. Years later, an American journalist picked up the story that after a particularly terrible attack Guevara was given up for dead, that someone told Fidel as much, and that the latter answered: "If he's dead, throw him overboard,"

On Wednesday, November 28, the boat was still taking on water, but the general outlook brightened up a little. *We discovered that the water pipe on the boat was no such thing, but an open valve leading from the toilets.* Two other versions were to crop up over time. According to Chuchú Reyes: "One of the toilets was blocked by the comrades being sick all the time; it overloaded, the flap through which it flushed was jammed open, and seawater began to enter the toilet, too." Fidel's version was this: "We were desperately bailing out, but the problem was quite simple, we found out later. The boards that were normally above water were less watertight [than those normally below] and at first began to leak, but as the boat sank under the weight and they got wet, they expanded and thus plugged their own gaps." Whatever had happened, the fact is that the men had spent the three previous days bailing the boat out in shifts.

On November 29, the fifth day at sea, the boat drew away from Mexico and the west of Cuba to steer a course toward the Cayman Islands, *to the south of Cuba, skirting Jamaica.* Some fishing boats appeared in the distance, and Fidel ordered the decks to be cleared, readied for combat, as weapons were raised from below. It turned out to be a false alarm, however.

What the expeditionaries on board the *Granma* could not have known was that the Batista dictatorship was mobilizing forces all over the island, and the air force was under orders to search for suspicious-looking boats in coastal waters; also, the U.S. Navy, without apparent reason, was gathering forces in Santiago de Cuba, where a submarine, several destroyers, a frigate, and an escort ship had anchored.

The next day Friday, November 30, the boat's radio began to pick up alarming news. An uprising had broken out in Santiago, and there was fighting in the streets. There were sporadic shoot-outs and acts of sabotage in other Cuban cities, but it was in Santiago where the uprising seemed most extensive. There were reports of fighting in the police station and at the maritime police headquarters, and of snipers on the city's rooftops.

On board the *Granma* there was a feeling of anguish, of being out of it, stranded in the Gulf of Mexico while their comrades were fighting. The uncertainty, the delay, were like a dark pall drawing over the invaders. Then, as the hours went by, reports seemed to confirm that the affray was dying down and the rebels were being beaten.

Fidel and the pilots discussed a change of plan: instead of trying to land near the port of Niquero, which by now would be under close military surveillance, they would try to approach a beach called Las Coloradas, to the southeast of the original spot. From there they would travel by truck to attack some nearby towns and then head for the Sierra Maestra.

By December 1, Batista's army's sources had managed to confirm (doubtless thanks to their informant in Mexico) where the revolutionaries intended to land, and sent the following communiqué to the navy' and air force:

> Begin search by Air Force planes, white yacht 65 ft., chain running almost whole length boat, nameless, Mexican flag, sailed Tuxpan, Veracruz state, Mexico, 25 November. Estimated heading Oriente province. Report results CEN. General Rodríguez Avila.

After circulating the same wire dozens of times, they happened to correct it: for "chain" read "cabin."

Meanwhile, on board the boat, according to Haul Castro's diary: "a cigarette butt was priceless." *In the night, we set a head-on course for Cuba, desperately looking for the Cabo Cruz lighthouse, lacking water, oil, and food.* There were only ten fourteen-gallon drums of fuel left, the *Granma* was taking on "a lot of water," and, *at two in the morning, with a storm blowing, the situation was worrying. Lookouts took turns peering into the darkness for a shaft of light on the horizon, which never appeared. Roque climbed the little lookout post, to the see the light from the cape, but lost his footing and fell in the water.*

A frantic search began in the dark, which lasted for hours. They turned in wider and wider circles, failing to locate the comrade among the high waves in the choppy sea. Fidel insisted and ordered the boat to turn back. It was a moonless night.

Leonardo Roque had spent an hour on his own in the middle of the sea, thinking of his mother and father and how nice it would have been to die some other way than by drowning, for instance in a real revolution, when the yacht appeared in front of him and he heard Fidel shouting for him. After a thousand and one mishaps, they managed to fish him out of the rough water, and the two doctors, Che Guevara and Faustino Pérez, gave him artificial respiration.

Just after we set off again, we could see the light, but the boat's erratic progress made the journey's final hours seem endless. At dawn on Sunday, December 2, after 172 hours at sea, a journey of more than seven days instead of the planned three, the expeditionaries could see the outline of something that looked like day land.

Fidel asked one of the pilots, Onelio Pinto: "Is that the Cuban mainland? Are you absolutely sure we're not in Jamaica or some key?"

"Yes."

"Then let's have the motors full steam ahead and let's head as fast as we can to the nearest coastline,"

They did not get very far, as the boat ran aground on a mud flat that they figured was some two-thousand yards from shore. Visibility was only fifty yards, and they could just make out the contours of land masses with sparse vegetation.

The day was warm, seventy degrees.

A short while later, they would know they had landed in front of a mangrove swamp, at a place called Belic, a mile and a half from their intended destination at the Las Coloradas beach. . . .

In the early hours of January 1, 1958—at 3:15 A.M., to be precise—four Aerovías Q civilian aircraft took off from the Columbia military base on the outskirts of Havana. Before climbing into the first one, Fulgencio Batista told General Eulogio Cantillo he was putting him in charge of the country, the business, the whole kit and caboodle. Then he vanished into the skies. Batista was off to exile in Miami, although his entourage changed its flight plan on the wing and instead landed in Santo Domingo, home to that other blood-thirsty dictator, Leónidas Trujillo. The Havana newspapers carried an Associated Press wire report that "government troops, with tank and air support, have routed rebel troops in the outskirts of Santa Clara and thrown them back toward the east of Las Villas Province."

Day had yet to break in Santa Clara; the guards in No. 31 Squadron headquarters had stopped shooting. Víctor Dreke cautiously drew near. A white flag was waving from a window. Rolando Cubela, back with the troops after a lightning visit to the hospital, had just received a brief note from Che: *Rolando. Demand unconditional surrender. I will support you with the necessary forces. Greetings. Che.* No. 31 Squadron now surrendered. A rumor that Batista had fled made the rounds of the soldiers who had given themselves up. The rebels looked at each other in amazement. Was it all over? Captain Millán, in charge of the troops who had surrendered, was granted permission by the Directorio to use a microwave relay to contact the Leoncio Vidal barracks; the officer in charge there answered him with insults. The civilians came out onto the streets and, overjoyed, looked at the defeated soldiers in front of the barracks, which was pockmarked by hundreds of bullet holes. The prisoners were taken to Che at the rebel command headquarters.

The Grand Hotel was also about to fall. The snipers cut off on the tenth floor had had to drink coffee from ashtrays and had looted the bar. Captain Alfonso Zayas posted a tank in front of the hotel and shot the windows to pieces. Lieutenant Alberto Fernández's troops attacked and the snipers surrendered. The dozen policemen, stool pigeons, and torturers came out with their hands up and were showered with insults.

Only the Leoncio Vidal barracks was left. Colonel Cándido Hernández had taken charge there, replacing the runaways Casillas Lumpuy and Fernández Suero. Lieutenant Hugo del Rio contacted the regiment from a radio in a patrol car captured from the police headquarters, and the officer who answered requested a truce. Del Rio answered that only Che could grant the request but agreed to look for him to inform him of it. He found Che in the command headquarters in a meeting with the geographer, Antonio Núñez Jiménez, and Dr. Adolfo Rodríguez de la Vega. He and Che went to the patrol car and contacted the regiment by radio again. Che agreed to send Núñez Jiménez and Rodríquez de la Vega to talk with Colonel Hernández. Shortly afterward the latter requested an indefinite truce, to which the emissaries replied that the only available option was unconditional surrender. Colonel Hernández, arguing that his brother and his son had already lost their lives in the fighting, that he had done more than enough to serve his country, handed over the command and the decision to his next in line, a Commander Fernández and his superior officers. Fernández then insisted on speaking with Che.

Just as the negotiations were about to begin, a broadcast by General Cantillo, speaking from the high command headquarters in Havana was received at the Leoncio Vidal barracks.

The news was very contradictory and extraordinary. Batista had fled the country that day, and the armed forces command came tumbling down. Our two delegates established radio contact with Cantillo, advising him of the offer to surrender, but he reckoned it was not possible to accept as it constituted an ultimatum and that he had occupied the army command under the strict orders of its loader Fidel Castro.

Hernández asked Núñez and Rodríguez to talk to Cantillo, who offered them a truce. They repeated that there could be only unconditional surrender. Cantillo tried to trick them, saying he had nominated a provisional government under Fidel Castro's orders and that under such conditions he could not hand over the barracks. The conversation ended amid insults.

A few hours earlier, at 7:30 A.M. at the main quarters in the America sugar mill, Fidel Castro went to the door to drink a cup of coffee, cursing the irresponsible rebels for wasting ammunition by shooting into the air to celebrate the new year. The surprising news of Batista's flight, picked up by Radio Rebelde, made Fidel angry; the dictator had escaped and the event smelled like a coup d'état. He began to gather his captains together to march on Santiago.

The news was confirmed. Supreme Court judge Carlos Piedra was now president. Cantillo, who had been conspiring with the aid of the U.S. embassy to find an easy way out of the revolution, was army chief.

Fidel set a piece of paper on a wardrobe and wrote: "Revolution, yes, military coup, no," Then he wrote a call for a general strike. He took a jeep to the Radio Rebelde station to record the message. It was on the air by ten A.M. and was later relayed by dozens of radio stations across the country and in Latin America.

Che heard Fidel's message at about the same time as he received the latest information from the besieged barracks.

We got in touch with Fidel immediately, giving him the news but telling him our opinion of Cantillo's attitude, which was just what he thought, too. To create a military junta would just waste the revolution by forcing it to negotiate with the remains of the dictatorship.

Commander Hernández insisted on speaking to Che. Núñez and Rodríguez went with him. Che was very sharp with the regiment's new commander. He reportedly said:

Look, Commander, my men have already discussed this matter with the high command. It's either unconditional surrender or fire, but real fire, and with no quarter. The city is already in our hands. At 12:30 I will give the order to resume the attack using all our forces. We will take the barracks at all costs. You will be responsible for the bloodshed. Furthermore, you must be aware of the possibility that the U.S. government will intervene militarily in Cuba; if that happens, it will be even more of a crime as you will be supporting a foreign invader. In that event, the only option will be to give you a pistol to commit suicide, as you'll be guilty of treason to Cuba.

Commander Hernández went back to talk matters over with his officers. Soldiers were already deserting their posts and fraternizing with the rebels. The military hesitated. With a few minutes left before the appointed time and with the rebel rifles primed and ready to fire, they agreed to a negotiated surrender: they could leave the barracks unarmed and be sent to Havana via Caibarién. Those who had committed violence against the population would be excluded from the agreement.

As the negotiations proceeded outside the barracks, and with ten minutes left before firing would resume, the soldiers began to throw their weapons down of their own accord and walk unarmed over to the rebel lines. It was 12:20 P.M. on January 1, 1959. With the fall of the Leoncio Vidal barracks, the battle for Santa Clara was over. The rebel forces took the airfield without firing a shot.

Photographs show the townspeople of Santa Clara looking in amazement at the smashed-up boxcars and the mass of twisted iron that are the wreckage of the armored train; the victorious rebels in front of immobile tanks; the bearded young rebels, the *barbudos*, in front of the pockmarked barracks, now in silence; groups of Batista's disarmed soldiers around a young rebel who is lecturing them; Che giving instructions beside a tank, holding his injured left arm up with his right. Below the beret with the metal crossed-swords badge on it, his eyes are glassy with fatigue; a cigar hangs loosely from his lips, and he's cracking a smile.

Fidel urged the final attack in a quick succession of communiqués over Radio Rebelde that demanded the surrender of the Santiago garrison and ordered Che and Camilo Cicafuegos to advance on Havana. Che was to take the La Cabana fortress and Camilo Batista's stronghold at Columbia. Visor Mora's column was ordered to take the cities of Guantánamo, Holguín, and Victoria de las Tunas. The general strike in Santiago was called for three P.M.

Entique Oltuski, the July 26 Movement regional coordinator, who had been frantically traveling, with one mishap after another, as to bring a message to Che from Fidel, arrived at Santa Clara in the midst of street parties. He found Che in the operations room at the public Works Building:

> Che was standing behind a large bureau, opposite me. He had one arm in a cast and a sling made from a black rag. We briefly exchanged greetings. He waved at me to wait while he gave instructions to a rebel who, too young for a beard, had let his hair grow.
>
> The room was small and completely closed in. I began to feel hot. Then I could smell the clinging odor of Che's body. The time went by very slowly. I took Fidel's message out of the lining of my pants; it was the order to advance on Havana. Finally, the rebel left and I handed the paper over to Che.
>
> When he'd finished reading it, he turned to the window and looked outside:
> *Yes, I already knew. We'll set off in a few hours.*
> "But how?
> *We managed to establish radio contact with Fidel.*
> I felt enormously frustrated.
> *He has already designated a civil governor of the province.* He was referring to a man from his column (Captain Calixto Morales), but at the heart of the matter was the political mistrust in which Che held us, the representatives from the Plains.

In Havana, meanwhile, as soon as the news broke

that Batista had fled the country, students began to gather at the university, and M-26 banners were unfurled on the university hill. The population crowded the streets. There was looting in the Biltmore and the Sevilla Plaza hotels and the casinos. M-26 militias took over newspapers sympathetic to Batista. The police machine-gunned the boroughs; political prisoners in the Príncipe prison were freed. The Resistencia Cívica group took over the CMQ radio station. In the midst of the turmoil, urban M-26 and Front II cadres began to fill a very precarious power vacuum, as there were still thousands of Batista's soldiers in the barracks who might rush in to set up a military dictatorship. The police abandoned various stations, and only a few precincts fired in response to the growing crowds on the streets.

At two P.M. U.S. ambassador Earl T. Smith, accompanied by the rest of the diplomatic corps, met with Cantillo (not with president Piedra; they were under no illusions about where power really lay). The United States was looking for a way, with the departure of the dictatorship, that would avoid backing Fidel and the M-26 but would also exclude forces loyal to Batista and keep up the appearance of neutrality." The takeover sector was the "good military" group, headed by Colonel Ramón Barquín and Borbonet, who had conspired to overthrow Batista. They were in jail, but Cantillo gave way to U.S. pressure and at seven P.M., released the officers from Pinos Island, along with M-26 leader Armando Hart.

The people were out on the streets. Street parties were engulfing Santa Clara with cheering and shouts, and the rebels were the crowds' booty. Singing and dancing were the order of the day in the liberated city, but there were also demands that captured torturers be sent to the firing squad.

Oltuski also recalled:

> The news that the dictatorship's army had surrendered spread throughout the city and thousands closed in upon the building where we were. They knew that Che was there and no one wanted to miss the opportunity to meet him. We had to put guards at the entrance to keep from being overwhelmed by the mass of humanity.
>
> On the floor above was an improvised prison for war criminals from the forces of repression who, one by one, were being uncovered and caught by the people.

The sources contradict each other concerning names and numbers, but there is no doubt that in the hours following the liberation of Santa Clara, Che signed death warrants for several of Batista's policemen whom the people accused of being torturers and rapists, beginning with detainees who had acted as snipers in the Grand Hotel, including Casillas Lumpuy, who was captured by Victor Bordón's men while attempting to leave town. *I did no more and no less than the situation demanded—i.e., the death sentence for those twelve murderers, because they had committed crimes against the people, not against us.* As it happened, Casillas was not executed but died in a struggle with one of the guards taking him to the firing squad. The photo of Casillas in a short-sleeved checked shirt, trying to take a rifle from the soldier guarding him, was to go around the world. Police chief Cornelio Rojas, who had been arrested in Caibarién while attempting to escape, was shot a couple of days later.

Whereas Che's and the Directory's fighters kept a tight grip on weapons and the situation on the street in Santa Clara, the crowds in Havana were exacting a long-delayed justice. A sort of reasoned and selective vandalism took hold of the crowds, who attacked the gas stations belonging to Shell, which was said to have collaborated with Batista by giving him tanks. They also destroyed the casinos belonging to the American mafia and the Batista underworld, trashed parking meters—one of the régime's scams—and attacked houses belonging to leading figures in the dictatorship. (They threw Mujal's air-conditioning unit out the window.) There was no control by the repressive apparatus of the dictatorship, which was falling apart by the second with the massive exodus of Batista's cadres; neither Cantillo nor Barquín could fill the resulting power vacuum, because the revolutionary forces refused to enter into negotiations. Television studios were taken over, and witnesses gave spontaneous testimony to the horrors of the now-ended Batista régime.

The surrender of Santiago was agreed to at nine P.M. Fidel entered the capital of Oriente province; Judge Manuel Urrutia swore him in as president; and he announced his march on Havana and reiterated his call for a revolutionary strike. Radio Rebelde declared a liquor ban in the occupied cities.

Che began to regroup the separate platoons in his column

in Santa Clara. Victor Bordón's and Bamiro Valdés's forces were called up. Cars with loudspeakers cruised the streets, calling the rebels to rejoin the column. Che found out that some fighters were taking cars abandoned in the streets by escaped Batista supporters; he angrily ordered the keys to be handed over. *They were not going to ruin in one second what the Rebel Army had maintained as a standard: respect for others. They were going to Havana—by truck, bus, on foot, but it was the same for everyone.* He really chewed out Rogelio Acevedo, who was still a teenager and had requisitioned a '58 Chrysler.

During this time, Che received a communiqué from Eloy Gutiérrez Menoyo, placing the Front II forces at his disposal. *There was no problem. We then gave them instructions to wait as we had to settle civilian affairs in the first major city to be conquered.* A fighter named Mustelier asked Che to grant him leave to go and see his family in Oriente province; the commander tersely told him no.

"But, Che, we've already won the revolution."

No, we've won the war. The revolution begins now.

The Doñas, a Girl's Memory

V*IVA LA REVOLUCIÓN!* Those words droned in my ears like the buzz of angry bees whose hive has been disturbed, like a twisting tornado, its long black tail just ready to touch the ground. Though I was very young when the Cuban revolution began in 1956, it has had a lasting impact on my life. Four decades later, I still freeze when I hear the sounds of a helicopter. The deafening noise of the engine, the thwack of the blades evoke images of terror I can't control, even today. *That sound! They're coming back!* In an instant, I am a small child covering her ears to shut out the terrifying noise. My stomach forms knots thick as a rope, my eyes search for a place to hide . . . my heart pounds against the walls of

FLOR FERNANDEZ BARRIOS's *1999 book* Blessed by Thunder *vividly portrays the reality of growing up in Cuba during the early days of Fidel Castro's leadership. Beginning as a journal, Barrios's heart rending tale successfully captures the joy and pain of her Cuban girlhood.*

my chest and I begin to sweat. My legs shake so hard I feel any minute I may drop to the floor and be swallowed up by my terror.

My early childhood unfolded in the swirling storm of political change. The nation was weary of money-hungry politicians and their broken promises. All around me, revolutionaries dreamed of creating a new Cuba free of dictators. I was a year old in December 1956, when Fidel Castro and his brother, Raúl Castro, along with Ernesto "Che" Guevara and seventy-nine other revolutionaries disembarked from the cruiser *Granma* in the province of Oriente to start a revolution.

Most of these guerrillas were soon killed by government forces. The group that survived escaped to the mountains and established a base in the Sierra Maestra. From there, they launched a campaign of insurrection against Fulgencio Batista, the dictator who had controlled Cuba since the 1930s. Radio Rebelde was inaugurated, from which Fidel spoke to listeners all over the country. From his distant and isolated territory, Fidel, a charismatic leader, was able to move people deeply with his speeches of hope and promises of changes that would transform our island for the betterment of all.

I can still recall snippets of intense conversation that floated around me like soap bubbles when I was three and four years old. Fidel Castro was going to help poor children and their families. He was going to let black people go to all the places where the whites went. Fidel had his two best friends helping him—Ernesto or El Che, and Camilo Cienfuegos. The tension in the air was no less than if a hurricane were about to hit the island.

At that time, Fulgencio Batista was widely despised—even the wealthy wanted him out. But many people felt uncertain about Castro and his band of revolutionaries. Like my father. He said Castro made too many promises. Our neighborhood was equally divided in its opinions. During the evening domino games, loud arguments could be heard from the street. Occasionally these heated discussions were interrupted by Radio Rebelde, with a special broadcast of Fidel Castro direct from the Sierra Maestra. All activities would immediately stop, and even the children would gather around the radio to listen to Castro's speech.

Toward the end of 1958, the winds of this so-called hurricane gathered intensity, and the domino games were stopped by frequent blackouts that left the town in darkness for hours. I overheard the adults say that the blackouts were the work of Castro's men so that they could pick up food supplies and weapons from their allies.

During one of those long nights, my father was almost shot by the Batista militia. As my father told the story, he was walking home around 9:00 P.M. after a game of dominos, when the lights went out. Aware of the danger, he began to hurry, but as he turned a corner, a soldier shot at him. Father ran toward a tall brick wall that surrounded an old convent, and with the swiftness of a cat, jumped over to the other side, landing on the tall grass of an unkempt garden.

Unfortunately, two soldiers posted along the tall columns of the building went after my father and captured him. Father was accused of being one of Castro's allies and was sent to jail, where he was interrogated. I was not quite four years old at the time, but my memory of the night remains vivid. Mother and a group of neighbors went from door to door, asking if anyone had seen my father. These conversations were conducted in hushed tones. My mother was thinking the worst. During those times, it was not unusual to find people dead on some abandoned road or on the outskirts of town.

Mother tried very hard to keep calm, and she reassured me that "Papi was coming home soon," but I knew something very serious had happened. Then I heard Uncle Manolo say, "If Pepe is dead we should find him soon, but if he is in jail we might not get any information for awhile. They'll torture him, especially if they think he's involved with the revolutionaries." I was terrified. I couldn't imagine my Papi dead, alone somewhere. *Papi . . . Papi, come home soon.*

Two days later, a pair of well-armed Batista officers appeared at our door. They brushed us aside and began searching the house. I was so frightened by their rudeness that I moved into a corner of the playroom and hid behind an old brown leather chair. From my hiding place I could hear things being thrown on the floor, drawers and doors being opened and then slammed. I could hear Mother's voice asking, "What are you doing? Tell me what you're looking for! Where is Pepe?" She had Jose, my two-year-old brother, in her arms as she followed them around the house. There were no answers.

The soldiers poked into our things till they had searched every room and every corner of the house. Finally, I heard them say to my mother, "Listen, lady, if you have any guns in the house, you better tell us now. Your husband is in jail under suspicion of involvement with those rebels in the mountains." Mother cried, "Oh, thank God, he is alive! Look, I don't know who you are, but my husband is no revolutionary, and we have no guns in our house."

When the soldiers finally left, I ventured out of my hiding place. The house looked as if a tornado had upended it. The contents of our closets, cabinets, and night tables had been emptied out on the floor.

Mattresses had been pulled from the bedframes, pillows were cut open and their stuffing strewn all over the bedroom. I walked around, picking up some of my toys, and found my mother standing in the middle of the living room. She held Jose in her arms wearily as she cried, "Teresa, come here, my baby, your father is going to be home soon. Come . . . come, my baby, don't be scared!"

Father came back home that same day. He was pale, with dark circles under his eyes. The white shirt he wore was torn and stained with brown dirt and blood, probably from his bottom lip, which was swollen and purple. The right side of his face was badly scratched. He hugged and kissed Mami and then lifted Jose with one arm and came toward me. Kneeling on the floor, he put his other arm around my shoulders, holding the two of us close to him. He wept. I'd never seen my father cry.

"I thought I'd never see you again, my little children, *pequeños de mi corazón.*"

After my father's disappearance, I was constantly worried about my parents. I didn't want to leave their sides.

Any time they went out of the house, I feared they would be killed. I began having stomachaches and developed chronic constipation from my anxiety.

For weeks my mother had to give me painful enemas. The minute I saw her coming toward me in the morning with that horrible red rubber bag, I ran and hid under my bed. Mother would beg me to come out: "This is for your own good, Teresa. You're constipated, and this will make you feel better. Come on, don't be scared. It won't hurt as much this time," Lies! I knew it was going to hurt—the terrible cramps doubled me over and sometimes left me crawling the bathroom floor. The ordeal would last for almost an hour, leaving me exhausted and limp. I hated that red bag, much as I came to hate Fidel Castro and his red communist insignia years later.

During the next few months, as the revolution moved closer to our town, new fears were added to my world. One morning, we were awakened by the staccato of machine-gun fire. My mother came rushing into my bedroom, holding Jose in her arms.

"Come, Teresa . . . come, get down on the floor!" Her voice sounded harsh and shaken. Mami pulled me down with her and Jose and covered both of us with her body. Jose was screaming, terrified by the noise of the gunfire. I curled up and held my breath, thinking if I remained quiet, a stray bullet wouldn't find us.

The shooting went on and on. Then, everything was silent, the only sound a fly buzzing somewhere in the room. We were all still trembling but Mother got up and turned the radio on: Batista's army and Castro's revolutionaries had skirmished. We were regaining our composure when a loud siren sounded down the street. Jose ran and hid behind my mother.

"Felicia, Felicia!" A neighbor called my mother from the street.

"*¿Qué pasa?*" my mother asked, walking to the door.

"Felicia . . . Miguelito was killed on his way to work just around the corner from here."

"*¡Oh, por Dios, qué desgracia!*" My mother put her hands to her head. Miguelito was the son of Carmela, my mother's best friend.

From that morning on, I became very familiar with the refrains of "so and so was killed" and "so and so is in jail." Terror hung thick in the air. It became the monster under my bed, sneaking out at night and chasing me in my nightmares. Death invaded the fragile world of my childhood games as my dolls got "shot" and were rushed to the hospital.

One afternoon, Jose and I were playing with his wooden blocks in the living room when, again, we heard the sound of helicopters followed by machine-gun fire. We automatically stopped our games and Jose crawled toward me, seeking the protection of my arms. The shooting continued. Through the large window that faced the street, we could see people running in all directions, seeking refuge wherever they could. I saw one woman hide with her young child under a milk truck. Bullets hit the asphalt, the trees, the trash cans in front of the houses. Suddenly, there was a break in the fire. The streets became silent, so silent one could almost hear the pounding hearts of those hiding.

The sound of a motorcycle and then an explosion

unexpectedly broke the silence. Our whole house shook. At first, I thought we had been hit by a bomb. But out the window, I saw a ball of flame racing down the street and then drop to the ground. After a few moments, I realized in horror that the burning mass was the body of the motorcyclist being consumed by fire.

Pieces of the motorcycle were scattered all over the street. The pungent smell of burned rubber and of incinerated flesh filled our nostrils. The woman who was hiding under the milk truck dragged herself out and ran to the scene. Her young child, left behind, began to scream. The woman didn't look back. She took off her skirt and tried to stop the fire from destroying whatever was left of the motorcyclist. A neighbor from across the street came outside with a big white blanket to cover the remains.

My view was blocked by the neighbors as they formed a circle around the dead man. But it didn't matter. The image of the scorched body was forever fixed in my mind. Jose, poor Jose, he was still holding on to me, his little arms wrapped around my body so tight I could hardly breathe. I pulled him closer. I don't remember if we cried. With our eyes closed, we stayed entwined and rocked each other back and forth. After that, every time we heard a helicopter we ran and ducked under our beds.

On the morning of January 1, 1959, revolutionaries under the command of Che Guevara invaded Santa Clara, the province where we lived. According to my father, we never went to bed that New Year's Eve. Our traditional family dancing and *arroz con pollo* dinner were interrupted by a bulletin on the radio. The voice vibrated with excitement as it informed us that General Fulgencio Batista had deserted and left the country.

Glasses of wine went up in the air, toasting the long-anticipated freedom from Batista's rule. Family and friends gathered around the television to watch images of an island in a state of euphoria over the victory of the revolutionaries: People were out in the streets celebrating, waving Cuban flags and posters of Fidel Castro, Che Guevara, and Camilo Cienfuegos, singing the national anthem and shouting, "¡Viva la Revolución!"

As I grew older, I heard the details of that day from my mother. Her recollection always begins: "Neighbors were coming and going from one house to the other, drinking coffee and talking about how many Cubans who didn't like Castro were rushing to the airports with the hope of getting to Miami." During one of the quiet breaks between visitors, Mother was in the kitchen while Father sat in the living room, glued to the radio. I was playing with my set of plastic army soldiers next to Papi when our next-door neighbor and friend, Nena, came rushing through the front door.

"Felicia! Innocent people are getting killed by the *milicianos*."

"What are you talking about?" my mother asked as she dried her hands on her apron.

"Right by the big wall at the entrance to the cemetery. They're killing all those who don't like Castro, anybody under suspicion for counterrevolutionary activities."

When describing this part, Mother never forgets to

mention how Nena's hands trembled as she held the tiny cup filled with coffee that Mother had handed to her friend.

"Oh, Felicia, you should have seen how those poor men were lined up, blindfolded and then sprayed with bullets from the machine guns of those criminals. Oh, my God!" Nena broke down in sobs. "The white wall turned red with their blood. I couldn't believe what my eyes were seeing."

Afraid for our safety, my mother and father decided it was best for us all to go and stay at my mother's parents' farm until things settled down in town. Without wasting any time, she packed a small suitcase with clothes and we started out on the eight-mile walk. "It is not safe to travel by car with all these crazy shootings," she said firmly. She thought the revolutionaries were targeting the "fugitives" driving to the airports to escape to the United States with their fortunes and families.

As we set out, Mother and Father took turns carrying Jose, while I held one of their hands. To me, our walk was an adventure at first, but as we reached the edge of town, the scenery changed. What had been a sugar cane plantation was now a cluster of still-smoldering ruins. A rain of dark gray ashes began to drift down on us and the air smelled of burned grass and cane juice. "There goes Luis's fortune. This year he won't need to worry about finding cutters; the fire took pretty good care of his plantation," Father said. We continued walking down the main road, occasionally meeting other people on their way to town who greeted us with "¡Viva la Revolución."

About a mile from my grandparents' farm, as we

approached an orange grove, I saw the bodies of two men, each hung from the long branch of a big *ateje* tree on the side of the road.

"Papi, look! Those men are swinging from the tree," I said, not quite understanding what I was seeing.

Both Father and Mother stopped and I realized something was very wrong. The men's faces were swollen and purple, their features twisted, their tongues hanging from their mouths. Each man's head was tilted somewhat to the side, the eyes wide open, looking up at the sky.

"Oh, God!" I heard my father say.

"Pepe, please let's go," Mother pleaded, and with her free hand she pulled me to her side. Father didn't respond but walked straight to the men.

"Poor souls," Father said, and he took his hat off.

One of the men wore gray twill pants and a shirt, with a wide leather belt around his waist that held a machete on the right side, the dress of a local farmer. His white straw hat had fallen to the ground. My father commented that the man was no older than forty. The other man was younger, maybe twenty. His white *guayabera* was stained with blood that was still dripping from his nose.

"Don't look, Teresa," I heard my mother say, but I couldn't pull my gaze away from the men. All I could see was their faces, the strange look in their eyes. I wondered if the men had children like Jose and me. My heart withered with the thought of a little child waiting for her Papi to come home, as I had waited for my father the night he was thrown in jail. Young as I was, I knew these men would never return home.

My father stood motionless beneath the men for a moment. Then he pulled his knife from his pocket and tried to reach the rope from which the older man was suspended, but it was too high. He looked around for something to step on but finally had to climb the wide trunk of the tree and crawl out on the big branch from which the men hung. Holding on to an upper branch with one hand and the knife with the other, he cut each rope and one by one, the bodies dropped to the earth, hitting the ground with a dull thud that still echoes in my ears.

"Mami . . . are they really dead?" I asked. It took her a few seconds to find her voice. "Yes, *mi hijita*, they are dead." I wanted to go and touch them, but my mother's arms held me fast.

Father kneeled down in front of the older man. He lifted his right hand and, with a slow and tender motion, closed the man's eyes. Then he did the same with the younger man. During the years that followed, I comforted myself with the thought that these men had been tucked in their deathbeds by my father, and that, perhaps, he had helped them not to be so afraid of whatever dark places lingered near the stars.

Father picked up his hat from the ground and walked back to where we were waiting. Silently, he reached out for my small hand, and we began the final mile to the farm. Behind us, the dead men were no longer hanging from the tree. Thanks to my father, they were at rest on the warm Cuban earth.

But to me, they are always there, hanging in the darkness of my nights. I can see their tongues, long and purple, and their eyes, wide open to the sky.

THE
CULTURE

LOUIS   A.   PÉREZ   JR.

Image and Identity

T HINGS NORTH AMERICAN arrived in Cuba in many forms, in ways that were always changing and hence serving as a source of further change. . . .

Air travel began in 1921, when Aeromarine Airways, Inc., inaugurated daily air service between Key West and Havana. In 1928 Pan American Airways scheduled daily flights from Key West to Camp Columbia Aviation Field. Havana thus became one of the first cities in the world to operate an international airport. Air service increased dramatically in the decades that followed. Pan American Airways, National, Brannif, Chicago and Southern, and Cubana Airlines scheduled hundreds of flights weekly

LOUIS A. PÉREZ JR. *is the J. Carlyle Sitterson Professor of History at the University of North Carolina at Chappel Hill. A recipient of a Guggenheim Award, he is also the author of* Cuba: Between Reform and Revolution. *This piece was excerpted from 1999's* On Becoming Cuban.

between Cuba and points north, including Miami, Tampa, New Orleans, Houston, New York, and Chicago.

Changes within the United States also enhanced the appeal of travel to Cuba. Postwar prosperity and economic growth had expanded the ranks of the middle class. The work week shortened and vacation time lengthened. More people had more disposable income and more leisure time for the pursuit of personal pleasure and entertainment. The 1920s were years of cultural transformation, shifting moral boundaries, and changing lifestyles. Change did not always come easily, of course. Popular tastes often outran official morality; in fact, at times it seemed that they were running in different directions. State legislatures had banned horse track betting during the 1910s, and tracks were eventually closed in New York, Louisiana, and California. The Volstead Act of 1919 ended the legal sale and distribution of alcoholic beverages.

It was precisely these activities, outlawed in the United States but available in Cuba, that gave tourism one of its defining characteristics. Travel in the 1920s shaped a larger narrative of choice and free will. Much of the North American fascination with Cuba then and thereafter was as a place to work through the contradictions of competing moral imperatives. This was Cuba as site of negotiations, as means and metaphor for liberty and license, independence and indulgence. What made this contact so decisive in Cuba was that as a result of their overwhelming presence, North Americans were able to establish as dominant discourse the concept of "Cuban" as a function of their needs, around which much of what subsequently developed as "Cuban" assumed form.

From the outset the Cuban tourist industry was driven by North American tastes and preferences. Under the circumstances it probably could not have been otherwise, for the principal impulse behind the development of tourism originated from among North Americans themselves. The travel market was obviously North American, around whose needs the tourist infrastructure developed its definitive characteristics.

Travel to Cuba began slowly and increased steadily, from nearly 33,000 visitors in 1914 to 36,000 in 1915 and 44,000 one year later, reaching spectacular levels in the decades that followed: from 56,000 in 1920 to 90,000 in 1928, to 178,000 in 1937. Between 1920 and 1940 more than two million U.S. tourists visited Cuba. Travel resumed after World War II and escalated in the 1950s: from 120,000 in 1946 to 194,000 in 1950, to a record 356,000 in 1957.

This travel included a visible high society: the rich and the famous, visitors whose presence conferred on Cuba the status of chic, glamour, and fashion. This was Cuba for the socially prominent and the smart set: trendsetters like Gloria Vanderbilt, Dwight Morrow, and Mayor Jimmy Walker; celebrities such as Charles Lindburgh, Amelia Earhart, Irving Berlin, and Will Rogers; film stars like William Powell, Norma Talmadge, Gloria Swanson, and Gary Cooper.

Tourism was not limited to the well-to-do and well-known personages, however. On the contrary, what made travel to Cuba noteworthy was its appeal to the mass market, the large number of middle- and working-class North Americans who found Cuba accessible and affordable. Havana became a popular site for conventions and trade meetings: the Brotherhood of Locomotive Engineers, Allied Traders of the Baking Industries, Alabama Press Association, Southeastern Laundrymen's Association, National Editorial Association, and Shriners were among the many U.S. organizations to meet there. And, of course, periodic inundations of sailors and marines on liberty filled the streets of Havana and Santiago de Cuba with a boisterous presence. "The day of our departure a great fleet of American destroyers landed:" Hart Crane wrote of his last day in Havana in 1926. "The streets immediately became torrents of uniforms."

Cuba offered an ideal vacation spot: a foreign country with Old World charm and a felicitous winter climate located close to the United States. This was the background and setting, always conceived as ambience. In fact, the success of tourism depended less on the allure of things foreign than on the availability of things familiar. Indeed, herein lay the immediate impact and the long-term significance of U.S. tourism: its power to modify setting and meaning of ordinary life around North American familiarities to which vast numbers of Cubans had become accustomed.

Changing moral codes and lifestyles in the United States during the 1920s implicated Cuba almost immediately. Prohibition, for example, had sweeping consequences. Unemployed bartenders and saloon keepers found jobs in Havana as bars and cabarets that closed in the United States were reopened in Cuba. William Caldwell's Neptuno Bar advertised "choice American food and the best liquors money can buy. A favorite gathering place for Americans." Harry McGabe's Gold Dollar Bar presented "60 beautiful dancing girls?" Tom Morris from Cleveland owned the American Busy Bee Bar—"open day and night"—promising the "largest glass of beer in Havana for to cents.' When Prohibition forced Ed Donovan to close his bar in Newark, New Jersey, he packed up the chairs, tables, mirrors, hanging sign, and the bar itself and relocated on the Pradeo. Pat Cody also reopened his New York saloon, Jigg's Uptown Bar, in Havana. Peter Economides, formerly chief barman at the New Orleans Café in midtown Manhattan, became proprietor of the Café Suzerac. John Moller from Brooklyn opened Ballyhoo Bar, and George Harris operated George's Winter Palace. Harry McGabe opened the Rialto Café, also on the Prado. Other establishments followed: the New Orleans Café, Winter Garden Bar, Muldoon's Café. The Seminole Café offered "nothing but genuine American and Scotch whiskey. Best draught beer in town."

Bars multiplied prodigiously, and there seemed no limit to the number that could remain in business. By the 1920s about seven thousand bars operated in Havana. "If there is any city with more bars than Havana," commented U.S. consul Carlton Hunt, "I have still to see it. Literally hundreds of them crowd the smaller thoroughfares especially at the street corners, often in connection with grocery stores, and are surcharged with bottles of every kind."

Liquor distributorships also proliferated. So did distilleries and breweries. W. A. Kennerly relocated his Roanoke,

Virginia, distillery in Havana. The Havana Distilling Company—"which represents considerable American capital," reported the U.S. chargé d'affaires Edward Reed—opened a large plant at El Cano to manufacture rye whiskey, Scotch, and other liquors. In 1920 the Cuba Cervercera Company purchased the entire factory of the U.S. Brewing Company of Chicago, increasing its production capacity to five million liters of beer daily.

The familiar world of North America was reassembled in Cuba: familiar brand names, familiar food, familiar language, and familiar amusements. This was one more way that North American cultural forms were transmitted to Cuba. "The home lover," the *Havana Post* asserted in 1924, "those who think they cannot get along without just what they have been used to all their lives can find it right here in Havana?" The paper observed: "Time was when it was difficult to find what they termed 'good American cooking' here. Now there are plenty of places. . . . One may go out in the great open spaces or he can remain in the thickly crowded districts and mingle with his own kind. . . . A man may see the American baseball. . . . One is not deprived of his own form of religious worship, whether he be Catholic, Protestant, Jew, Christian Scientist or Oriental."

Hotels owned and operated by North Americans were designed for the comfort and convenience of North American guests. Old hotels were refurbished and passed under new management. The old Seville was acquired by John M. Bowman, head of the Biltmore chain, and reopened in 1919 as the Seville-Biltmore. The new Havana Biltmore appeared in 1924, becoming the twelfth Biltmore of the Bowman group. Walter Fletcher operated the Hotel Plaza, modeled on the New York Plaza and using the same suppliers for its silverware, china, and glassware.

The number of new hotels increased. W. T. Burbridge opened the Miramar Hotel; Dwight Hughes, the Albany Hotel; and John A. Richardson, the Hotel Lincoln. Following in quick order were the Hotel Vanderbilt, Hotel Packard, Hotel Cecil, St. Louis Hotel, Hotel Biscuit, Hotel Bristol, Savoy Hotel, Hotel Saratoga, Hotel Pacific, Hotel Palace, Boston Hotel, Miami Hotel, Hotel Parkview, Hotel Ambassador, and Hotel Washington—all sounding familiar and always referred to in English. George Koenig from Miami promised that his Hotel Seminole would be a "first-class American café, lunch, and restaurant." The New Ritz Hotel advertised "American management." Roy Wake operated the Clifton House, "making a specialty of American home cooking and baking."

Mrs. H. Weidemann called her Hotel Brooklyn the "American headquarters" for "strictly American cooking." The Riverside House in Vedado was a "strictly up-to-date American house with all modern improvements and home comforts." J. E. Harrigan, proprietor of the Hotel Harrigan on Neptuno, provided "all American beds." The Hotel Royal Palm promised its guests a "homelike home for those away from home": "At the Hotel Royal Palm you will find all those little comforts that tend to make you feel at home. All help . . . speak both English and Spanish, and therefore can intelligently interpret your desires. Beds have American springs and mattresses. All rooms have telephones with direct connections with any phone in the United States or Canada. . . . Restaurant serving American food at reasonable prices. Meals like mother used to make."

U.S-owned hotels reached across the island, including the Hotel New York in Camagüey, the Hotel Burnside in Nueva Gerona, and the Castle-Pullman Hotel and Hotel Happiness in Varadero. The Cuba Company operated La Casa Grande in Santiago de Cuba, the Hotel Antilla, and the Hotel Camagüey.

New restaurants appeared in Havana almost as quickly as hotels. The New American Restaurant opened in 1920 on San Rafael. The Havana Tea Room—"under the management of American women"—offered "homemade pies, pastry, cakes, and waffles . . . in quiet and pleasant surroundings." Fanny's Place on O'Reilly advertised itself as "famous since 1917 for its American home cooking." Anita Carter operated the Green Parrot: an "American dining room offering pancake and waffle breakfast 6–10 A.M. and businessmen's lunch 11–2 P.M." Geyer's American Restaurant assured prospective customers that "only English speaking waiters [were] employed." The McAlpin Café proclaimed itself "a real American cafe: not an imitation, but a spacious, beautifully appointed AMERICAN eating place. The large dining room is socially favored for dancing and cabaret each evening until midnight. . . ."

Entertainment reached new heights of grandeur with the opening in 1928 of the Gran Casino Nacional in Marianao. Nothing quite like it had ever been seen before. Designed by

New York architects Schultz and Weaver and interior deco-
rator Renee Lewis, the Gran Casino represented the North
American rendering of tropical opulence. Capable of seating
one thousand people, the palatial restaurant-nightclub
included an immense gambling room as well as an elaborate
dance floor and stage area from which extravagant floor
shows alternated with dance orchestras. The casino immediately acquired an international reputation as the "playhouse
of the Caribbean" and set the standard for elegant dining and
fashionable nightlife. The dining area, wrote Consul Carlton
Hurst, "is always crowded with beautifully gowned and
bejeweled women. The center of the floor is cleared for fancy
dancing by professionals and the space is then retaken by the
public. . . . In the rooms beyond are the roulette tables
where thousands of dollars change hands in the course of the
evening. People walk out at intervals on the broad terrace to
see the fountain with colored lights playing on the marble figures of the dancing nymphs."

The Gran Casino Nacional underscored the salient feature of tourism in Cuba: the capacity of North America to
arrange the physical environment of Cuban life around its
own needs. What passed for Cuban was, in fact, often of
North American origin. From the Havana Biltmore in the
1920s to the Havana Hilton and the Riviera in the 1950s,
U.S. motifs dominated hotel construction. The Seville-
Biltmore Hotel and the Concha Beach Club were designed
by Schultz and Weaver. The Hotel Nacional, completed in
1930 and hailed as the "quintessential Cuban hotel," was
designed by New York architectural firm McKim, Mead

and White; construction was supervised by Purdy and Henderson Company. The Nacional's Grand Ball Room was decorated by New York designer Robert E. Locker; the floor plan was completed by Hasbrock Flooring Company of Long Island.

Never before had the exaltation of things Cuban so thoroughly passed into the popular imagination. Cuba was chic, Cuba was in vogue: morning golf at the Country Club, afternoon races at Oriental Park, evenings of formal dining at the Casino Nacional and dancing at the Plaza Hotel roof garden. Travel writer Joseph Hergesheimer proclaimed Havana "a city both fashionable and rich." Sydney Clark described the times vividly: "Cuban articles, Cuban music and that vague substance known as Cuban atmosphere became the rage of smart circles in both hemispheres."

Comparisons were perhaps inevitable, and they too accentuated the vogue of things Cuban: the "Cuban Riviera," the "Riviera of the Caribbean," and the "Nice of the Atlantic"; the Gran Casino Nacional was the "Monte Carlo of Latin America" and the Prado was the "Champs Elysee of the winter time." Havana was described variously as "a little Paris," the "Paris of the West Indies," and the "Paris of America." It was "the substantial rival of resorts like Monte Carlo and the Venetian Lido," asserted one travel writer.

Havana seemed to have cast a spell over North Americans. It was "a paradise on earth" (Olive Gibson) and a "veritable fairyland" (Pauline Bychower), a sensation echoed by Anaïs Nin—"I have been transported to Fairyland"—and Hart Crane: "It's a funny little metropolis, more like a toy city than a real one." "Days there fly by as if on wings and one feels as if living in a land of enchantment," wrote tourist Nina Hawkins. "I thought I'd died and gone to heaven," was National Airlines flight attendant Alcyone Hart Barltrop's first impression of Havana.

Images of Cuba were transmitted in newspapers, magazines, and periodicals, in travel articles and tourist books, and in advertisements of travel agencies, railroad companies, steamship lines, and airline carriers. Havana was the subject of motion pictures, poems, odes, and songs. The sights and sounds of Cuba-real and imagined—served as a Hollywood staple for decades. Between the 1930s and 1950s Cuba was the setting of scores of films, including *The Girl from Havana* (1929), *Under Cuban Skies* (1930), *Cuban Love Song* (1931), *Havana Widows* (1933), *Weekend in Havana* (1941), *Moonlight in Havana* (1942), *Cuban Pete and Club Havana* (1946), *Holiday in Havana* (1949), *Havana Rose and Cuban Fireball* (1951), *Santiago* (1956), *Affair in Havana* (1957), and *Pier 5 Havana* (1959). Cuba appeared in the fiction of Burnham Carter, James Gould Cozzens, Graham Greene, Ernest Hemingway, Josephine Herbst, and James Street and in the poetry of Hart Crane, Theodore Dreiser, Robert Frost, Langston Hughes, and Wallace Stevens.

But it was in the lyric of popular music that the North American narrative on Cuba acquired its greatest resonance. The lyric could celebrate the most fanciful notions of the island through wistful yearnings and wishful thinking. Indeed, few countries in the world have been the subject of more popular songs than Cuba.

Cuba entered the North American imagination in many forms, but principally as a place of pleasures unavailable at home—where one could do those "things" that usually were not done anywhere else. Access to alcoholic beverages during Prohibition was an early tourist attraction. "Never has so much beer, rum and Daiquiri been consumed in so short a time," a tourist wrote home. Visitors availed themselves of the opportunity to drink immediately on arrival. "I have seen people leaving incoming ships," commented Consul Hurst, "who have stopped at bars on their way to the hotel taking alcoholic drinks. By the time they reached the hotel they could scarcely ask the reception clerk for a room."

It was not merely the availability of alcoholic beverages, however. The opportunity to drink carried a subtext of individual freedom and indulgence. It implied license for excess. "Here the tourist finds that touch of the tropics of which he has read," the *Havana Post* proclaimed:

> The somber mantle of Volsteadism is not draped over this happy island, where personal liberty is something to be enjoyed openly and not spoken of with bated breath within the murky precincts of an evil smelling speakeasy. Here the tourist . . . may, if he chooses, "take a whirl" at the lottery or other games of chance prohibited by an element which in his homeland seems desirous of removing the spice of life from the reach of the worker and relegating it to those able to pay for the luxury of violating popular laws.

Correspondent J. J. Van Raalte extolled Havana as the "paradise of the cocktails," the "ideal country of personal liberty," adding: "When we come here again next year we should bring with us the Statue of Liberty, to place in the port of Havana, where it properly belongs." Cuba was the "land of the free," affirmed one visitor, where "all forms of pleasure will flourish until the sun advances along the meridian and the mighty throng of visitors turn their faces northward again." Among the major appeals of Cuba, Basil Woon declared, was "personal liberty carried to the Nth degree," by which he meant: "You may drink as much as you want to . . . you may lose as much money as you desire in the Casino, you need not carry your marriage certificate with you, and you may stare at the pretty señoritas." Isabel Stone agreed: "Three hundred years ago our forefathers came to America in search of "life, liberty and the pursuit of happiness. . . ."

The most enduring North American images of Cuba were formed during these years and served as the principal narrative depicting the island: Cuba evoked romance and exuded sensuousness. Romance was everywhere, for the taking. Havana "was made for romance," proclaims the narrator of Burnham Carter's short story "Journey by Moonlight" (1940). It was "hyper-sensual and mad," concluded Hart Crane, "i.e., has no apparent direction, destiny or purpose; Cumming's paradise." "Havana is a veritable city of romance," exclaimed one visitor; "the last refuge of romance and romantic living," insisted another. In 1924 a tourist rhapsodized: "It seems that in this part of the world the moon shines its brightest and the spirit of romance that breathes in the air on a moonlight night in Cuba is irresistible. The tall graceful palms swaying in the breeze; the stillness of the night, undisturbed except by the sound of the ocean, washing the shores, the luxuriance and fragrance of the vegetation, all combine to lend a complete sense of enchantment and contentment."

Romance was the staple of the lyric of popular music: "Havana, gay rendezvous for romancers," affirmed "Cuban Cabaret"; "Cuban Moon" proclaimed Cuba "the Island of romance," and on the "Sidewalks of Cuba," one would be "intoxicated by romance."

The notion of romance was, in fact, a euphemism for sex and seduction, the rendering of Cuba as a setting for amorous adventures. The "air was instinct with seduction" as Joseph Hergesheimer described Havana. "Cuba—the very name conjures visions of romance, beautiful women, soft music-filled nights and cigars," Hyatt Verrill wrote. *House and Garden* was slightly more circumspect: "A certain amount of sin, naturally, is to be expected in a city as whole-heartedly devoted to love and romance as Havana. . . . All this Latin temperament and the beauty of Cuban girls, who are well aware of their enticements, having a tendency to unsettle susceptible Americans and induce erratic behavior." Helen Lawrenson attributed Havana's appeal to "atmosphere," a condition "so toxic, so insidious, so hypnotic" that it "casts a spell over the hearts of men." She was convinced that "something in the air" had "a curious chemical effect on Anglo-Saxons, dissolving their inhibitions and intensifying their libidos": "Travelers . . . find in Havana a seduction more potent than anywhere else, even though much of the time they are unaware of its exact nature. The intrinsic basic quality of Havana is a deadly magic which permeates the very air which flows through the city, inescapable and inseparable, and which can only be defined, in the last analysis, as Sex. It is, without any doubt, the sexiest city in the world. . . ."

Prostitution flourished. Sex shows and live pornographic theaters proliferated. The Shanghai Theater and the Tokio Cabaret offered nightly pornographic performances; the Tokio advertised: "Come when you like, do what you please, and let your conscience be your guide." The estimated number of prostitutes in Havana increased from 4,000 in 1912 to 7,400 in 1931. By the late 1950s about 270 brothels operated in Havana, with more than 11,500 women working as prostitutes.

Descriptions of brothels routinely appeared in tourist guidebooks. Adolphe Roberts recommended the "refined prostitution" available on Virtudes Street, "institutions" that were air-conditioned and well furnished and offered drinks at moderate prices. Here the visitor would find the "tapestried and mirrored rooms where the salaciously-inclined may witness startling scenes in the flesh or by means of moving pictures." Roberts specified that the "girls constitute the main attraction. . . . Any one of them maybe taken from the premises." *Terry's Guide to Cuba* gave tourists precise directions to Havana's waterfront red-light district—"the prurient spot resorted to by courtezans, varying in complexion from peach white to coal black; 15-year-old flappers and ebony antiques; chiefly outlanders who unblushingly loll about heavy-eyed and languorous, in abbreviated and diaphanous costumes; nictitating with incendiary eyes at passing masculinity; studiously displaying their physical charms or luring the stranger by flaming words or maliciously imperious gestures." Sydney Clark recommended Oficios Street: "many prostitutes, most white or near-white ply their trade here with conscientious zeal, greeting any in-coming male as though he were a dear friend from childhood days."

Not for the first time, Cuba insinuated itself into the North American imagination, became implicated in North American transformations, and was in turn shaped by those transformations. This was an environment summoned into existence for North Americans. They did not "discover" paradise, they created it. Cuba met North American needs so fully that it had to have been invented by them. They found in Cuba the perfect Other: foreign but familiar, exotic but civilized, primitive but modern, a tropical escape only hours from home in which to flout conventions, a place to live dangerously but without taking risks.

Cuba became associated with indulgence and abandon, and visitors were rarely disappointed. Ernest Hemingway liked Cuba because it had "both fishing and fucking." Tennessee Williams would reminisce about his "riotous weekends in Havana," and Ava Gardner fondly recalled the Havana of her honeymoon in 1951 as an "American playground, complete with gambling houses, whorehouses, and brightly lit cafés, every other one boasting a live orchestra. Traffic, lights, bustle, cigar smoke, pretty girls, balmy air, stars in the sky, they all combined to form a Latin town that

aimed to please." Hoagy Carmichael remembered everything as "tropical"—"tropical nights, tropical beer, tropical
music, tropical girls, tropical moon, tropical mood"—and
was unabashedly nostalgic about the "strangely blonde
Havana B-girl" who "danced divinely." Carmichael wrote:
"The beer was strong. The rumba music, the first I had
heard, gave me a tingle . . . it was a wonderful cruise."
Graham Greene delighted in Havana "for the sake of the
Floridita restaurant (famous for daiquiris and Morro crabs),
for the brothel life, the roulette in every hotel, the fruit
machine spilling out jackpots of silver dollars, the Shanghai
Theatre, where for one dollar and twenty-five cents one
could see a nude cabaret of extreme obscenity with the bluest
of blue films in the intervals." When bored with the bars and
brothels, Greene went in search of "a little cocaine," and
nothing "was easier." Historian Neill Macaulay also
recounted his time in Havana: "The whorehouse I
visited . . . was furnished with spotless, linoleum-topped
tables and chairs arranged around a small dance floor. There
was a brightly bubbling jukebox with rock-and-roll records,
and a bar. The girls, all teenagers, were dressed in shorts
and halters. All were white and several blonde, though their
eyes were unmistakably Latin. It was a place where American high-school and college boys of the 1950s came to
relieve their sexual tensions in surroundings that were not
forbiddingly foreign." This must have been what John
Sayles had in mind in his novel *Los Gusanos* (1991) when he
wrote of "the Casa de Rock, where boys from the University of Miami would come to fuck little blonde Cuban girls

who spoke good English and wore ponytails and blue jeans just like the little blonde girls they were afraid to fuck back home." In Havana, U.S. ambassador Arthur Gardner could only observe with mounting incredulity and lamely lament: "The masses of people who come here are bent only on pleasure and think of Cuba except in terms of fun, rum and nightclubs."

North American tourism was at once the cause and effect of other changes. As nightclubs and cabarets expanded, nightlife assumed extravagant proportions. Big-name performers arrived from the United States to play for North American audiences. In 1939 Martin Fox purchased the Villa Mina estate in Marianao and constructed the Tropicana nightclub. Small clubs, bars, and dance joints proliferated bearing such names as Dirty Dick's, Hollywood Cabaret, Pennsylvania, Johnny's Dream Club, Tally-Ho, High Seas, Skippy's Hideaway, and Turf Club.

In the 1950s more than twenty new hotels were completed, and gambling establishments increased. In 1951 Florida developer Jerry Collins opened a greyhound racetrack in Miramar. In the same year a new, modern amusement park called "Coney Island" operated in Havana. The Riviera and the Hotel Capri introduced casinos in 1957; these were followed by the Montmartre, Sans Souci, and Tropicana nightclubs. The Capri hired actor George Raft as the casino host. Other casinos were installed in Havana at the Hotel Nacional, Plaza, Seville-Biltmore, Deauville, and Comodoro; in Cienfuegos at the Jagua motel; in Varadero at the Internacional; and on the Isle of Pines at the Colony Hotel.

The U.S. underworld was also attracted to Cuba. Indeed, the reach and range of organized crime on the island increased dramatically in the 1950s with the hearings of U.S. Senator Estes Kefauver, which had the net effect of forcing criminal elements to relocate their gambling operations elsewhere. "It was the chill of the Kefauver hearings which to a large measure induced the Americans to seek warmer and more hospitable grounds to the south," reported *Variety* in 1953. Once again, like Prohibition, North Americans seemed content to exorcise their demons by exporting them to Cuba. The Fulgencio Batista government obligingly modified existing gambling regulations to permit any nightclub or hotel in Havana worth $1 million or more, and more than $500,000 outside the capital, to operate gambling casinos. The stage was set. "These are wonderful things that we've achieved in Havana," proclaims Hyman Roth (Lee Strasberg) in the film *Godfather II*, "and there's no limit to where we can go from here. . . . We have now what we have always needed: real partnership with a government. Here we are, protected, free to make our profits, without Kefauver, the Goddamned Justice Department and the FBI—90 miles away, partnership with a government."

By the late 1950s, organized crime had assumed control of the major hotels and casinos in Cuba. Tens of millions of dollars were invested in luxury hotels, nightclubs, and gambling casinos. The "famous Cleveland gambling syndicate," *Life* reported, including Sam Tucker, Moe Dalitz, and Wilbur Clark, operated the Parisién Casino of the Hotel Nacional. Norman Entratter from Las Vegas controlled the

Venecia in Santa Clara. Harry "Lefty" Clark, described by the *Miami Herald* as "the dean of the U.S. gambling underworld," went to Havana in 1956 and immediately took over the Tropicana casino. Norman Rothman operated the Sans Souci and later passed it on to Santo Trafficante, who also managed the Capri. Meyer Lansky provided most of the $14 million used to construct the luxurious Riviera Hotel. Lansky operated the Montmartre, Seville-Biltmore, Internacional, Comodoro, and Havana Hilton.

In the 1950s gambling receipts exceeded $500,000 monthly. "This is going to be another Las Vegas," an anonymous gambling promoter boasted to *Life* correspondent Ernest Havemann, "only like Las Vegas never imagined." The *Havana Post* concurred, observing that Cuba was bidding for the title of "the Las Vegas of Latin America." During these years Lucky Luciano was planning to transform the Isle of Pines into the "Monte Carlo of the Western Hemisphere," with luxury hotels, lavish gambling casinos, and elegant brothels. "Without any question," recalled mob attorney Frank Ragano on the CBS news documentary "The Last Revolutionary" (July 18, 1996), "there wasn't a better place in the world for a mobster to operate a business than in Havana, Cuba. That was a great time there, anything you wanted was there, was available."

North American crime figures became a familiar sight in Havana, ranging from the high-profile mobster to the small-time hood and hustler. "In fact, the underworld presence assumed the proportions of a migration. Mobsters "have moved into Havana in such force," reported one observer, "that the town looked like a haven for the underworld in exile." The *Miami Herald* described an "invasion of Cuba by the U.S. underworld." "You walk into one of these new gambling joints," reported *Newsweek*, "and it's like walking onto the set of a Grade-B gangster movie. Every thug you ever saw east of Las Vegas who can get up the plane fare is walking around one of these casinos in a white silk evening jacket acting like a head waite." Longtime Havana resident Milton Guss also noticed the change. "The tide of gambling has washed a lot of American undesirables ashore," he observed ruefully. "There is no shortage of American hoodlums in Cuba." In 1958 former prime minister Manuel Antonio de Varona appealed directly to Estes Kefauver for assistance. The introduction of big gambling," Varona explained, had resulted in the arrival of "several well-known American racketeers," adding: "These strange elements are extremely dangerous to the Cuban people, since they are not only fostering many vices among my fellow citizens, but acting as potential instruments in the hands of an unscrupulous tyrant. Nobody can fix a limit to these characters, once they have enough power to act. They could become a powerful force to undermine or destroy any person or institution firmly determined to fight corruption on the island. . . ."

In the late 1940s and early 1950s the *mambo* seized hold of the North American imagination. The origins of the new Cuban dance were variously attributed to Orestes López, Antonio Arcaño, Arsenio Rodríguez, and Israel "Cachao" López, but it was pianist Dámaso Pérez Prado's arrangements of the mambo, presented in a big, brassy band sound with trumpets, saxophones, and trombones, backed by a powerful rhythm section—all influenced by Stan Kenton—that captured the *afición* of the North American public. Pérez Prado's treatment of the mambo in the 1950s was similar to the approach adopted by Cugat and Arnaz for the rumba and the conga in the 1930s and 1940s: to popularize by means of showmanship and theatrics. His audiences were taken by his onstage antics, his high kicks that soon developed into high jumps, loud grunts of "Uh!" as he spun in the air. "Prado is a natural showman," wrote Johnny Sipel in 1951, "combining his batoning with dancing and kicking. His enthusiasm projects to the payees as well as sidemen, who work standing up and weaving and bobbing in rhythm."

The mambo overnight became a national phenomenon, riding a wave of popularity that swept across the United States. Pérez Prado drew overflow dance audiences nightly. "The largest crowd the Zena Ballroom [Los Angeles] has ever seen went wild in its enthusiasm over Pérez Prado and his band," wrote *Down Beat* in September 1951. Two weeks later Ralph Gleason reported from San Francisco: "Pérez Prado has swung into Sweet's Ballroom and 3,500 people followed. Prado's audience dances, my friends—young and old they kick out."

The mambo was in demand everywhere. "Dance hands drifting in from the hinterlands report loud and persistent requests to "play a mambo," reported Bill Simon. "Mambo-mania!" proclaimed *Newsweek* in 1954, adding: "The mambo is the biggest exotic dance craze to sweep the country in a quarter century." Walter Waldman agreed: "In terms of dedicated hypnosis, nothing like the effect of the mambo on its exponents has ever been witnessed in contemporary America." From Chicago *Variety* reported: "Mambo fever has gripped the windy city"; from New York it announced: "New York is beginning to shake from the hips down as the mambo fever continues to spread around town."

Mambo became the dominant motif at nightclubs and in dance rooms nationwide. The Encore Room in Chicago changed its name to Mambo City. Another Mambo City opened in Los Angeles. Other new clubs included the Mambo Club in New York, El Mambo in Miami, and the Mambo Room in Cleveland. When Roseland sponsored "Mamborama," the Palladium countered with "Mambo-Scope." The Hartford Statler featured a weekly dance program called "Mambo at the Statler." Carnegie Hall presented the lavish stage show "Mambo Concerto," and the Los Angeles Shrine Auditorium promoted the "Mambo Jambo Revue." The Savoy Ballroom and the Apollo Theater declared Mondays as "Mambo Nights." Dance studios rushed to add mambo lessons to their offerings. "Dance studios find a course in mambo these days is as essential as a time payment plan," reported *Down Beat* in 1954. The Palladium hired dance instructor Joe (Killer Joe) Piro to offer free mambo lessons on Wednesday evenings. Mambo also received more airtime on radio. "With the rapid spread of the mambo heat in the last year," observed *Variety* in 1954, "pop disc jockeys are now programming an increasing number of such platters on their shows." Increasingly bands adopted "mambo" as part of their name. Cal Tjader reorganized his group as the Modern Mambo Quintet. Others included Carlos Molina and the Mambo Men, the Charlie Velero Mambo Band, and the Peacock Mambo Combo. Record revenues soared. By the mid-1950s mambo record sales topped $5 million. In 1955 Paramount released the movie *Mambo* starring Silvana Mangano and Shelly Winter.

The mambo influenced virtually all genres of popular music. The dance was such a commercial success that in mid-1954 RCA Victor limited its weekly single record releases exclusively to mambos. "Music publishers and record companies have caught mambo fever," reported *Variety* in 1954. "They've opened up all the valves in the current mambo push and are flooding the market with variations on the theme, hoping to cash in on some of the gravy before the law of diminishing returns sets in." There seemed to be no end to mambo recordings. Jazz musicians were among the first to record mambo titles. Errol Garner made an album under the title *Mambo Moves Garner*, Cal Tjader released *Mambo with Tjader*. Others included Sonny Rollins (*Mambo Jazz*), George Shearing (*Cool Mambo*), Billy Taylor (*Early Morning Mambo* and *Mambo Inn*), Shorty Rogers (*Mambo del Crow*), Stan Kenton (*Mambo Rhapsody*), Duke Ellington (*Bunny Hop Mambo*), and Count Basie (*Mambo Mist*).

Dance orchestras released scores of mambo recordings, including the Duke Jenkins Orchestra ("Mambo Blues"), Woody Herman ("Woodchopper's Mambo"), Sonny Burke ("More Mambo"), Ted Heath ("Manhattan Mambo"), Les Brown ("St. Louis Blues Mambo"), Pete Terrace ("Invitation to the Mambo"), and Lester Young ("Another Mambo").

Popular recordings with mambo titles reached the top of the charts in spectacular fashion, although it was never clear that they had much to do with the Cuban rhythms from which they presumably derived inspiration. Vaughn Monroe's "They Were Doing the Mambo" rose to number one on the charts and was followed almost immediately by Perry Como's "Papa Loves Mambo." Rosemary Clooney sang about the "Mambo Italiano," and the Honeydreamers recorded "Irish Mambo." Other recording artists with successful mambo titles were Eartha Kitt ("Mambo de Paree"), the Five DeMarco Sisters ("Mambo Is the Word"), Mel Torme ("The Anything Can Happen Mambo"), Gary Crosby ("Mambo in the Moonlight"), and Sophie Tucker ("Middle Age Mambo"). Ruth Brown climbed to the top of the rhythm-and-blues charts with "Mambo Baby," which encouraged other entries in that category, such as Big Maybelle's "New Kind of Mambo" and the Sheppards' "Cool Mambo." Bill Haley and the Comets recorded "Mambo Rock." Country and Western versions included Darrell Glenn's "Banjo Mambo" and Sheb Wooley's "Hillbilly Mambo." In the category of children's music, the Lennon Sisters recorded "Mickey Mouse Mambo." Classical music was represented by Jan August's recordings "Bach Mambo," based on a Bach fugue, and "Minuet in Mambo," inspired by a Paderewski opus. Sonny Burke recorded "Longhair Mambo," based on a Mozart composition. The Melion Orchestra made "Mambo á la Strauss." Among the stock of Christmas releases in 1954 were Pete Rugolo's "Jingle Bell Mambo," the Smith Brothers' "We Wanna See Santa Do the

Mambo." Jimmy Boyd's "I Saw Mommy Do the Mambo with Santa Claus," and the Billy May Orchestra's "Rudolph the Red Nosed Mambo." Novelty items included the Frankie Yankovich Orchestra's "I Don't Want to Mambo Polka" and the Irving Fields Trio's "Davey Crockett Mambo."

The mambo entered all show business venues. "Almost all dance halls and night clubs now require its band to have at least some mambos in their books," reported *Down Beat* in 1954. In the Las Vegas Thunderbird, Les Barker fronted a flashy *Mambo Cuba Revue*, complete with chorus and dancers. In New York, the Chateau Madrid, Latin Quarter, Stork Club, and El Morocco booked mambo bands. Leonard Bernstein incorporated a mambo sequence in *West Side Story*. Las Vegas stripper Lili St. Cyr used a mambo number for a "Latin" act in her stage show. Radio City Music Hall included a mambo for the precision tap line in its *Noche Caribe Revue*. The *Sonja Hene Ice Revue* staged a "Songs of the Islands" production featuring mambo numbers on ice. The *International Revue* at the Las Vegas Desert Inn included a pair of chimpanzees, Tippy and Cobina, who played the maracas and miniature timbales, and Ringling Bros. and Barnum and Bailey Circus in New York introduced mambo-dancing elephants.

Demand for the mambo had not yet fully waned when another Cuban dance captured the North American imagination: the *cha-cha-chá*. Developed by violinist Enrique Jorrín, Orquesta Aragón, and José Fajardo in the early 1950s, the cha-cha-chá was in many ways the opposite of the mambo: rather than brass, it relied on strings and flute; it was

light, crisp, and melodic. The rhythm was catchy and, compared to the pulsating mambo, simple. Most of all, the dance
was eminently learnable. . . .

North American tastes demanded commercialization of
the rumba, conga, mambo, and cha-cha-chá to the point where
the music was transformed beyond the reach of Cuban com-
posers and musicians. Many of them dedicated their talents to
commercial forms in an attempt to gain access to this market.
Nevertheless, it was a market in which they could not compete. Simply put, they could not produce credible adulter-
ations such as "Papa Loves Mambo" and the "Davey Crockett
Mambo." In the process, much creative energy went into the
development of execrable material, little of which succeeded
but had the net effect of subverting the authenticity of the
genre. Cuban music was transformed as fully as it was transforming. The U.S. market turned the rumba into a genteel
ballroom dance almost beyond recognition. No Cuban musician could have discerned that the mambo compositions of
Antonio Arcaño and Arsenio Rodríguez bore any relationship
to "Hillbilly Mambo" or "Mambo Italiano."

The vogue of "Cuban" transcended music. During these
years, Cuban no doubt acquired its most enduring represen-
tation in the character of Ricky Ricardo. *I Love Lucy* debuted
in 1951 and continued until the end of the decade. It may
have been inevitable that the Desi Arnaz role was shaped by
the rendering of Cuban most prominently fixed in the North
American imagination: a rumba orchestra leader at the Tropicana nightclub who periodically performed renditions of
"Babalú Ayé." In the episode "Lucy Meets Bob Hope"

(1956), Ricky buys "a piece of the Tropicana" and changes the name to "Club Babalú."

Although it is impossible to fully comprehend how this image of Cuban was understood or otherwise contemplated by the public, the series clearly attracted a huge audience. Indeed, *I Love Lucy* was one of the most-watched programs in television history—by the mid—1950s it typically drew 50 million viewers weekly. By one reckoning, everyone in the United States had seen at least one episode of the show. "It's unlikely that anyone between the ages of 6 and 60 . . . hasn't been able to identify Desi," affirmed Down Beat in 1953. "Lucy and Ricky were not merely characters in a domestic comedy," TV critics Donald Glut and Jon Harmon insisted. "They were real, they were loved. . . . They would become an American institution."

Ricky Ricardo as "real" and the Cuban as an "American institution" suggest the reach of *I Love Lucy*. An entire generation derived, in varying degrees, its image and impression of "Cuban" from the television program. Ricky Ricardo conveyed all the information that many viewers would ever know about Cuba. He easily reinforced the dominant images: rumba band leader, heavily accented English, excitable, always seeming to be slightly out of place and hence slightly vulnerable, perhaps even childlike and non-threatening. Ricky was "a combustible combination of cockiness and stubborn authority," wrote Michael McClay in an official history of the series, "mixed with a fiery Latin temperament tinged with vanity—and a hilarious accent." He served as an easy foil for Lucy's schemes; Ricky as an object of mockery and mimicry was one of the series' recurring thematic elements. Embarrassed by Ricky's English in one episode, Lucy hires a tutor for their baby and pleads with Ricky: "Please promise me you won't speak to our child until he's nineteen or twenty."

Whatever else *I Love Lucy* may have been about, it possessed a subtext about Cuba. Cuba always seemed to be implicated in Ricky's behavior. In "Be a Pal" (1951), Lucy seeks to surround Ricky with "things that remind him of his childhood" and proceeds to decorate their apartment in what she imagines Cuba to be: palm trees, Mexican *sombreros*, a flock of chickens, and a mule. In another scene, Lucy breaks out into song, lip-synching to a Carmen Miranda recording. In the episode "Lucy Meets Bob Hope," after Ricky performs an energetic dance number, Bob Hope asserts: "That'll set Cuba back a hundred years." In "The Ricardos Visit Cuba" (1956), Lucy manages to cause havoc in the Ricardo household and the next day laments: "After what I did last night, Cuba might cut off America's sugar supply!" In "Lucy Is Enceinte" (1952), Ricky has had a bad day at the club and frets: "Oh, what a business. Sometimes I think I go back to Cuba and work on a sugar plantation." In "Ricky Needs an Agent" (1955), Lucy encourages him to consider a movie career by remaking old films: "Gone with the Cuban Wind," "Seven Brides for Seven Cubans," and "Andy Hardy Meets a Conga Player."

The most successful Cuban performers in the United States were types, musicians who shared several traits in common. Xavier Cugat, Pérez Prado, and Desi Arnaz, in his brief motion picture career and as Ricky Ricardo, played off their antics and accents, lending themselves to caricature and self-parody, and implicated their music in novelty in ways that would have been inconceivable for Tommy Dorsey, Benny Goodman, or Stan Kenton. Along the way, they created an image of Cuban that others would be obliged to conform to as the price of success in the North. They possessed finely tuned commercial instincts and showed remarkable talent in adapting Cuban idioms to North American tastes. "I am accused of not playing Cuban music the 'way it is,'" Cugat once defended himself in an interview in Cuba. "Fine. That is exactly the reason for the great success of Cuban music there. Without immodesty, I can say that the rise of our music is due to my efforts. Don Azpiazu, for example, played our music 'as it is.' I can assure you that he reached a very small public, and nobody remembers his orchestra. Has the same thing happened to me? Oh no! In any city of the United States they know the Cugat orchestra. . . . In that way, Americanizing the Cuban somewhat, which continues being Cuban, I can answer you, one reaches the mass audience."

Things and ways Cuban, once under the sway of U.S. market forces, were transfigured as a function of commercial imperatives. A people for whom, the proposition of civilized and modern was central to national identity were cast in the role of the North American Other, as exotic and primitive. "The tourist is a type . . . who has become tired of civilization and seeks the primitive," observed Eladio Secades. "To create the primitive where it does not exist is one of the ways to promote tourism." Chilean Tibor Mende, on visiting Havana in the early 1950s, readily understood the drama unfolding before him: "In exchange for [North Americans'] dollars, *habaneros* obligingly provide them all the illusions of the tropics. Cuban orchestras . . . play on a lavishly decorated stage, the black rhythm palpitates amidst the rays of light and bodies continue the playing of the sinister sound of the drums of the Congo; heard in the darkness are the sounds of exotic *rumbas*, of *congas* and *mambos*."

Cacharros

HERE IS A NAME FOR THE GORGEOUS old American cars that continue to hum, rattle, and roll through the Cuban landscape: *cacharros*. Normally the word means a broken-down jalopy that requires its owner to push it up bumps in the road. But in the case of these Yankee beauties—the white '49 Plymouth convertible at Varadero Beach, the eggplant-colored '52 Chevy Styleline Deluxe before the Hotel Nacional, the sleek black '59 Fleetwood Cadillac with minor roles in major motion pictures—cacharro is whispered softly, tenderly, like the name of a lost first love.

When Fidel Castro marched into Havana on New Year's Day of 1959, nearly thirty-five years ago, he could not have imagined

CRISTINA GARCIA *was born in Havana and grew up in New York City. She has worked as a correspondent for* Time *magazine in San Francisco, Miami, and Los Angeles. Her first novel,* Dreaming in Cuban *(from which this piece was excerpted) was nominated for a National Book Award.*

that his triumph would ultimately create the greatest living American car museum in the world, a hunk of Americana not even available the United States. But the severance of relations between Cuba and the US. in 1961 virtually assured the preservation of these marvelous mechanical dinosaurs. Cut off from the supplies and automotive evolution of the mainland, the cars, like any transplanted and isolated species, were forced to adapt. Flash frozen and tinkered with to perfection by Cuban mechanics legendary for their ingenuity and expertise, these automobiles are heroic testaments to their era: a time when gas was cheap and plentiful, the Space Age was imminent, and the future—if you didn't look too far into the atomic horizon—was so bright, you had to wear (3D) shades. How else to explain those fabulous, faux-aerodynamic, wildly fun and flared-out fins?

In Cuba, these grande-dame Packards, Oldsmobiles, Lincolns, Buicks, De Sotos, Dodges, Pontiacs, Hudsons, Studebakers, Cadillacs, Fords, and ever-present Chevys are pampered and fussed over like first grandchildren. Their owners are unabashedly passionate about them. They make declarations of *amor* one would expect more from lovesick adolescents than burly grease-creased mechanics. The cars are buffed and polished, patched up and troubleshot, intestinally reconstituted with parts from Russian jeeps, trucks, and motorcycles until the owners wake up one fine Saturday morning reveling in the sounds they love to hear: vroom, purrr, roar, mmmmmmm. It's working! They save up for gas, wait endlessly in lines for a few liters at best, and then: *Silvia! Pepito! Manolo! María! Get dressed! We're going for a ride!*

Un paseito. A little ride. That is all most of these gas-guzzlers can go for these days. Even with more fuel-efficient carburetors torn from Volkswagens or Russian Ladas, even with the most brilliant mechanics on the face of this blue-green planet, they cannot self-manufacture gas. Until recently, Cubans were allowed only about forty liters (roughly ten gallons) a month, down from three-hundred liters a month in 1991. This does not get them far; maybe to the next province for the obligatory visit to the in-laws on Sundays. Maybe for one blow-out drive to Havana or Varadero Beach. Maybe only for the month's essential errands. They bargain, trade, save, cajole as much gas as they can on the black market (going prince: ninety U.S. cents a liter, which comes to about $3.40/gallon), or from friends of friends, or contacts in the government, or the "industry"—and then they're off! Freedom, wind, the open road, at least for an hour.

Every Cuban, the saying goes, is a mechanic. One wonders if this trait is born of necessity or is somehow genetically coded, like a propensity for *cafecito* so sweet it makes your teeth ache. Everyone who owns a vintage American cacharro in Cuba seems to know how to fix it. These men (it is always men) gather in their neighborhoods after work, fixing and tinkering, swapping tips like kerchiefed housewives from another epoch. This is their social gathering, their kaffee klatsch without the kaffee, the one place they don't have to worry about meeting quotas, pleasing their boss, or being good communists. This is not work but leisure of the purest kind, undiluted joy.

Very few of these cacharros are 100 percent original. While the degree of originality is prized—*Mira, señora*, they crow, taking your elbow and leading you to the treasure . . . a smooth, dentless chassis, perfectly preserved upholstery, two-tone paint as bright as the spring day in 1957 when it was applied—the ingenuity in adapting replacement parts is what separates the men from the boys. Despite the many advances of women in Cuba, despite the Family Code of 1975, *machismo* still reigns under the palms. And there is nothing quite so macho as bringing to life one of these goddesses.

José de la Paz, a retired mechanic in Pinar del Río province, boasts that the engine in his cream and pink '49 De Soto is so perfect that it doesn't burn oil. Okay, maybe just the tiniest amount, barely enough to grease a skillet. But no way could you fry plantains. De la Paz, who bought the automobile brand new for 2,500 pesos from the Dodge agency in Havana, was recently offered 40,000 pesos for it. He indignantly refused. His De Soto hasn't needed a repair since 1984. What would he do with the money, anyway? In Cuba, for Cubans at least, there was, until recently, no place to spend the cash. Besides, he's nicely rigged up the radio to run from a battery in the trunk. And, oh yes, in case you haven't noticed, his house is painted the exact same colors as his car.

But don't think for a moment that these automobiles are treated like delicate hothouse orchids. Most are not hermetically sealed in temperature-controlled security garages the way they would be in the U.S. These cacharros, whenever humanly possible, are put to work. They are exotic cash cows, a source of foreign exchange. Good for tourists and tours, weddings and *quince* celebrations. No underemployment here. Go to any big resort hotel on the island and you'll see these beauties parked in the lots, one after another, shining like so many sun reflectors. Dare to walk by them. Something primal and indescribable will force your hand into your pocket. Twenty dollars buys gas enough for a decent spin. Seventy dollars gets you a day in a top-of-the-line Cadillac convertible with fins so big they block the rearview mirror. Forget about renting from Hertz or Avis ever again.

Filmmakers from around the world feature the *créme de la créme* of these automobiles in movies, television shows, and commercials. The owners get paid in hard currency, which is what everyone in Cuba is after. Dollars, francs, and deutsche marks are their ticket, if not to the good life, then to a better, more comfortably upholstered one. A few well-placed dollars go a long way on the island, secure little luxuries like toilet paper or seafood or hammers obtainable no other way. One woman, offered a bar of Ivory soap in exchange for a photograph of her '57 Ford, burst into tears of gratitude.

Lily Galainena, an enterprising *viejita* of seventy-plus years, drives foreign visitors on architectural tours of her beloved Havana in a '53 Chevrolet. Another gentleman, the owner of a spectacular white '55 Cadillac convertible, charges four hundred pesos for a wedding in his hometown of Cotorro, nine hundred for nuptials in the capital. Along the Malecón, that sweet curve of road where Havana meets the sea, the Rum Boys are cruising big time in a sleek '50

Chevy. Despite the fact that the car belongs to one of their mothers, they are genuine bad bays, the kind everyone else's mother warns you about. They're draped inside the cacharro with studied nonchalance, hustling up rides for a bottle of rum. If they manage to score, say from crazy Canadian tourists wanting a spin in their car, they disappear for days, too soused to drive. Tita Lazara Vilela also makes a good living from his '59 Mercury. He used to drive a truck before the gas ran out and his salary was cut to seventy-five pesos a month. Tita's extended family put their heads together and decided to trade their rundown '56 Chevrolet plus 36,000 scrounged-together pesos for the pristine Mercury. The investment has paid off. This one car, this Yankee anachronism, this flamboyant product of fat cat American corporatism, is keeping the Vilela tribe in Cuba happily fed and clothed three and a half decades after it bumped off the assembly line in Detroit. Talk about capitalist tools.

Tourists are not the only ones smitten by these dazzling behemoths, although in many ways the rising influx of tourists during the last decade has sparked a renewed appreciation of the American cacharros. For a while in the 1980s, the Cuban government attempted to cash in on the vintage cars in Europe, North America, and Japan by buying up as many of the local cacharros as possible. In exchange, they promised owners a brand new (and widely scorned) Russian Lada. The dearth of parts and gas forced many a heartbreaking decision. After all, to many families, their cacharros were family. How could they turn in their automotive *abuelitas* for mere transportation? Cuban officials collected the cars on huge lots, enticing foreigners starved for a little felicitous form in a world gone to hell with function. Many of the island's best automobiles left the tropics in this desperate bid for foreign exchange. The exodus came to an abrupt halt in 1989 when the government discovered its apparatchiks diverting profits into their own pockets.

What is it about these cars that makes the hearts of even confirmed subway riders do a little cha-cha-chá in the chest? Is it that irresistible stretch of grinning grillwork? Those low-slung trunks you want to throw luggage into? Those acres of chrome, hoarding a hog's share of sunlight? In the early 1950s, car stylists actually measured chrome by the square inch, making sure they had enough. Longer, lower, wider. That was the ethos of the day. Gadgets like flip-up gas fillers, push-button gear selectors, and swivel seats became de rigueur. Automobiles, more than ever, became blatant extensions of the personality. Sex was linked to horsepower. The boxy models of the thirties and forties gave way to a potent new curvaceousness. Dr. Jean Rosenbaum, a well-known psychiatrist of the time, pronounced that for men: "See what a big car I have," could be translated as "See what a big penis I have (or wish I had)."

So *that's* what this is all about? In a world where sex can be scary and four-cylinder cars rumble out of international factories with a ho-hum gumdrop likeness, these old cacharros positively explode with a riotous sensuality. Get within ten yards of one and it is impossible, literally impossible, to keep our hands to yourself. You close your eyes and take in the catch and growl of the motor. You open them and follow those sinuous lines like silver trajectories to your past and future. You yearn for a letter sweater and a chocolate malt to share with your sweetheart. (So what if she just deserted you and you never played sports? So what if you grew up in Manhattan and failed your driving test nine times?) You slip in behind the steering wheel. Suddenly you understand why you were born. Stop everything. Find some gas. Let's drive this baby to Santiago!

In Cuba, it's that way for everyone: a cacharro with a working battery and a full tank of gas is a holiday in itself. Forget Christmas. Forget Carnival. Forget the Forty-First Anniversary of Fidel's Attack on the Moncada Barracks. It's party time! Somehow, through a dizzying chain of bartering, string pulling, and back slapping, the fixings for a cook-out materialize. Twelve people of assorted length and girth climb into a just-resuscitated '49 Plymouth convertible and head straight for the beach. The water is bath warm, the wind stirs just enough to keep the mosquitoes disoriented, and the radio blasts a salsa so hot it nearly overcooks the pork. *Sí, hombre, así vivímos* [Yes sir, this is living].

Public transportation, a necessary evil, just doesn't cut it. Neither do the tin cans-on-wheels from the ex-Soviet bloc. Emilia Fernández understands this. He owns three cacharros himself—a Dodge, a Ford, and a Chevy, all from the forties and fifties—but only one working battery. A Mother Teresa among mechanics, Emilio lends this single battery to fellow cacharro owners stranded with dead batteries. One neighbor needs it to go visit his mother for her birthday (heaven help him if he doesn't show up). Another wants to take his family an a long-delayed trip to another province: Emilia always obliges. His is the pure spirit of the revolution.

To repair a cacharro in Cuba you need:
A. imagination
B. connections, and
C. mucho chutzpah.

You can't just walk into an automotive store or drive up to a reputable garage and request a new muffler or a brake job. If you are sufficiently unenlightened to actually take your car to a state-run repair shop, you might as well bid farewell to the decent parts you do have. Theft is a big problem both inside and outside the official garages. Cars are stripped for parts or stolen for illegal resale. Consequently, many of the finest cacharros are kept under tarpaulins, a sure sign that there is something underneath worth stealing. Some car owners have gone so far as to inscribe their initials on the windshields in a vague attempt at security. It doesn't stop the crooks.

The black market for spare parts, especially old American spare parts, is enormous and highly lucrative. The market's machinations are a mystery to all but the initiated. Yet the persistent (and Cubans are nothing if not persistent) can always find a way to tap into the network. One man, the owner of a white Studebaker, complained that some *desgraciado* had stolen the tail lights right off his car. His annoyance was tempered somewhat by the fact that he'd heard there was a source in Viñales, 130 miles west of Havana, who might be able to supply him with another set, possibly original. That is how he would spend his Sunday.

When a repair problem goes beyond the talents of a particular car owner and his little neighborhood group, the names of brilliant mechanics around the country are reverentially whispered. There are usually a couple of these men in every province, über-mechanics in a land of technical aces. Men whose thick, blackened hands should be enshrined along with other totems of the revolution. Men whose miracles of mechanical verve and inventiveness render fellow craftsmen weak with admiration. Outside their country, they might be hopelessly lost in a world of all-electronic ignitions, air bags, anti-lock brakes, and automatic cruise control. But in Cuba, their services are absolutely required. These mechanics usually work out of their homes, on the sly, charging exorbitant fees far exorbitant solutions. No one begrudges them a centavo.

Others get around car trouble by machining their own parts. Antonio Aguilera of Santiago de Cuba converted his garage into a sideline business producing parts for American automobiles. It is as much a labor of love as profit since he, too, is the owner of a beautiful cacharro—a '56 Hudson Hornet Hollywood, green and white with yellow trim, so perfect it could suck nectar from wildflowers. A familiar scene: Aguilera is reviving a dead cacharro for an increasingly restless group of young men. They mill about, drinking beer, looking over Aguilera's shoulder. It's getting later and later and there's a party somewhere. The prettiest girls will already be taken. Suddenly, the engine springs to life. Cheers break out all around. Before they can hail Aguilera a genius, they're halfway down the road.

The scarcity of original parts has forged thousands of exotic mechanical marriages. Russian Gaz jeeps are particularly sought after for parts since their engines were copied from an American engine and adopt very nicely to many cacharros of the fifties. The Lada's carburetor, while no gem by any stretch of the imagination, is frequently grafted inside vintage American cars to improve mileage in gas-lean times. Organ donations from Volkswagens and other vehicles also come to the rescue of the cacharros. Rigoberto Ramírez Pérez of Havana cannibalized an entire Ford Falcon to resurrect a blue '36 Chevy. He and others on the island do what they can with the limited resources at hand. Who says the spirit of sacrifice is dead in revolutionary Cuba?

One hears of beer cans doubling as pistons (although no one ever admits to actually having seen this with his own two eyes). "Bolts" made of baling wire apparently are not uncommon. Cuban exiles in Miami sneer that it is the paper clips they left behind years ago that keep the body and soul of these cars intact. Mechanics in Cuba repeat the same joke with a certain amount of pride. One thing is certain: long before the Cold War thawed, cubanos were employing their own practical form of mechanical détente.

Paint is nearly as hard to get as spare parts. One year, pink may be all that's available—not a decorous pastel pink but a Tropicana showgirl neon pink—and suddenly, it seems, every car in the capital is in flamingo drag. Some cars have had so many paint jobs that a minor amount of sanding and scraping yields peeling frescoes of confetti colors.

Cubans also love to gussy up their cacharros with a myriad of knick-knacks and decorations that would horrify purist vintage car owners anywhere else. In Cuba, historic preservation is a luxury few can afford. Sleek hood ornaments (streamlined birds in takeoff positions are particular favorites) are traded and mounted and extolled. Painted flames arch back from front wheels. Flashy metallic stars, made by local artisans, are frequently bolted to the sides of the automobiles. Blue glass side windows turn backseats into soothing sanctuaries: Mercedes-Benz emblems ironically adorn the dashboards of many garden-variety Chevrolets. And stickers of all sorts enliven even the most beat-up cacharros with a little humor: T-U-R-B-O-C-H-A-R-G-E they scream across the windshield. Yeah, right.

It is a shock to learn how many cacharros are still in the hands of their original owners, or have been passed down from one generation to the next like cherished family heirlooms. Pedro Pérez Vega, of Pinar del Río province, bought his blue and white '57 Ford brand new. In all these years he's put only 140,000 miles on it. He stores it under a thatched roof carport and swears it's never given him more than a half-day of trouble. Manuel Mario Aguilera also bought his '50 Oldsmobile direct from an American dealer. He estimates its mileage at 400,000 miles. Reading odometers is not a precise business in Cuba. *¿Quién, carajo, se recuerda?* Does it really matter how many times the thing's gone around? The car is running, isn't it? Rolando Urquiola, a

---

Havana mechanic, inherited his immaculate '51 Chevy from his father, also a mechanic. He claims it is the best-maintained car on the island. It is impossible to doubt him.

Cacharros are the quintessential ice breakers in contemporary Cuba. People who might otherwise be too shy or frightened to speak with foreigners turn positively garrulous when it comes to their beloved antediluvians. There is none of the usual looking over the shoulder to see who might be watching or listening to their conversation. They give their names freely and do not fear repercussions. When they praise their cacharros, owners lose track of time, superlatives, anecdotes. They engage in fleecy reminiscences. Boasting is part of the good-natured fun of it all.

When the maître d' at the Hotel Nacional, once the swankiest hotel in Havana, bought his Chevrolet Deluxe Power Glide in 1952, he claims it was one of three cars in Cuba that had air conditioning. He had the world by the tail in those days, driving around with his windows rolled all the way up. He never had any trouble giving a good-looking woman a ride. Forty-two years later, the air conditioning still works perfectly. And women still point at him, impressed.

Cubans love having their cars photographed. One owner of a black '38 Buick became so excited at the prospect of having his fifty-five-year-old baby immortalized in this book that he worked two days straight getting it running again. Even his wife got all dressed up for the big event. Others proudly recount their cars' milestones like parents of precocious children. The owner of a navy-and-white '59 Dodge Coronet gleefully relates how his automobile has already "killed" two Russian Ladas. It is clear he expects the death toll to climb. Car homicides aside, there is virtually no overt politicization of these vehicles. Although many of the vintage car owners are certainly intrigued by America, their interest, more often than not, happens to coincide with a love for the cars, but it is not necessarily connected to it. Yet there is something of a residual emotional link to the United States, especially among the older generation of cacharro owners. Is it possible, after all, to be in love with such an unmistakable icon of America without feeling the slightest stir for its popular culture?

Hector Fernández and his family live in a graceful old mansion in the Miramar section of Havana. Fernández, an avid disciple of General Motors, keeps his three vintage cars, a '50 Chevy, a '55 Olds, and a '56 Dodge, in impeccable condition by the courtyard fountain. He bought the cars in happier times. These days, his family is ostracized for having applied for a visa to leave the country for Panama. His son-in-law, Rodolfo, a lunatic Yankees fan and former world-class marathoner, has been demoted to teaching running to elementary school children. Rodolfo's son, Steve (he insists on being called Steve, not Estéban), is mad for Jack Nicholson. The family has erected a shrine to the actor—an autographed glossy obtained through an American friend is the centerpiece—in a corner of the living room, right over the ancient television set. It is one of their most prized possessions.

The Cuban government seems oblivious to the irony and

symbolism of having all these American fossils revving up their motors under its nose. In fact, several of the more famous American cacharros are displayed in a museum dedicated to automobiles that have played a prominent role in the revolution, like the car that Raúl Castro, Fidel's brother, drove during the attack on the Moncada barracks in 1953. Or the Maximum Leader's mother's Ford. Although the car's contribution is not specified, one is tempted to speculate how Cuba's history might have changed if Alina Ruz had driven, say, a Peugeot. Another vintage car, a '56 Buick Special, stands as a monument to all the heroic *compañeros* of Santiago who died fighting for the revolution. People actually make pilgrimages to these cars, bearing wreaths and roses. There is no tongue-in-cheek involved.

Pilgrimages of another sort occur among the cacharro owners themselves. Many make a hobby or holiday out of visiting the finest vintage American automobiles on the island. Invariably, those with great cars know or have heard, at least, of everyone else with a great car. They've seen each other driving around town, worked together on movies or televisions shows, thumbed the pictures taken by fellow enthusiasts on cross-country trips.

In fact, something of a cacharro hierarchy has developed in this socialist land. In the absence of Jaguars, BMWs, and Lexuses, the old fifties order still dominates. The owners of good Cadillacs are the elite, the automotive royalty. A '59 Eldorado Biarritz convertible—with fins that could slice the island in two—is as desirable a camp classic in Cuba as it is in the United States. (Perhaps it is no coincidence, then, that the revolution was ushered in at the height of this stylistic excess. Subsequent years saw the fins devolve into smaller and smaller appendages—mere scales, really—before disappearing altogether. A more sobering age was dawning on both sides of the Straits of Florida.)

General Motors cars are prized next after Cadillacs. Ask any cacharro owner in Cuba who made the best American cars before 1960 and the response, invariably, is GM. Now they may have an oddball or sentimental favorite, like the '53 Studebaker Starlight Coupe, one of the most sensational-looking cars ever built. But this has nothing to do with engineering. Studebakers are referred to locally as Studedesgracias, which translates roughly as: "Sure they look nice, but forget about going anywhere."

In Cuba there are about ten General Motors cars for every three Chryslers and two Fords. Chevrolets are far and away the most popular, probably because they were the most affordable automobiles of their time exported to Cuba. Currently, there are 5,413 registered Chevys on the island, most of them '51 to '57 models. One wonders if other American accoutrements of the time also abound in long-forgotten drawers—saddle shoes and poodle skirts, Brylcreem and Elvis Presley's Sun recordings. Or was it all mambo mambo mambo fever?

Today, while Americans are squeezing themselves into stingy econo-boxes, Cubans, who have far less in material goods and certainly much less fuel, continue struggling to preserve these grandiose, octane-gobbling boats. Only in

Cuba is the flagrance and pleasure of the American automobile phenomenon thoroughly savored—a direct expression of individuality in a sea of government conformity. The cars themselves have gone native in Cuba, thoroughly tropical, a little soft in the head from the heat. They're like a bunch of deliriously happy Michigan retirees in paradise, complete with daiquiris and tiny paper umbrellas. They have the best care in the world (Hell, with Cuban mechanics they'll live forever!), move around quite a bit for their age, and take in the sun with other old fogeys. What more could they possibly want?

Indisputably, the Cubans, over the years, have made these cars—these ultimate Yankee artifacts—their own. It's not just the multi-colored flags waving from the antennas, invoking the protection of Changó or Obatalá or another one of their favorite *santería* gods, or the little leather armrests that prevent blisters from too-hot chrome, but the Cubans' total reclamation of these automobiles. Sure, it's wonderful if the original tuck and roll is in good condition but if not, old clothes or burlap sacking will do just fine—for now. What, there's no gas for the guzzler? Bueno, let's go around to that young gas station attendant's house and see if he can't sell us just the tiniest bit to get us going (many station attendants do a brisk black market business siphoning off a liter of gas here and there).

The truth of the matter is, that despite the restrictions and privations of their society, despite a future that promises only uniform goods and a constant shortage of them, despite highways overrun with those downright dowdy Ladas, there is still plenty of energy to worship these old cacharros. Perhaps it is only fitting that their owners hold the keys to these perfect American symbols of nostalgia and hope. Now if they could only get their hands on those few drops of gas. . . .

SUSAN ORLEAN

Rough Diamonds

MOST OF THE TIME, the boys in *categoria pequeña*—the Cuban equivalent of Little League baseball—play on days when there hasn't been a coup in Latin America, or at least not in a country that supplies a lot of oil to Cuba. Unfortunately, the Ligeritos, a team made up of kids from the Plaza de la Revolución neighborhood of Havana, had a practice scheduled for the Sunday in April after the President of Venezuela was deposed. The uprising evaporated in a matter of days, but when I went to watch the Ligeritos play it was still fresh news, and many people were staying home and watching television reports on the crisis. Kids who wanted a ride to the practice had to wait out the developing story of the coup.

SUSAN ORLEAN, *called one of America's most original journalists, is a frequent contributor to* The New Yorker *(where this piece originally appeared in 2002),* Outside, *and* Rolling Stone, *and is the bestselling author of* The Orchid Thief *and* The Bullfighter Checks Her Makeup.

The practice was supposed to start at nine, but when I arrived there were only a few boys at the ball field. The Ligeritos play at a big and fitfully grassy park called El Bosque, at the end of a narrow neighborhood road. The park is flat and open, bracketed by tall, weary trees, and it has an unevenly paved basketball court at one end and enough room for a few baseball games at the other. That day, a loud game between two government ministries was already under way on the best diamond, and a couple of military police officers were on the basketball court taking foul shots with a flabby orange ball. The handful of boys who'd managed to get to the field had gathered on an overgrown area near the basketball court. One had a ball, one had a bat, and another had the most important equipment for playing baseball in Cuba—some sixteen-inch-long machetes, for grooming the field. While the boys played catch, a few of their fathers stripped to the waist and started slicing through the tall grass.

I had obtained an introduction to Juan Cruz, the Ligeritos' shortstop, through a friend in Havana. Juan is a slip of a kid, eleven years old, with dark, dreamy eyes, long arms, big feet, and the musculature of a grasshopper. His thirteen-year-old brother, Carlos, plays for the Ligeritos, too, but it is Juan who woke up at four every morning during the 2000 Olympics to watch the baseball games and who cradles his glove as if it were a newborn and who always wears a baseball cap, indoors or out. When his stepfather, Victor, is asked about Juan, he says, "Oh my God, this one dreams in baseball." In spite of the morning's news, Juan had persuaded Victor to drive Carlos and him to the ball field at nine. He popped out of the car almost before Victor had finished parking, and ran onto the field.

The morning was soft and wet, just on the verge of summer. In Havana's Parque Central, a daily assembly of old men were arguing fine points of Yankee and Red Sox history and the likelihood of Havana's Industriales sweeping the upstarts from Camagüey in the national series. The Havana baseball mascot—a fat, placid dachshund wearing a baseball shirt, sunglasses, and a Greek fisherman's hat—was brought to a spot near the trinket market every afternoon for souvenir snapshots. And everywhere boys were playing baseball. They were playing in the parking lot of Estadio Latinoamericano, home of Havana's two teams, the Industriales and the Metropolitanos; and alongside the Malecón seawall, observed by the snobby young hookers who like to line up there and smoke; and in the dense downtown of Old Havana, wherever some building had finally completed its gradual and melodramatic collapse, opening up just enough room to field a pickup game. Every time I came in or out of my hotel, a group of boys were in the street, dodging potholes as big as washtubs, and, whether it was the bright start of the morning or the half-darkness at the end of the day, they were always in the middle of a game.

There has been baseball in Cuba almost as long as there has been baseball anywhere. Introduced in the 1860s, it has been the dominant sport in the country ever since; volleyball and basketball are distant seconds, and soccer, the prevailing sport in the rest of Latin America, is hardly played. From the start, baseball has been strangely tangled up with politics.

Cubans embraced it as a statement of rebellion because it was a modern and sophisticated export from democratic America, rather than an imposition of imperial Spanish culture on the island. It was also played by people of all races, not just the white elite, which added to its political allure, and Cubans fleeing Spanish oppression took it with them to Venezuela, Puerto Rico, and the Dominican Republic.

In 1911, the Cincinnati Reds drafted two Cuban players, the first of more than a hundred to be recruited to the American major leagues over the next fifty years. In the 1940s and 1950s, some teams even had full-time scouts in Cuba. It has long been rumored that, in 1942, a scout working for the Washington Senators met with a promising teenage pitcher named Fidel Castro, a rangy right-hander with velocity but no technique. Castro claims that the team gave him a contract, which he turned down; baseball historians say the Senators never made him an offer. It has also been rumored that he passed on a five-thousand-dollar signing bonus from the New York Giants in order to go to law school. There is no dispute, however, that he remained passionate about the game.

After the revolution, Castro banned most aspects of American popular culture, but baseball was so embedded in Cuba and in his own life—he sometimes pitched for an exhibition team called the Bearded Ones—that it persisted and even expanded, although Castro remade it in the revolutionary spirit. In 1961, he enacted National Decree 83A, which outlawed professional sports in Cuba. Henceforth, all competitive sports would be played by amateurs, the best of whom would receive a small government stipend equivalent to a worker's salary. This would end, as Castro took care to point out, American-style "slave baseball," in which players were bought and sold like property, and in which players and owners—especially owners—were enriched at the expense of the public. Cuban players would represent their home provinces, would never be traded, and would never get rich. The first Cuban national series, in 1962, was, according to Castro, *"el triunfo de la pelota libre sobre la pelota esclava"*—the triumph of free baseball over slave baseball. Cuba's gold medals in the 1992 and 1996 Olympics were celebrated as vindication of revolutionary baseball, and the loss to the United States in Sydney was regarded as a calamity. Castro has said he would like two major-league franchises in the country, so that Cuban teams can regularly prove themselves against Americans. "One day, when the Yankees accept peaceful coexistence with our own country, we shall beat them at baseball, too," he said in a 1974 speech. "Then the advantages of revolutionary over capitalist sport will be shown."

Baseball, with its runs to home, its timeless innings, its harmony between the lone endeavor and the collaboration of a team, has always implied more than athletics. In Cuba, it has also come to describe a social history: the version of baseball you are part of is also the version of Cuba you are part of. There are still scores of retired ballplayers in Cuba who remember the game before the revolution, who hosted American players in the Cuban winter leagues, who might have played a few seasons in Texas or Florida, and whose superstar teammates were scooped up, legally, by American teams. There is a middle generation, players in their twenties and thirties, who were born after Decree 83A and grew up knowing only *la pelota libre*, who saw friends defect to play up north, and who have Castro as an occasional pitching coach and de-facto commissioner of the game. Finally, there are the kids like Juan, in *categoria pequeña*, who are now learning to play. Unless Castro lives to be a hundred, these kids will reach their prime without him—the first generation in three who will have baseball without having Castro telling them how to play the game.

Juan dreams about both Cuban and American baseball. It is illegal to watch American games in Cuba—that is, it is illegal to have satellite television on which you could see the games. But for years Cubans have been sneaking small satellite dishes into the country by painting them to look like decorative platters, and those people who haven't managed to get their own dish often barter for tapes of the major leagues at *categoria pequeña* games. As a result, Juan is now equally loyal to the Yankees and to the Industriales. "My favorites are, for the Cubans, Omar Linares, German Mesa, and Javier Mendez," he says, "and, for the Americans, Derek Jeter, Tino Martinez, and Baby Ruth." When I asked him whom he had rooted for during the Olympics, he just grinned and said, "My team."

That morning, he was wearing the Ligeritos' uniform, a white jersey with purple raglan sleeves and the team's name in jazzy blue letters across the front, and his favorite hat, an old Albert Belle Cleveland Indians cap that he had got from a friend. I asked him if he was an Albert Belle partisan. "No,

I don't really even know him. I just like the picture on the hat," Juan said, referring to the Indians' Chief Wahoo logo. The Ligeritos' neighborhood rivals are the suspiciously counterrevolutionary-sounding Coca-Colas, and the Brigada Especiales, a team sponsored in part by the Special Brigade police, whose barracks are across the street from El Bosque. Even teams with sponsors just squeak by when it comes to equipment. You rarely see wooden bats in Cuba, because of their cost—until two years ago, even the major-league teams used aluminum ones—and new leather gloves are a luxury. Many of the kids I saw playing on the street were bare-handed or had gloves that were so limp and splayed that they looked like leather pancakes. The most popular street game in Cuba, four corners (or its variant, three corners), is super-economy baseball—you play it without gloves, and it involves whacking a round thing (rock, bottle cap, ball, wad of tape) with a long thing (tree branch, broom handle, two-by-four) over the heads of your opponents.

While Juan and Carlos took turns swatting at pitches and fielding grounders, Victor and I sat on a concrete beam lying at the edge of the field. "When I was a kid, I always played four corners," Victor said. "We had some sewers on our street, and they had those round metal covers, and we just used them as our bases. With us, it was always baseball, baseball, baseball, all the time." He smiled and shook his head. "With these guys, with Juan especially, it's the same. I can't wait to get him a bike so he can take himself to his games."

For some boys in Cuba, it really is baseball all the time:

every child in the country is evaluated at the age of five and steered toward a particular sport, and boys favoring baseball begin playing interschool tournaments and join a *categoria pequeña* team. The talented kids are usually well known to the national scouts by the time they're ten. (Presently, there is no baseball program for girls, although a *categoria pequeña* is planned for next year.) At thirteen, the outstanding athletes are admitted to one of fifteen Sports Initiation Schools, the first rung in the Soviet-model athletic program that Castro established in 1961. The very best of those are sent to an Advanced School for Athletic Perfection when they turn sixteen. Castro is especially proud of the system. A billboard in the Havana stadium carries one of his favorite declarations: "Cuba has developed a real and healthy sports culture."

The Ligeritos' coach, Maximo Garcia Cardenas, was at El Bosque when I arrived, and, after greeting the parents, he called the boys together for some drills. Cardenas is sixty-five years old. He played professional baseball in Cuba from 1955 to 1960—the last five years that pro ball existed in the country. In 1961, he left for the United States and pitched in the Double-A Texas League; he spent the next fourteen years with various teams in Mexico. When he returned to Cuba, he went to work for the National Commission of Baseball as a pitching coach for the Cuban national team. He has been coaching the Ligeritos for four years. He has known baseball before and during Castro, and likes to keep his hand in the baseball that will come after him. "Some of these boys are very, very good," he said during a break. "Watch Hector, this one." He gestured toward a wiry boy wearing the team jersey, Snoopy socks, and black Nike sneakers. The boy noticed Cardenas pointing toward him, so he crouched and put out his glove and got a tough look on his face. "That one might really be something," Cardenas went on, keeping his eyes on the boy as he spoke. "He could really be something."

By ten, the news from Venezuela must have been drying up, because a dozen more boys appeared, fanned out, and started throwing to each other, ducking around the men who were still clearing the field with machetes. The kids were dressed in an international array of T-shirts advertising Mexican rock groups, Korean cars, Canadian concert tours, and American baseball teams; all of them were slight and tan and excited, too earnest to horse around much, and yet old enough to affect a little bluster. Now that most of the team was in place, Cardenas started another series of drills, hollering at the boys to move quickly and watch the ball. They practiced for ten minutes or so, and then Cardenas called them together near the scrap of cardboard that was marking third base. He divided them into two squads for the practice game, and then turned to Hector, who was the captain of the team. Hector stood at attention in front of him, and the rest of the boys lined up to the side. "Are you and your colleagues ready?" Cardenas asked him.

"My colleagues and I are ready," Hector said.

The boys yelled, "Ready!"

"Are you ready to play for the good of the team?" Cardenas asked.

"We are ready," Hector said.

The boys again yelled, "Ready!" They jostled each other and crowded closer to Cardenas.

"Who owns the right to sports?" Cardenas asked.

The boys chanted, *"El deporte es un derecho del pueblo!"* (Sport is the right of the people—one of Castro's trademark slogans.)

"Tell me again?"

"Sport is the right of the people!"

"Once more?"

"Sport is the right of the people!" they yelled, and then scrambled to their positions on the field.

Juan says that if he doesn't get to play baseball professionally he would like to be an investigator, a policeman, a doctor, or a hero. "Those would be OK," he says, "but I would like to be a baseball player." He says he would be happy to have his career either in Cuba or in the United States, although he likes Cuban baseball more than American. "The Cubans play for fun, not for money," he explained to me between innings. I asked him what he thought of American athletes, and he said, "They play only for the millions. A real player plays because he likes baseball and doesn't need that much money to live a normal life."

At the top of the second inning, Javier Mendez, an outfielder for the Industriales and one of Juan's heroes, stopped by El Bosque with his four-year-old son, Javier, Jr. Mendez is broad-chested and sturdy, with meaty arms and legs, and he has a goatee and a buzz cut and big dimples. That morning, he was wearing Oakley sunglasses, an Olympic website

T-shirt, and a cast on his right hand. Mendez is thirty-seven years old and a huge star in Cuba. He had been on pace to tie the Cuban record for lifetime doubles and to get his two-thousandth hit—something only ten other Cuban players have managed—when he was struck by a pitch and had to end his season. He had hoped to retire this year, but he wants to polish off those records. "Next season," he said, flexing the fingers of his injured hand, "if all goes well."

Mendez had come by to visit a friend whose son played for the Ligeritos, but it was also a chance to let Little Javier take a few swings. The boy was dressed in a tiny, spotless Industriales uniform and an oversized batting helmet. When he swung, the bat nearly toppled him. When he finally hit a pitch, he toddled straight to second base. "Javi, tag first! Tag first!" Mendez shouted. He yelled something to Cardenas, and they both started laughing. "Oh my God, look at him," Mendez said. "Well, I wasn't any good when I was young. I was weak and really small. I just practiced and persevered. I grew up in a fishing village but I didn't know how to fish, so I played baseball. But I wasn't any good until I was sixteen."

Mendez has been on one Olympic team and won a slew of national championships. The Cuban government allowed its players to take sabbaticals in Japan in the early nineties, and Mendez and a few other Cubans played there for two seasons, but he subsequently returned to his team, at around the time that the pitcher Livan Hernandez defected to play in the United States. Just a few years later, Mendez's team-mate (and Livan's older brother) Orlando Hernandez also defected, and signed a multimillion-dollar contract with the

Yankees. Star athletes in Cuba often receive gifts from the government—cars, houses, equipment—but most of the time their compensation is measly. A few days after the Ligeritos' practice, when I took Juan and Carlos to a major-league game between Havana's Metropolitanos and Camaguey, a vender offered to sell me not only coffee, cigars, and potato croquettes but, for fifteen dollars, any of the players' hats or shirts—as soon as they were done using them in the game.

Mendez has played one game in the United States. On May 3, 1999, the Cuban national team played the Baltimore Orioles at Camden Yards, as part of a cultural exchange that had begun in March, when the Orioles played the national team in Havana. The Cubans won the game in Baltimore, 12—6, suffered an interruption during the fifth inning when an anti-Castro protester ran onto the field, and lost one pitching coach, who defected afterward. The game was nevertheless considered a success—the beginning of what was being called "baseball diplomacy." Mendez loved playing in Baltimore and said it was a shame about the defection, especially since it might interfere with any future games. "You know, it's hard when anyone on the team leaves for other countries," he said. "It's hard on the team. It's hard on the fans. It makes people very depressed."

I asked him if it was a good life, to be a Cuban baseball star.

He watched the next boy come up to the plate and slap at a pitch. "It's a good life," he said, "in a sense."

The boys drifted over to see Mendez, most of them too shy to get close or say anything when he asked them how they were doing. He watched the game intently, applauding the good bits and the good catches, shouting encouragement and corrections along with Cardenas, as if this were the most important game in the world, a big-league game, a game he might play in now, or one that Cardenas starred in forty years ago, rather than a matchup between gawky boys on a ragged field on a quiet street in Havana.

It was now midday and the game was over. Juan had had a great morning: not only had he hit a single and a double and made one flashy catch—a hard-hit bad-hopping shot from Hector—but he had got up the nerve to ask Mendez to pose with him for a photograph. Even after the other boys had headed off, Juan wanted to keep hitting, but his father said it was time to go home.

NANCY STOUT

The Story of the Cigar

T HROUGHOUT THE WORLD AND throughout the history of the existence of cigars, there has been one, and one only, that has been recognized by the true connoisseur as the ultimate cigar, the legendary and peerless one, the *ne plus ultra*, and that is the *habano*. *Habanos* are cigars produced only in Cuba, shipped only from the port of Havana, made entirely of special varieties of Cuban-grown tobacco, and marketed only by the designated name *habano*.

They are smoked by the most famous people and sold for the highest prices. They are imitated and counterfeited. And, always, as the true sign of a rare luxury item, supply sometimes cannot meet demand, and they are often simply "N/A," not available.

NANCY STOUT *is a writer, editor, historian, and photographer. Her books include 1997's* Habanos: The Book of The Havana Cigar *(from which the piece was excerpted),* Homestretch: A Celebration of America's Greatest Tracks, *and* The Colvins: Oregon Pioneers.

Havana cigars have been N/A in the United States since the imposition of the blockade by President Kennedy in 1962. We get to smoke the imitated and counterfeited ones, or fine cigars from other countries. The irony is that Cubans do not smoke them either; *habanos* can only be purchased in Cuba in U.S. dollars, and most Cubans don't have extra dollars. On the other hand, Cubans are not cigarless; they are able to buy four national cigars per month at their local bodega, in pesos, on a ration card. These are called *tabacos*, which simply means "cigars" in Cuba, and they are made of rejected leaf. All other tobacco, that is, the very best, goes into cigars for export, the *habanos*.

Officially, *habanos* must meet five conditions. *Fundamental:* That the cigars be manufactured of tobacco, cultivated on a large scale, of particular varieties grown in Cuba. *Origen:* That the cigars are manufactured in Cuba. *Materia prima:* That the tobacco used is of high quality and the filler is necessarily of large leaves. *Proceso industrial:* That the product is made entirely by hand. *Garantía Oficial:* That the product is presented in foreign markets as guaranteed by the Cuban government, bearing a legal seal.

Knowledge of *habanos*, for a whole generation of Americans and Cubans, whether for political or financial reasons, is still a pretty nebulous thing. What, for instance, does a Cohiba cigar—a brand so sought after that it is rare and expensive even in Havana—taste like? You cannot rely entirely on the older generation who "knew" Havana cigars before the revolution because some of the blends have changed. The heavy, sweet cigars of the 1950s are anathema to the dry, distilled power of the Cohiba developed in the 1960s. Now, every cigar smoker wants a box of Cohibas, but there are not enough produced to fill the demand. They are a luxury item in limited supply, and the same is true for the Montecristo and Romeo y Julieta blends. The European, Middle Eastern, and Asian cigar market pretty much dictates their availability and taste.

If *habanos*, with their mythical status and rarity, remain largely unknown, then cigar factories remain largely unseen. People in Havana do not know much about the famous factories and often confuse them with places for cigarette production, except for the La Corona factory, which is open to the public, and Partagás, which is not. These are hard to miss, though, since one is located at the base of the Presidential Palace, now the Museum of the Revolution, and the other is behind the Capitol Building, now the Academy of Sciences. But where were all the other factories? I had earlier roamed most of the streets and neighborhoods of Havana for months, photographing its architecture. Yet I felt that a certain mystery surrounded the cigar industry. I searched the streets convinced that there were unmarked cigar factories everywhere; I just had to find them.

The year I began to study *habanos*, exceptionally heavy rains fell during the growing season. Industry officials, preoccupied and fearful of the effects of the weather, encouraged me to delay my research until another season. Not wanting to wait, I argued that tobacco leaves were just one part of the story. I found an ally in Eusabio Leah, the Historian of the City, who understood my obsession with the streets and buildings of Havana and my desire to discover what lay behind these world-famous cigar factories. He admitted that he, too, had always felt a fascination for the industry but only knew it secondhand. He gave me a letter of endorsement and assigned a translator, Nuria Oquendo Arroyo, from his office to get me over the rough spots in the research libraries and at the factories. Thus equipped, and with the required licenses from the U.S. Treasury Department, I was given an opportunity rarely available to North Americans: I could snoop around Havana and its environs unimpeded.

I scoured the libraries for books about Havana cigars and was surprised to find only one, *Havana Cigars* by William Gill, similar to what I had in mind. It was written in 1910, so I thought an update would be timely.

In Cuba, there have always been official tobacco historians: in this century, José Rivero Muñiz wrote three books between 1946 and 1964; José Perdomo compiled a wonderful lexicon in 1940; and Antonio Nuñez Jimenez currently produces books for Cubatabaco and Tabacalera, Madrid. In addition, two scholars have looked at the industry: Gaspar Garcia Gallo, in a two-volume work produced in 1961; and an Englishwoman, Jean Stubbs, whose 1985 doctoral dissertation examines the agro-industrial complex between 1860 and 1959. Everybody's favorite book, including my own, is *Cuban Counterpoint: Tobacco and Sugar* by Fernando Ortiz, published in 1936.

Most of these authors have an obsessive interest in defending Cuba's claim as the creator of "rolled leaves" and as the earliest recorded place where tobacco was found. There are volumes of history analyzing fifteenth- and sixteenth-century references. On the other hand, there are style books on smoking by tobacco connoisseurs such as F. W. Fairholt, an Englishman writing in 1859 when cigars were still relatively new in London In all the books two things are clear: one, cigars made of Cuban-grown tobacco are legendary because of their superior flavor and aroma; and two, there have always been imitations, which all the authorities admonish readers to avoid.

I learned to ignore imitators' labels, no matter how gilded. The twenty-dollar boxes of Cohibas in the streets of Havana are not genuine. Counterfeit *habanos* date back to the sixteenth century when Cuban tobacco was the exclusive privilege of Spanish kings; all other cigars were unauthorized and usually contraband. Pirates and buccaneers craved the lucrative *habanos* and would do anything to obtain it in their raids along the Cuban coasts In fact, until fairly recently, tobacco was part of an illicit trade outside the official relationship between Cuba and Spain. In the United States, the politics of trade agreements intrude on our smoking habits even today; in New York one could overhear in conversation, "I get tobacco from a reliable source smuggled directly from Havana." Such a statement could also have been made in Elizabethan England four hundred years ago.

For centuries the world hungered for well-crafted cigars, and around 1820, when the Spanish finally let the Cubans export *habanos* to countries other than Spain, Europeans and Americans were instant buyers. Those shipped directly from the port of Havana have always been guaranteed to be authentic. Better still are cigars boxed, sealed, and bearing a label with the exporter's name and address, which promises accountability.

Cubans themselves rarely claim they have the best tobacco in the world. Rather, they wisely let the rest of the world say it. Cuban literature on agriculture simply quotes the references, the U.S. Department of Agriculture among them, that come to this conclusion, and first-place medals garnered in competitions all over the world during the nineteenth and early twentieth centuries confirm it.

In the early days of the export cigar, women smoked as well as men. We know this because tobacco connoisseurs compiled albums of watercolors and engravings of snuff-taking and pipe-smoking men: suddenly, around 1830, these began to depict women with cigars. Women, also, have traditionally been key players in the cigar industry, though this has not always been recognized. Although black women were tobacco sellers in Columbus's day, and women played an important role when the cigar market billowed in the nineteenth century, and were leaf selectors in the growing areas, only men were in the rolling departments. In the 1960s, Celia Sanchez brought women in as rollers, and today they make up over half of the rollers in Havana. The Cohiba factory is the outcome of one of Sanchez's many projects to employ women. One of her missions was to find professions for the ninety thousand maids—and probably as many prostitutes—in Havana during the first decade of the revolution.

In my frequent and inquisitive trips around Havana, I

have never been asked where I was going or what I was doing. This does not mean that the bureaucratic arm of the export cigar industry, the state-owned company *Habanos*, S.A., was not curious about what I was up to. I knew that I was breaking some rules. For instance, I visited some factories normally off-limits to outsiders; but after conferences and phone calls to *Habanos*, S.A., I was always welcomed. Looking back, I feel that this had very little to do with security. It is more likely that visitors are seen as disruptive to the manufacturing process, especially now, when there is an all-out effort to increase production. As G. Cabrera Infante says in *Holy Smoke*, "To make a cigar is a devil of a skill, but to roll so many in a day's work is sheer sorcery." Even though the rolling rooms are the size of gymnasiums, they seem intimate and have a family atmosphere that is easily disturbed, especially since Cubans have an immense curiosity about outsiders.

As it happened, I was visiting the Romeo y Julieta factory just days after the Cubans had shot down two small planes that had flown into their air space from the United States. Our two countries were firing hostile accusations toward each other hourly. I held my breath as I was introduced over the microphone as a North American writer. The rollers broke into applause. For an instant I felt my throat tighten and thought tears would come into my eyes. Later, I decided they were delighted that I'd come with a letter from Eusebio Leal. People love his weekly television program, on which he walks through the city and talks about its history; they want to be, like him, aficionados of Havana's history. Leal also secures resources from institutions throughout the world for restoration of Old Havana, and, perhaps because of this, is a friend of Fidel.

I have met Fidel. At a reception, I shook a hand softer and better manicured than my own, and with slightly longer nails. I am tall, but I had to look up. Fidel is perhaps six feet seven inches in his military boots, and was by far the tallest person in the room. I was introduced to him in 1992, while working on my book on Havana architecture. Cubans noticed in that book that I often ignore the usual landmarks. Consequently, Habanos, S.A. didn't expect me to stick to their view of the cigar industry and didn't try to make me follow it. I frequently stopped by their offices to ask questions. I knew they were keeping an eye on my progress and assumed they were monitoring my routes as I worked the city with my lists and map.

Each day I methodically traveled to addresses I had taken from a 1940s list of cigar manufacturers. I also had a short list of factories from the 1978 telephone directory, the most recent one until a new edition was published in 1996. I annotated my map with ink spots, except when I found holes in blocks where a building once stood. Some days I came across ghosts of the past—buildings standing empty as though waiting for something to change. Other times I discovered factories that are now tobacco warehouses. Good days revealed vital, efficient factories that have never changed. I also located a group of buildings, not on any list, that are tobacco warehouses.

In most of the literature on smoking, cigar smokers go to

private clubs, drink, and smoke one good cigar. This may be how they used to do it, but in reality private clubs were banned with the revolution, food on occasion is scarce, wine is a luxury, and if only one cigar is available, Cubans smoke it after breakfast, not dinner! In the morning rush hour, commuters on bicycles and policemen on motorcycles smoke cigars. In my months in Havana, I learned all the nuances of cigar-smoking behavior.

One hot morning, en route to the farmers market, I walked down Paseo, an avenue that has very large trees in the center and old iron and wood-slatted benches left over from the Republican period. I stopped to rest and shared a bench with a man smoking a cigar. He was reading a novel and didn't look up. His cigar was bigger than a government-issued breva, but not an expensive export model either. It seemed to be of little concern to him. Much of the time it rested in his hand, which was on his knee; then it was brought to his mouth, puffed gently several times, and returned to rest. At one point the cigar stayed in the reader's mouth and both hands held the novel, *Gallego* by Miguel Barnet.

A man came up and interrupted the reader to ask for a light for his cigarette. The reader didn't offer his cigar, but reached into his pocket for a lighter and quickly returned to reading. Alter the man went away, the reader removed the ashes from his cigar. Had the man had a cigar and not a cigarette, the reader very well might have raised his eyes, searched the man's face, put the novel down, if only briefly, knocked the ashes from his cigar and offered it for a light. He might even have spoken a word or two, but that he did not

INSIDE CUBA

illustrates that cigar smokers are seen as superior in Cuba. Based on the smoking hierarchy, it is understood that the one would ignore the other; this is, after all, still the country where the first cigarettes were made from sweepings from cigar factory floors and referred to as "dirty."

I had been so dazzled by wrapper leaves, after seeing the tall plants grown under the shade of acres of gauzy white cloth in the Vuelta Abajo, that I couldn't conceptualize the rest of the cigar. Then Esther Luisa Hernandez, one of Cuba's great rollers, explained that each cigar is both recipe and ingredients, outer brocade and inner lining, and that the roller is both chef and tailor. The cigar is an object and a symbol. Therefore, I begin this book with Esther. In the first chapter. "The Art of the Cigar," she explains the slow and very careful process of making each cigar, which I hope will fill your mind with the aroma, the taste, and the feel of tobacco leaves, and evoke a sense of the cigar's extraordinary five-hundred-year history.

A word of caution, though. After five hundred years, the Cuban cigar industry has packaged its story very smoothly. I have tried to give you an appendix to that story. If I had not read historian Jean Stubbs, I would not have known how precarious the industry had become at the turn of the century. If I had not read ethnographer Fernando Ortiz, I would not know about the intrigues among sailors and women, Indians and blacks, to popularize tobacco. If I had not seen an illustration of a lynching—tobacco farmers hanging from trees—in a book of poetry and later in a child's history book, the legacy of the tobacco monopoly would not have sunk in.

Discovering the *Cartilla Rústica*, which I found in the

Rare Book Room of the New York Public Library after searching every library in Havana, gave me the most pleasure. If there is a bible of tobacco growing, this is it. Written in 1840 as a dialogue between a father and son, it contains all of the myths and practices of tobacco in one little treatise. It is a primer of growing practices and a key to much of the symbolism on cigar box labels. My visit with Alejandro Robaina, Cuba's preeminent grower, only confirms that very little has changed in the way that Cuban tobacco has been grown and cured since the *Cartilla Rústica* was written. This is perhaps the main reason why Havana cigars have maintained their legendary place throughout history. . . .

Esther Luisa Hernandez is one of Cuba's great tobacco rollers. She is a tall, slender, African-Cuban woman. Her hands are delicate, with glossy skin like polished wood, and her nails are painted light pink, the color of summer roses. She wears large glasses that sit in the middle of the bridge of her nose. She was in the process of making a julieta, a fairly large cigar, when I met her at the Romeo y Julieta factory.

The room she works in has fluorescent light overhead and natural light from a long wall lined with opened windows. A soft breeze sweeps across the rolling tables. Unlike most cigar factories, which are dim places where dark green window blinds are drawn so the tobacco stays damp, in this one the cinnamon leaves mix with a fresh breeze. I fuss with my camera and try to put the three feet of my tripod in a place where they don't fit. Finally, I simply stand in front of Esther, my elbows leaning on her table, and watch. She smiles at this decision.

As she worked she told me that she had been rolling cigars for twenty-five years and had been awarded a commemorative cigar in recognition of her work. "My mother rolled cigars in a factory, in Pinar del Río." She told me that her mother had been recognized for her skill as a roller as well.

"Let me show you how I roll cigars." It is a simple invitation.

"There are three varieties of leaves that make up the filler, the *tripa*, of a cigar." I'd seen this done a hundred times before. Was it the sunlight that made the leaves on her table look so different? The rolling appeared to be in slow motion.

"I take two leaves of *el seco tripa*, dry filler, for flavor. I add half a leaf of *ligero*, light, to give the cigar strength," and she tore one leaf in half and pressed it into her palm along with the two dry filler leaves. I understand that she is teaching me a recipe—she is telling me how cigars are blended.

"You also need one leaf of *volado* for combustion."

She wraps a binder around the julieta, trims it, and puts it into a mold. Now she turns her attention again to me. "You wanted to know about the cigars I smoke?" I tell her that I'd been learning about smoking habits in Havana by asking a lot of questions.

"My own cigars are softer; the ones I make for myself." She pauses. "I'll make one for you." We start again. She chooses two leaves from the Romeo y Julieta blend on her table. They are thick, but soft and spongy. She takes the other half-leaf left over from the julieta, then picks up two dark and thick *volado* leaves. I watch the *volado* go into the center of the leaves already cupped in her hand.

"Those are two *volado*," I protest, and ask for clarification, thinking, "How can she use two leaves of fire?"

Then she put the long filler leaves down on her table lengthwise, folding and compressing them together in a roll. "This does not change the flavor. I've reduced the *ligero* proportionately by adding more fire. A roller may add more of any of the three ingredients. It depends on the leaves before her." I like the way she speaks as though all rollers are women.

I smoked one of her cigars later that day. It burned comfortably fast, easily and well, and it certainly was *not* a bland cigar, despite her "soft" description. Although bigger than a panatela, and a little smaller than a breva, I smoked it in about twenty minutes.

She returns to making julietas. I concentrate on the *capote*, the binder. This is one of the two outer leaves on the cigar, similar in texture to the outer wrapper.

"This leaf is like an inner lining in a dress." She takes a knife and trims the well-shaped body to size. The filler leaves left over from the cut are brushed aside.

Esther takes the *capote*-wrapped cigar—called a "bunch"—and puts it into a mold, a *tabla*. Every table has a stack of molds shaped for the type of cigar being rolled. A young man comes by to pick up the molds and carries them to a press.

"Is every cigar put in a mold?"

"Depending on the *vitola* [the size and shape of the cigar]. All large cigars are put in a mold. They remain there for a period of time, not particularly long—in some cases only ten minutes. They settle and shape." We look at the molds stacked up in a press. The young man tightens the press by hand.

"The press is not about shape, it is about good density. The press makes internal combustion of the tobacco good."

Other women join us for a few moments from time to time. We are mother and daughter, teacher and student. There is a hum in the factory, but not from machines. People converse quietly, from table to table and along the aisles, with their supervisors and friends.

Esther opens a package of *capa*, or wrapper leaves. In the Romeo y Julieta factory these are distinctly brown, flecked with gold. In Havana, unfolding squares of plastic containing *capa* leaves is rather like seeing gems uncovered at a jeweler. It seems impossible not to stare for a moment. She gently smoothes a *capa* leaf, spreading it out on her table, then trims along the outer edge of the leaf.

I think about what I'd learned in Pinar del Río. Nearly all the energies of growing shade tobacco—developing these big, pale green leaves, grown under miles of cheesecloth, tied up with thousands of yards of string so the plants stand perfectly straight, like ballerinas—go into these wrapper leaves. Good wrappers are like silk, extremely soft, with fine veins more like delicate webs than a vegetable structural system. Esther's wrapper felt like oiled tissue paper.

"The *capa* is the cigar's outside dress." I know that the *capa* is a leaf that is selected for visual appeal, an expensive outer layer. She takes the body of the cigar from the pressed mold and lays it down on the *capa*.

"Begin at the end of the cigar that is lighted and finish at the end that goes in the mouth." She rolls the *capa* in a spiral around the body. Then with her knife she cuts out a little circle of tobacco, about the size of a nickel. She touches a tiny dot of vegetable paste to the circle, and then, placing it over the head of the cigar with her thumbs, she smoothes the completely enclosed head, the *casquillo*. She holds the cigar for a moment, then compares it to a gauge on the table to check its length. With a *chaveta*, a knife without a handle and with a short, moon-shaped blade, she trims the end to the proper length, pushing aside the spare tobacco.

The cigar is finished. It is unique. She, however, is proud that it looks like all the others. As if she knows what I'm thinking, the great roller sums up her work: "Of course, the art of the cigar is always about individual perfection achieving uniformity."

In the quality control department the cigars will be sorted by color and shape, and men and women will select the twenty-five nearly identical cigars that go into a box. Each row will be carefully arranged so that no two cigars will contrast sharply. The ringer will lift each cigar out of the box, never changing the order, never rotating the cigar, and will paste the paper ring around the head of the cigar and return it to the box, exactly as found. All this is done in the name of individual perfection achieving uniformity.

ANDREI CODRESCU

The Flowers of
the Revolution

JACK'S BREAKFAST-AND-LUNCH-ONLY eatery in the central business district in New Orleans has checkered tablecloths. The menu has forty soups and sandwiches, including the rarely requested Cuban sandwich: pork, tomatoes and chicken. There is a wine list, but few people drink wine at lunch anymore; it's a mineral water and Fruitopia crowd. And let's not even talk about smoking, though Jack, talking to me after closing time, is puffing on a long Romeo y Julieta, $30 in Canada, acquired for $3 in Santiago de Cuba, the second-largest city in Cuba.

"I met her when she was 14," he says. "She'll be 15 this year. Here is her picture."

From a billfold stuffed with credit cards, he pulls out a snapshot. It's a girl in a green miniskirt

ANDREI CODRESCU *was born in Sibiu, Romania. He is a poet, novelist, essayist, screenwriter, and frequent columnist on National Public Radio. His books include* Messiah *and* Wakefield. *This piece originally appeared in* The New York Times Magazine *in 1998.*

standing in water up to her knees. She's doe-tender, chocolate-hued, looking with uncertain flirtatiousness at the camera. Around her neck is a Pioneer neckerchief, testifying to her schoolgirl status and devotion to socialism.

"I started going to Cuba in '93," Jack says. "It was unbelievable. At this fiesta in Santiago, I had one girl waiting outside by the rum truck and I was by the wall with this other girl I just met. But then Yasmina showed up with some high-school friends. I told them all, "No more, I met the one." "So, it seems, have increasing numbers of foreign, middle-aged men, including many Americans.

In December 1995, Fidel Castro announced a crackdown on prostitution and private businesses, but the crackdown never materialized. What the writer Pico Iyer reported in 1994—"Prostitution, which was scarcely visible (if only for security reasons) five years ago, is pandemic now: the tourist hotels are filled with Cuban teen-agers reddening their lips with children's crayons"—is still true in 1998. The U.S.-Cuba Trade and Economic Council estimates that 84,000 American citizens visited Cuba in 1997, at least one-fifth of them illegally.

Tom Miller, author of *Trading With the Enemy: A Yankee Travels Through Castro's Cuba,* has been going to Cuba for more than ten years, for trips ranging from five days to ten months. "I don't think many Americans go to Cuba with sex as their primary reason, as Mexicans, Spaniards, Bahamians and Italians do," he says. "But I do think some of them come home with sex as the primary incentive to return. The romantic range spreads from lust and money to love and marriage."

Jack met Yasmina in Santiago de Cuba, outside a salsa bar called Casa de las Jovenes, a state-run place that draws big crowds most every night. Jammed in front of the gates are gaggles of girls hoping to find a tourist to pay the $3 entrance fee. Three dollars in Cuba is one-fifth the monthly salary of a skilled worker. Doctors make $20 a month.

There are also doctors in the crowd of would-be *jineteras*. The word is Cuban for hustler, and it can mean anything from prostitute to self-appointed tour guide to penniless dance lover. The women are young, beautiful, barelegged, dressed in short skirts or body-hugging spandex. The sounds of salsa have them on the move, hips wiggling, torsos shimmying, hands playing invisible maracas.

"You have to be careful when you pick a girl," Jack advises, "because once you pick her, she's yours. She won't move from your side. She'll stay the night, whatever."

Yasmina wanted to stay the night with Jack, but Cuban girls aren't allowed in tourist hotels. Instead, they went to the all-night Club 300, where they swayed the night away and saw the pink dawn rise over the cathedral in Parque Céspedes. By dawn, Jack had found love. He asked Yasmina to go to the beach with him for the weekend.

Jack, fifty-two, with a ponytail and a silver-dollar-size bald spot, twenty pounds overweight, twice divorced, a restaurateur and member of the Rotary, bought a red rose from a tired flower girl dozing on a park bench.

"You'll have to ask my parents," Yasmina said. Hand in hand, they walked the mile or so from Parque Céspedes to a solario at the edge of the Old City and found Yasmina's mother, grandmother, four sisters and four little brothers still sleeping. A solario is a seventeeth-century building recast for the needs of large families into small cubicles lining long, dark corridors. A pig was tied to a crumbling wall just outside the low entrance covered by a frayed yellow curtain. The mother gave her permission.

For three days, Jack says, they lay on the beach lost in their own little world. When they returned, Jack was determined to make Yasmina his and to prevent her from becoming a *jinetera* or a prostitute. To that end, he began sending her $100 a month through a Canadian bank. They speak on the telephone every week, which isn't easy, because Yasmina's family doesn't have a telephone. The closest is at her uncle's house, two streets away. But every Friday at a predetermined time, the two lovers, who still don't speak each other's language, coo in the international tongue of passion and assure each other of their fidelity.

"I always say to her, '*Hasta la victoria siempre,*'" Jack confesses with a grin. To victory always. That phrase, along with Che Guevara's picture, is the most potent symbol of the revolution in Cuba, and it means "victory" for socialism, of course, but there you have it: *amor vincit omnia.*

Jack says he's looking for a house, in case the embargo should unexpectedly be lifted. It is illegal for a foreigner to buy a house in Cuba, but a permanent resident married to a native can buy a house in her name. Jack is in love, but about marriage . . . well, he has been around the block twice.

Jack gave me a package of clothes and an envelope stuffed with the photographs he took last time in Cuba, to take to Yasmina.

Santiago de Cuba is in Oriente province, at the eastern end of the island. It is the heart of Afro-Cuba: the sun is hotter here, the people darker and, everyone believes, more passionate. Santiago is also the birthplace of the revolution and the home of the Virgen del Caridad del Cobre, Cuba's most revered saint.

The Virgen del Caridad has left her perch in the mountains above Santiago only four times in the history of Cuba: at the successful conclusion of the War of Independence from Spain, at the emancipation from slavery, and during Castro's triumphant march from Santiago to Havana in 1959. And she was carried once more out of her shrine to meet Pope John Paul II on January 21.

After Havana's big-city hustle and bustle, Santiago seems like an oasis of tranquillity. A Christmas tree—legal since December 14—stands in front of the cathedral, and Christmas carols blare from a loudspeaker. A steady flow of Chinese-made bicycles, pedicabs, burros, lead-spewing Ladas and a few vintage American cars streams past the church at a leisurely pace. In the park across from the Casa Grande Hotel, several long-limbed young women look longingly at the terrace where middle-aged tourists drink mojitos and swallow pork sandwiches. Mojitos—rum, lime juice, sugar and mint—were Hemingway's favorite drink, and by coincidence, all the men on the hotel terrace this scorching tropical afternoon look a lot like Hemingway (in his later years).

One of them is a Canadian farmer who tells me that every fall, after the harvest, he and a couple of pals pack suitcases full of Salvation Army clothes ("nothing over a dollar") and head for Cuba, where "for a shirt you can have a beauty." As I sit there, contemplating both his parsimony and his lust for life, another red-bearded Canadian Hemingway comes up and says, "Let's have another one for Quentin."

Quentin, it turns out, was the third musketeer. He had a heart attack a week ago. There is a moment of silence, then red Hemingway says, "He died happy."

The image of a Canadian farmer expiring in the arms of an Afro-Cuban in the newly eroticized socialist island of Cuba is totemic. The last stage of communism is surrealism. Instead of "Workers of the World, Unite," the new slogan might as well be "Eroticize the Proletariat!" And kill the capitalists in bed.

My taxi driver has to ask several times for directions to Yasmina's house, but after some wrong turns through the twisted hillside streets, we arrive in front of the solario. The whole family, augmented by a dozen neighbors, pours out of the house as my 1959 Oldsmobile taxi comes to a stop.

Alas, Yasmina has just left with her Pioneers group to pick coffee in the mountains. Nonetheless, I am warmly welcomed. Yasmina's mother, who looks no older than thirty, and her grandmother, also very young-looking, kiss me on both cheeks and invite me inside. I sit on a small stool, surrounded by the bright eyes of ten family members who query me closely about Jack. The photographs he has taken are passed from hand to hand, and sighs of wonder and admiration fill the room as images of Jack and Yasmina at the beach—some of them quite risque—file past.

"Tell Jack," Yasmina's mother says, "that he shouldn't

stay away much longer. Yasmina is becoming more beautiful every day. She is waiting for him to come next month for her fifteenth birthday. He promised."

I am quite sure that Jack isn't coming next month: his business is suffering. But I say instead, "I will be sure to tell him."

I am awash in love thanks to my connection with Jack, on whom their hopes are so visibly pinned. I am also familiar enough with local hospitality to know that the reason I am not offered refreshments is there aren't any. These people are totally poor. I make them my own gifts of soap and candy, and they are grateful. Cuban families receive one bar of soap a month, two pounds of sugar, some cooking oil and two pounds of rice. Children up to age eight receive a milk ration. Everything else must be bought in pesos or dollars.

That same afternoon, on the terrace of the Casa Grande, I meet Bill. A gregarious Italian-American born in Brooklyn, he has been living in Cuba with his Cuban wife for a year. He misses speaking English and likes to come here to meet tourists, mostly Canadians and Britons, but now and then, to his delight, an American.

"I was raised in San Francisco, with two brothers and a sister," he says. "I had a bar in Jamaica, but just sold it. I had been coming to Cuba for fifteen years. Then one day I said to myself: 'That's it. Bill, you're fifty-seven years old, you have to settle down.' So I did. My wife is twenty-two years old. We have a baby. I brought all my Sonys here. We have the biggest TV on the block. We are popular."

Bill is full, equally, of contempt for United States policy toward Cuba and enthusiasm for the future. "I'd like every

American to come over. Helms-Burton is garbage. The potential here is unbelievable. But the authorities have tunnel vision. I want to open a bar. It will be the best bar they've ever seen. But they have trouble re-entering the business world. They need expertise. They need to know what tourists want. The bureaucracy is impossible."

What will happen, I want to know, when American tourists come?

"It could be terrible. If they come only looking for Cuban women, it's no good. That's happening now because there is no money. Money will flow here. My big fear is that the drug man will come right behind tourism. There are no drugs in Cuba now. There are family values here."

Take that, Jesse Helms.

Bill takes me home. His house sits on a hillside street of small, pastel-colored buildings, some with tiny balconies. There are flowerpots in front of the houses. Families are gathered outside on wooden stools and benches, playing dominoes, smoking cigarettes, gossiping. Kids play stickball on the street. The houses themselves look like toys to my American-trained eyes, but these are no solarios.

"This is Cuban middle class," Bill says. "The manager of the telephone company lives across the street, the head of the tourism bureau is over there. They are Yuckies"—Young Urban Cubans.

"On $20 a month?" I ask.

"Some of them get money from relatives in Miami. But everybody's pretty much the same. The only difference is their status."

Bill's wife, Sheila, whose given name was Jalin, beams when we are introduced. She is holding Bill Jr. in her arms, a gorgeous cafe-au-lait Cuban-American who seems most interested in my presence. Sheila's father, mother and brother are all smiles, too. We sit in a tiny living room dominated by Bill's twenty-seven-inch Sony television. Bill installs himself in the big papa chair—the only one in the room—and surveys his domain with satisfaction. Crouching at his feet is Hooker, the dog, brought over from Jamaica. "The only Hooker allowed in the bar," he quips. I sit across from Bill on a plastic bucket seat. Sheila remains standing, holding the baby.

"How did you meet Bill?" I ask.

She laughs a little-girl laugh and looks proprietarily at him. "He was so drunk. When he met me, I speak English the same. After six months he bring me to Jamaica. Then we plan to marry."

Bill says: "I met her at the hotel one night. She was the prettiest girl in the place. Married last year. My first marriage."

"Did you feel at home right away?"

Bill settles even deeper in the papa chair. "I was surprised at the treatment. You would think that after a forty-year embargo the Cubans would be mad. If my fellow Yanks came down here, they'd go home and tell Congress to end this nonsense."

Sheila, I notice, holds herself with the ease and pride of a dancer. I have noticed this in other Cuban women, who carry themselves with an un-self-conscious authority. I wonder aloud what Cuban men think of foreigners raiding their shores.

"Everyone is happy for me," Sheila answers, and if there is a school chum or a fellow Pioneer somewhere behind her bright eyes, I cannot see him. Well, maybe, just maybe, young Cuban women, unlike any other on earth, do love balding, middle-age men for themselves, not for their money.

"What did they teach you in school about the United States?"

"Only the bad side. No talking much about the people. I have plenty friends Cuban in the U.S.A."

And that, of course, is the other side of this story of love between Cubans and Americans. Almost every Cuban has family or friends in the United States. Loving and marrying an American may be a little like reuniting with loved ones on the other side of the water. On the street, every *jinetero*'s first question is: "Where are you from? Italy? Canada? Spain?" And when you say, "Estados Unidos," they shout for joy. "Estados Unidos? My father is in Miami! My brother is in New York! My sister is in Cleveland!"

There aren't many Americans living with Cuban women in Santiago del Cuba. Bill knows only two. "A guy from Philadelphia—an engineer—and a guy from Phoenix. But there are plenty with girlfriends who come for a week or two and send money."

This will surely change when the embargo comes down. Meanwhile, the Europeans, especially the Spanish, are finding romance here in great numbers. The Spanish Embassy in Havana runs a matchmaking service. Cuban girls bring their photos to the embassy to be forwarded to Spanish men wanting to meet Cuban women. Other Europeans have got the word on Cuba's latest export, but for the Spanish, something more is involved. They would like to recapture Cuba, once their colony, woman by woman. That is, if Americans don't get into the act, as they always seem to do at critical moments in Cuban-Spanish history. And then, Cuban boys and men find their national pride . . . and the wheel turns again.

I take my leave of Bill and Sheila, wishing them the best. They are still standing in the street, waving, as my '59 Oldsmobile, a contemporary of Castro's triumph, pulls out. This car, and others like it, was brought over in the heyday of American good living in Cuba, when the whole country was a cheap and bountiful mistress.

Later that evening, I retrace Jack and Yasmina's steps from Casa de los Jovenes to Club 300. Dozens of girls clamor for my attention. It's a sea wave of friendly gestures amid snippets of English and Italian. Before I know it, I am flanked by two willowy, miniskirted women on high-platform shoes who would be, unmistakably, prostitutes anywhere else in the world. But one claims to be a doctor; the other says she's a ballerina. It's probably true.

"What is the secret of Cuban beauty?" I ask. "Cuban women are so beautiful."

It is a stupid question, but the answer is real. The doctor says: "We eat very badly. There are no vitamins. We are beautiful because we are dying."

My whole macho world comes to a grinding halt. I look around. It is true. The most amazing thing about these women is their eyes. Their bodies are evanescent, nearly transparent. Fashion-model skinny, they are beautiful to my

American eyes accustomed to the death look of models and movie stars. There is no fat on them, no density. They glow because they are hungry.

It is a horrific revelation. The doctor laughs. "We just want to dance," she says. "Girls just want to have fun."

In my arms she feels weightless and sad. There is something feverish going on in the way she clings to me, real pathos. Her body gyrates like an electric eel in the disco light, but her eyes are black wells with gold lights shimmering in their depths like treasure at the bottom of the Spanish Main, eyes of coffee and night, rumba and the starlighted Oriente sky. There is ferocity and expectation in them, a kind of power that is barely contained. As she dances, I can see it. She doesn't merely dance; she is a flare. Cuba is sinking. Rescue me.

The Revolution Will Be in Stereo

D RIVING DOWN 23D STREET, Havana's main strip, in a Volkswagen convertible with David Calzado at the wheel is a little like cruising Sunset Boulevard with Puff Daddy. Every man, woman, and child waiting for the bus, pedaling a Chinese bicycle or just walking waves, smiles, screams, or tries to touch the leader of Charanga Habanera, the hottest and most controversial dance band on the island. Even the lucky few with cars honk.

Calzado takes his stardom in stride. He blows kisses. He waves and honks back. He high-fives with a man in a pre-Castro American jalopy and accelerates his silver convertible with the fat mag wheels. His VW is ten years

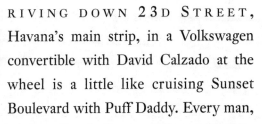

SILVANA PATERNOSTRO *is a journalist and senior fellow of the New York City-based World Policy Institute. Her work has appeared in the* New York Times Magazine, *the* Miami Herald, Spin, *and the* Paris Review. *This piece originally appeared in 1999 in the* New York Times.

old, but hip, rare, and luxurious in Havana. His new red-white-and-blue Tommy Hilfiger shirt sticks to his chest. "I love this country," he says. "If it weren't for the fact that I have to play outside to make money, I would never leave. But you know, I have gotten used to expensive things." He likes to dress in *ropa de marca*, designer labels, like the new Pelle Pelle jeans and the black Nikes he is wearing. He would like to buy a Mitsubishi four-door and install three TV miniscreens inside. "It would be the first car with television in Havana," he says.

Fidel Castro's government insists that Cuba is a socialist society. But with the blessing of the Central Committee, a small number of musicians today have more—much more—than the rest of the 11 million Cubans who live on the island. They are the first professionals in almost four decades—since Castro drove out the tobacco and sugar barons, the mafiosi and the American corporations—to accumulate wealth, the first Cubans allowed to be independent businessmen and rich capitalists, even if they are not allowed to invest in their own country.

This preferential treatment coincides with the country's loss of Soviet support. Before 1989, musicians were allocated good houses and had the possibility of traveling abroad and earning a per diem, but at home they were paid as "workers of the revolution," just like sugar-cane cutters, high-school teachers, or tobacco rollers. Today, a handful of them, particularly those who, like Calzado, play popular dance music, are treated like stars. Paulito FG, a self-taught singer and dandy who is turning Cuban teenage girls into screaming fans, Manol Gonzalez Hernandez, known as the Doctor of Salsa, a thirty-three-year-old physician turned salsa star; and Calzado himself are living extravagantly—in Cuban terms, at least.

———

In Havana, the billboards still proclaim Socialism or Death, but the streets seem more like an incipient Hollywood. Calzado is taking me to El Aljibe, his favorite restaurant, where an all-you-can-eat meal of delicious chicken in orange sauce, rice, beans, salad, and flan costs $14 a head, the monthly salary of a heart surgeon. It is the lunch spot of high-ranking government officials, foreign businessmen, journalists, and tourists. The waitress kisses him on the cheek and directs us to his regular table. Calzado removes his sunglasses and places them next to his car keys and a leather billfold. His cell phone does not stop ringing. His manager calls several times: the Music Institute wants Charanga to play twice this week—first for the employees of the Ministry of the Interior and then at Pabexpo, the convention center where the government is concluding the First International Construction Fair. These duties fall under the band's job description as state musicians, for which they are paid a monthly salary of about $30. But what Calzado really wants to know is whether the band is confirmed to play at El Palacio de la Salsa, the hot dance club where the cover charge is $20 and the patrons are, mostly, foreign men and Cuban women.

Calzado, at forty-two, is almost precisely as old as Castro's revolution. He grew up pledging at school every day to be a "pioneer for communism" and promising "to be like

Che." He fought in Angola. As he has a third serving of the chicken and asks the waitress for extra yuca sticks, I ask him how he feels about the noticeable differences between him and his fans, about reconciling his revolutionary education with his newly acquired lifestyle. He answers by quoting his Spanish producer, from whom he learns his capitalist cues: "We have to get used to the fact that some have and others have less. Equality doesn't mean that we all have the same but that we each have what we deserve, that we have what we work for," he says. "Plus, I have to be on top. My admirers want me to be the best, and that means I have to be the best dressed, to drive the best car. I cannot let them down."

The check arrives and I insist on paying. "Please," he insists. "This is nothing for me. Look, it's just $30. You should see what I pay when the music producers come from abroad and we are a big table. I like to do that. I don't like that everyone thinks that Cubans can't pay for their own lunches."

He opens his wallet with the mystery and mysticism of someone about to reveal something very illegal or very precious. "I always pay with one of these."

"A check," I say. "Not very many people in Cuba have them, right? I bet, fewer than those with cell phones."

He nods with satisfaction. "Yes," he says. "Next I would like a credit card. But, I don't really understand yet how they work."

Cuba has always been a musical cradle. It was here that the traditional son, as well as the mambo and the cha-cha-chá that took dancers by storm in the 1950s, were born. Beny More, Arsenio Rodríguez, and Pérez Prado, the forefathers of what is today known as salsa, were all Cubans. The famous Havana nights of the 1950s, usually associated with gambling, prostitution, and cigar-smoking mafiosi, were also filled with great music. One of Fidel Castro's first acts after seizing power was to undermine dance music, hoping to erase the image of Cuba as a party place for Americans. But communism was not able to kill music, and it might be the only thing left for many. The Special Period—Castro's euphemism for the years since the loss of Soviet subsidies—has brought hardship and discontentment. Gone are the days of Bulgarian baby food and cans of *carne rusa*, the Russian Spam that Cubans today recall with nostalgia. A recent Mexican poll reports that 76 percent of Cubans feel their economic situation has never been as bad as it is now.

There may be blackouts, shortages of gasoline, even rationing of rum, but there is still music. News is scarce on TV but there are plenty of music shows. Paychecks are meager but state-organized afternoon parties with live music abound. Calzado tells me that when his band plays in the countryside the only people who stay home are the elderly and the newborns. "Charanga drags as many people to the Revolution Square of Santiago as Fidel Castro," he says.

The music that Charanga plays is called *timba*, and it is a combination of jazz and rumba spiced with reggae, funk, and hiphop. Although rooted in the traditional elements of the *son* (a guitar-driven, brass-laced Cuban rhythm), it sounds as different from the music of old Havana as rap does from the Ronettes. *Timba* is the modern mambo, a hard-edged cha-cha-chá, designed to make the stiffest of dancers want to get up and try. "It is based on *son*, but it is more African, more percussive," says Ned Sublette, a Texas-born singer-song-writer who started one of the first American record labels for Cuban music. "It is sophisticated dance music."

Timba is the sound of the new post-Soviet Cuba; the music of the Special Period. It is the voice of average Cubans, of those who allow their cuban *alegría* —the Cuban identity that combines a joy of life, a sensuousness, a macho attitude—to seep out. "We are about *la alegría* that Cubans have even when they do not have anything," says Paulito FG as he puffs on a midmorning cigar and crosses his legs to display Mickey Mouse socks. "Here people sing all the time, even while they clean."

While *Granma*, Cuba's official newspaper, fills its pages with Castro's long speeches, party memorandums, and articles about the future of the sugar harvest, *timba* depicts everyday life in this new Cuba where dollars now compete with dialectics. Forty years of Marxism have not been able to strip the Cuban soul of its Afro-Cuban musical essence. *Timba* is playful, joyous, sensual. "The revolution wanted to make a new country, even with our music," says Manol, the Doctor of Salsa, one of the most outspoken and political of the timberos. "They tried to take away the *son* and impose on us *trova*." He is referring to *nueva trova*, 1960s-vintage folk-type music with messages of loving the revolution and hating *yanqui* imperialism. A society that once sang songs praising universal brotherhood, that inspired a whole generation from Mexico to Argentina, today sings superhits about women who prefer being kept. "*Trova* is the music of intellectuals, not the music of the people," says Manol. "Here we have to erect a monument to the *son*. The queen of this country is our traditional music. Here most people don't have the mind to decipher what the *trovadores* are trying to say. We do it in our street language—straightforward and direct."

The *timberos* sing about neighborhood gossip, about couples fighting, about consumption and materialism. One popular *timba* song is titled "The Shopping Maniac." Another is "The Supertourist," about a Cuban girl who only likes to go to expensive places, places that only a tourist can afford to take her to. In another, Charanga advises young women to find themselves a sugar daddy—"like Calzado, so that you can have, so that you can enjoy. A *papirriqui con wanikiki*"—a sugar daddy with dough. "I changed the name of money in Cuba," Calzado says. Today, when Cubans refer to dollars, they call them *wanikikis*.

When I asked eighteen-year-old Michel M. Marquez, Charanga's lead singer, what he thought about Che, he shrugged his shoulders. "I can't think anything," he said. "He was dead when I was born." That is very much the sentiment of the new generation, and *timba* songs reflect that apolitical attitude. But in a crucial way, these salsa stars are quite political, subversively so. Manol sings about "leaving behind the old mentality . . . let's take a chance on peace . . . times are a-changing, you will see. I already have friends in Miami." And Charanga uses an obvious metaphor in "El Mango": "Hey, you mango, we all loved you when you were green. Now that you are yellow and old, isn't it time to fall from the tree?"

Still, in the inchoate political atmosphere of 1990s Cuba, where free enterprise is supported one day and savaged the next, lyrics of nonconformity and protest, no matter how cleverly couched, eventually create problems, as Charanga was to discover.

"Charanga is a miracle," Calzado explains as we sit in his mother's living room, which contains a Russian refrigerator, a nineteen-inch Sony TV and an altar to Changó, her African god. He tells me the story of the band, created in 1988. Up to that point, Calzado was leading a comfortable if unremarkable life. He was trained as a classical violinist in a Cuba where money was not necessary. Everything was taken care of—Soviet-style and Soviet-subsidized. He grew up in a modest ground-floor apartment that the government gave to his father, a renowned musician, soon after Castro's victory. His education at Cubanacan, one of the best art conservatories on the island, was free. When he graduated from the institute, the government placed him with Orquestra Ritmo Oriental, one of the island bands that played the music known as *charanga*, which adds violins and flutes to the string sounds of traditional son. Calzado lived rent-free in a one-bedroom apartment with his wife and daughter. The couple worked at the famous Tropicana, where she was a dancer and he was the lead violinist for the preshow dinner hour.

One night, he was approached by a foreign businessman who offered him a $50 per diem to play in Europe, with a band he would form. His monthly state salary was less than $20. Within days, he had got together nine professional musicians, all trained with the rigor, discipline, and methodology of the music institutes established by the Soviet Union. For the next four years, from May through September, his group played in Monaco, opening with a show of Cuban oldies for pop luminaries like Whitney Houston, Barry White, Liza Minnelli, and Frank Sinatra, returning tò Havana in the fall with pockets stuffed with savings. "I lived like a king," Calzado says. But as popular as they were on the French Riviera, they were unknown and unwanted in Cuba—the average Cuban had no interest in bands that played "Guantanamera."

In 1993 the government, strapped for hard currency, legalized the dollar and began cultivating foreign markets in rum, tobacco, biotechnology—and music. Huge archives of unreleased recordings went on sale. And all musicians were extended the privileges of travel and the opportunity to save their dollar per diems that had previously been allowed only to a lucky few like Calzado. What really changed the musicians' fortunes, however, was a 1995 law that allowed them to negotiate with foreign record producers and tour organizers on their own. As Cuba opened its shores to tourism, a sizzling, dollar-fueled nightclub scene exploded in Havana. Overnight, everyone in Cuba wanted to be a musician.

Meanwhile, as Charanga's members sat and waited for the summer tour, Paulito and Manol were topping the charts. Paulito sang about breaking hearts, Manol about a girlfriend who left him for an Italian. Their concerts were jammed, and they were signing record deals. Calzado decided to move into *timba*. Charanga's first song, a playful come-on about a guy falling in love with a nurse, became an instant hit.

Francis Cabezas, a Spaniard who owns the record company Magic Music, saw Charanga playing at the Karl Marx Theater. He signed them up, then exchanged their frilly white *guarachera* shirts for overalls and baseball caps and added break-dancing and choreography to their act. In 1996, Charanga Habanera received the equivalent of the Grammy for best record of the year.

In July 1997, as the most popular band of the moment, they were invited to be the closing act for the XIV Youth and Students World Festival, a gathering advocating "solidarity, anti-imperialism, peace, and friendship." They played, outdoors, for thousands of young socialists from around the world. They performed as always—jokes with sexual innuendoes, Michel threatening to take off his pants, allusions to drug-taking. The next day, the curtain fell on Charanga. The hard-liners were furious: the Federation of Cuban Women was appalled, the Union of Young Communists was "deeply offended" and "greatly disappointed," and the Cuban Institute of Radio and Television banned them.

They were labeled the "kings of vulgarity" and forbidden to perform for six months. "They tell me that it was because it was a very capitalist concert," Calzado says. "But I don't know, when it comes to putting together a show, what makes a capitalist or a communist show?" Maybe the fact that they paid $5,000 to arrive at the concert in a helicopter, or maybe the way the lanky Michel was moving. "But four-year-olds in Cuba move their pelvis that way," Calzado protests. One American record producer says of the new groups: "There will be more confrontations with officials as they become a profitable subculture. The state will start looking for excuses to crack down on them because they represent freedom."

Today, there are approximately 12,000 state-salaried musicians, playing between twenty to thirty different genres—classical and jazz; every variation of traditional music such as *son*, rumba, and *guaguanco* and their dancing derivatives; even rock and rap. "There are more musicians than there is music," Luis Tamargo wrote in *Latin Beat*, a music magazine, "all commercially motivated." Last year more than a third of them played abroad and were paid in dollars. Charanga Habanera now charges up to $18,000 a week to perform in Europe and is said to have signed a six-figure recording contract with Universal in London.

Most likely, Calzado, Paulito, and Manol are not millionaires yet. But they make upward of $40,000 a year, which is a lot more than the $2,000 the Doctor would have made in his former profession. As a present to his singer, Michel, Calzado bought him a car—a beat-up white four-door Nissan—making Michel probably the only teenager with a car on the entire island. The Doctor lives in a freshly painted Art Deco apartment with locked gates, a black velour living-room set, and a modern kitchen stocked with a full set of wineglasses. Paulito drives a brand-new Mitsubishi with smoked windows, the kind Calzado wants to buy.

Last fall, the government shut down the dollar-based night clubs, including El Palacio de la Salsa. Just before that, I go to hear Charanga play. Housed in the Hotel Riviera, which was once owned by Meyer Lansky, the Palacio is in fact a dark room with old red-and-white checkered tablecloths and metal chairs, reeking of cigarette butts and stale beer. The sign on the stage is made of aluminum foil and the dressing rooms have no light bulbs. "People would take them home," says a member of Charanga as he buttons his shirt by the glow of a cigarette lighter. From midweek to Sunday, El Palacio offers Los Van Van, Manolin, Paulito, or Charanga Habanera live for a $20 cover charge.

It is one of Charanga's first performances after their six-month suspension. Everyone is nervous. The band knows it has been out of the game for months and knows it is being watched. They have prepared two new songs that they will try out tonight.

"What are they about?" I ask Calzado.

"Surprise," he responds.

The lobby hustles and bustles with women of astonishing beauty wearing more bright Lycra than I've ever seen outside of a gym. The men are mostly middle-aged foreigners and a few Cuban men, dressed in snappy clothes. One of the Cubans flashes a gold front tooth; another wears a thick gold chain with a dollar sign dangling on his chest. "They are *especuladores*," my friend Amaury, a disillusioned twenty-two-year-old former card-carrying member of the party, tells me as we walk by. "Cubanos who show off what they have. They drive cars and have gold. To do that you have to be a cigar smuggler, a pimp, or a timbero. No chance for me."

Inside, everything is for sale. I am offered bootleg tapes, bootleg beer, discounted cover charges, dance lessons for $2, and glossy head shots of Paulito for $5. Sitting at a reserved table, Calzado's seventy-two-year-old mother looks radiant, all primped up in the brand-new dress her son bought for her abroad. When she sees me, she lifts her plastic cup filled with Havana Club and tells me Charanga is ready to "come back and eat up Havana," quoting from one of her son's post-sanction songs.

Onstage, they mix their sophisticated musical prowess with Earth, Wind, and Fire and their own innocent version of gangsta rap. Their outfits are a mishmash: the horn section wears 1970s-type satin jumpsuits of carmine red, the percussionists baggy 'hood gear. One vocalist is dressed like Prince when he was Prince. Michel is shirtless, wearing the same black vest and plaid black-and-white pants he had worn all day long. Calzado's outfit is hard to peg—either funk, gangsta, or traditionally Cuban, for he has borrowed from each: a black-and-white satin ensemble of baggy pants and knee-length tunic, a woven cap on his shaved head and shoes of patent leather, black-and-white two-toned, like the ones his father wore. The choreography is campy; they raise their legs in unison. At one point, they all fall like dominoes. They announce the new songs. One, written by Michel, is a rant about mothers-in-law; the other one, by Calzado, is about a best friend who likes to party and pretends he doesn't. These songs have no political double meaning, no provocative allusion to money or drugs.

"Charanga is not operating at full speed," Calzado tells me. In a press statement he has proclaimed that they "profoundly regret that our performance created a disagreeable image, because that was not our intention." This is the equivalent of Marilyn Manson apologizing to Tipper Gore. Now that everything boils down to money, sanctions mean less money. Not being able to tour in Europe would destroy the lifestyle to which he has so rapidly accustomed himself. He would have to survive on the $30—360 pesos—he receives from the government every month, which right now he just turns over to his mother. "She still lives in pesos. I live in dollars."

Los Jardines de la Tropical is for Cubans with pesos. Los Van Van, the number-one dance band in Cuba for the last thirty years, is performing on a Monday night. "Van Van is Cuba," a friend tells me." But he discourages me from attending La Tropical. "This really is for Cubans. It really is too strong for anyone who is not Cuban." But Calzado offers to take me. "I can get us into the V.I.P. floor," he says. "I will reserve a table." La Tropical, far from a garden, is an open-air, dilapidated stadium with a stage and no bleachers. It offers the same bands that El Palacio de la Salsa does, except here the cover charge is in pesos, affordable to all. The exclusive room that Calzado mentions is the second floor of the con- crete building where musicians like Calzado can always count on a table and a bottle of rum at no cost. The second floor is sparsely populated, compared to the throngs of Cubans on the stadium floor. These are the Cubans who do not go to the Palacio—the women are not gorgeous and the men are not making dollars—but they are the ones who really vibrate to the music the timberos are making. Here they can forget about meager rations, about the buses they wait for endlessly. For a few hours they stop having to *resolver*, the most used verb in Cuba, where everything needs to be solved.

Through the static-filled speakers, Mayito, Los Van Van's young singer, dressed in baggy jeans and corn-row braids, invites everyone to join *el tren de la alegría*, the train of happiness. Music, it is clear, is what holds Cuba together; it is what keeps Cubans alive. Manol might be reprimanded for playing the song about Miami, but he is allowed to live like a diplomat, with immunity and privileges, because the government might just be aware of how much it needs him and the others.

Though ordinary Cubans now may make ground-meat dishes with orange rind instead of meat, women may dance with foreigners for a pair of new shoes, and most young men have no vision of a future, they all find solace in their music. Los Van Van is singing a plea to Orula, a *santería* spirit, to "protect all Cubans." Mayito is on his knees asking the audience to raise their arms and sing with him, and they do. What would happen in Cuba if the Government stopped providing them with music?

The concert is over at two in the morning. And as the crowd flows out of the stadium, I see that the only cars in the parking lot are taxis and Calzado's convertible. Most everyone here will walk home. Taxis are too costly and it is too late for buses to run. A couple in their early 1940s, walking hand in hand and looking content, even happy, tell me it will take them so long to get home that the man, who starts work as a security guard at seven, will have to go straight to work.

"Why come?" I ask him. "All this hassle."

"Because this is all we've got."

As Calzado drives me away, the sidewalks are full of

people and of life. Laughter resonates amid comments directed to Calzado as we whiz by. Jokingly someone asks him for a ride. Another one, quoting a song, yells out, "Oye, David, how would you like to be paid: in check or in cash?"

"In cash," Calzado calls back.

TODAY
AND
BEYOND

The Shipwreck

O N SATURDAY, NOVEMBER 20, 1999, fifteen Cubans ranging in age from five to sixty-five straggled through a cluster of mangrove trees to the marshy shoreline of Cárdenas, Cuba. There they huddled around a seventeen-foot aluminum handcrafted boat with a fifty-horsepower outboard motor, camouflaged by knee-high *pangola* grass. Swiftly and quietly they loaded the small craft with everything that they would be taking: cheese and crackers, hot dogs, water, and some blankets. All the money they had in the world was stuffed in their pockets.

The group was made up of two extended families, friends of long standing. There was the Rodríguez clan with their two

ANN LOUISE BARDACH *is an award-winning journalist who has covered Cuba for the* New York Times, Vanity Fair, *and other national publications. She is coauthor of the bestseller* Vicki *and edited the anthology* Cuba: A Traveler's Literary Companion. *This piece is from 2002.*

sons, a daughter-in-law, and a next-door neighbor. And there was the Munero family—Rafael, forty-nine, his wife, María Elena, forty-eight, and their two sons. One of their sons, twenty-four-year-old Lázaro Munero, called Rafa by his family, was the mastermind, boat builder, and driving force behind the escape. Accompanying him was his girlfriend, Elizabet Brotón, a shy, sweet-faced woman with long, dark hair and bangs running along her broad forehead, who was known as Elisa. With her was her five-year-old son, Elián González.

Then there was another couple in their early twenties— two fleeing lovers and the young woman's five-year-old daughter. The couple, unknown to most of the others, were the only ones who had paid Rafa for passage on the boat.

All of the fifteen aboard had their own reasons for leaving, their own expectations, their own dreams. Some were seeking more opportunity, some were fleeing a spouse or family in Cárdenas, some loathed Fidel Castro and communism, and some wanted better clothes and a better house. But the glue that bound the group together was love and family: the love of a spouse or a sibling waiting for them in America—the dream of family reunification.

More than half of the group could not swim and several had a dread of the sea. María Elena, Rafael Munero's wife, was recovering from recent heart problems and, like many working-class women from the country's provinces, had never learned to swim. For her, the splendid waters that enveloped Cuba's crocodile-shaped form were to be admired from the shoreline but never entered. María Elena had not been feeling well and had had an ominous presentiment about the crossing. But family was the cornerstone of her existence, and if her husband and sons were leaving, so would she.

Earlier in the evening, Rafael Munero had gone out alone to inspect the boat. Suddenly, he heard footsteps coming from behind him and, alarmed, swung around. Seeing that it was his brother Dagoberto who had secretly followed him to the boat, Rafael sighed with nervous relief.

Five days before, Rafael had confided to his younger brother that he and his family planned to flee the country and asked him to come. Dagoberto refused. He had had other opportunities to defect—when two other brothers had done so—but leaving was not for him. He lacked the ambition and energy of his siblings, and Cuba's socialism provided for his basic needs whether he worked or not. To prove his point, he boasted of having had laparoscopic surgery on his knee. "How much would that cost in the U.S.?" he asked knowingly. For days, the two argued and bickered. At times, Rafael would change his mind and say he wouldn't go, but after a pep talk from his son, he would recommit to the trip. On and off it went, even through their farewell dinner of roast pork in their cramped apartment, with Juan Gabriel crooning on the tape deck. Dagoberto had swung by around 9:30 in the evening. "The group was all gathered there," he would later recall. "I saw the couple there with her daughter. She was asking if the sea was rough. I asked her: 'You're going with that little girl?' And she told me yes. I told her: 'Here the waves are a meter high but out there they are four or five times more, up to ten meters high.'"

Dagoberto would not give up. He could not bear to lose Rafael, who had raised him like a son after their father had died when Dagoberto was still a teenager. "I was crying because when someone goes over there you always think the worst. My brother ate his dinner, then he left his place alone. I thought this was my last opportunity to talk to him again. I saw that he went for the brush that is all along the shore and I followed him. And when I got there I saw the boat."

Circling the narrow homemade boat, Dagoberto could see that parts of it were rusty and that holes in its bottom had been patched with packing materials. "I can't believe you're leaving on this piece of shit," Dagoberto bellowed to his brother. "This is not a boat. It's garbage! You're crazy." But, Rafael had made up his mind and didn't want to hear any more from him. "We're leaving on it," he said, his voice pitched with anger, "and if you're not coming with us, get out of here and leave me alone!"

There was nothing more to say or do. Angry and wounded, Dagoberto shuffled back to the main road, then made his way home. "I didn't say goodbye to him. I left him there alone maybe 10:30 that night," Dagoberto mumbled. "I left and I never saw him again."

Around 6:00 A.M. on Thanksgiving Day, Joan Ruiz and his friend Reniel Carmenate were coming ashore after an evening of fishing off Miami's Key Biscayne. Ruiz said that as they docked they could make out the forms of two people huddling and shivering on the shore by the water's edge. Nearby was an oversized Russian-made black truck tire. "They were in really bad, bad condition," said Ruiz. "Their skin was a sickly purple color, all ripply with wrinkles and covered in blisters. I wanted to help them take their clothes off because the material was welded into their skin but I was afraid that their skin would tear. The man was in the worse shape, almost going in and out of consciousness. They kept asking for water but I knew from experience that water could really hurt them unless it was given to them through an IV drip. We called the police and I ran to my truck and got some dry clothes."

The man was almost delirious; the woman's bones had decalcified from days of ocean immersion. Their bodies were latticed with the bite marks of fish. "The lady was the one who spoke and told us what had happened," said Ruiz. "She said they left Cuba with twelve others but that everyone had drowned—including a little boy." The young couple were the fleeing lovers—thirty-three-year-old Nivaldo Fernández and his twenty-two-year-old girlfriend, Arianne Horta.

Thirty miles farther north off Fort Lauderdale, Sam Ciancio was out in his cabin cruiser. With him was his cousin Donato Dalrymple, a housecleaner, out for the first time on his cousin's boat. Ciancio spied a large black inner tube bobbing in the Atlantic and thought he saw the outlines of a large doll inside the tire. But as they steered closer to the tire, they saw it was not a doll but rather a small child tied to the inner tube. Ciancio dove into the water and brought the boy aboard. The trembling child was five-year-old Elián González, who, in a matter of hours, would become the poster boy for both sides of America's forty-year-old Cold War with Cuba.

The three were the sole survivors of the group that had left Cárdenas in the wee hours of November 22. Elián's mother, Elisa, and her boyfriend, Rafa Munero, were among the eleven who had drowned-along with his brother, mother, and father. Not far from Elián's inner tube, the body of sixty-one-year-old Mérida Loreto Barrios, the matriarch of the Rodríguez clan, tethered to the end of a long rope, was found floating over the surface of the waves like bait. Stuffed in her undergarments was $210 in twenty- and ten-dollar bills. She had been the last of her family to die—after witnessing the drowning of her two sons, her husband and her daughter-in-law. Some of the bodies were found a hundred miles away from one another—swept by the driving currents of the Gulf Stream to Key West and as far north as Fort Pierce.

But the bodies of Elisa and her lover, his younger brother, and Mérida's husband were never found. They would join the thousands of others, failed seekers of a better life, in that immense aquatic graveyard—the Florida Straits.

Seeking to put faces on those who died, I went to Cárdenas, Havana, and Miami several times over the next two years. There were scores of pieces to find, identify, and jiggle into the puzzle. There were two extended families, eleven dead, two adult survivors, and two five-year-old children who would become estranged from their grieving parents. But clinging to the bare facts were conflicting stories to reconcile, and personal ambitions and political agendas to sort out amid a surfeit of grief, rage and shame.

In Key Biscayne's Crandon Park Marina, the shipwreck

survivors Nivaldo and Arianne, wrapped and shivering in blankets, told police detectives the saga of their deadly journey. Then they were whisked away to Jackson Memorial Hospital and later to Arianne's aunt in Hialeah—where they shut themselves in, rarely speaking about their ordeal. I first met Arianne and Nivaldo in early February 2000 at her aunt's small home on a torn-up and potholed street in Hialeah, the working-class Cuban community that borders Miami. The strains of their ordeal and their new lives were painfully evident. At the time, they had no money, no jobs, no clothes, and did not speak English.

Arianne is a small, dark-haired beauty with a sultry beauty mark on her chin. Outwardly, she seemed to have emerged from her ordeal entirely unscathed, her gaze riveted on the present and the future. Phoenix-like, she promptly enrolled in an English school in a Hialeah shopping mall, attending class every night from six to nine and charting out her life. Soon after her miraculous rescue, she made an appointment at the local *peluquería* in Hialeah and had dagger-length acrylic nails applied to her fingertips.

At our first meeting, Nivaldo seemed particularly stressed—his legs bobbing nervously, his face drawn and wounded. A light-skinned black man with translucent hazel eyes, he was still unable to sleep. Every evening, he said, be awoke over and over again—revisiting the shipwreck and the days they spent drifting in the water. "When we remember everything that happened, we feel it deeply," he said softly, "having seen so many people drown."

Nivaldo was besotted with Arianne, his eyes rarely leaving her. Although he too would like to learn English, he said that one of them had to sacrifice and he was willing to do so. And for the love of Arianne, he was willing to make many sacrifices. It was Nivaldo who had paid the entire fee for the two. He had left behind a wife, a good job, and a new house in Cárdenas. He rattled off the fine appliances he had in his home on Calle San José. "I lived a lot better in Cuba," he told me, "than I'm living here now." And while he thinks he would like Chicago, where his mother and other relatives live, he has contented himself in Miami because Arianne loves it so.

After surviving a perilous shipwreck and an excruciating ordeal in the raging Atlantic, Nivaldo found himself in a home feeling unwelcome. Indeed, when I spoke with her weeks later, Arianne's aunt couldn't have been more candid about her feelings. Repeatedly tapping her forearm with two fingers—Cuban for signifying that someone is black—she found my eyes and sighed. Racial prejudice is not uncommon in Miami's exile community, which is roughly 95 percent white. Local talk radio speculated that had Elián González been black—as are 65 to 70 percent of Cubans on the island—"he would have been tossed back into the sea." A close friend of the couple said that Arianne's aunt was uncomfortable with Nivaldo in her home. "Supposedly one room is for them but the aunt doesn't want Nivaldo sleeping with Arianne. So he has to sleep in the living room." Pushing back her red-blond hair, the aunt told me that Nivaldo's arrival had been difficult for her. "For us, it is a very big thing. He is the first black person in our family. We grew up in a time when parents brought us up right. We accept him," she said with another, deeper sigh, "because he is a good, hardworking man. What can we do?"

Sitting in a Hialeah coffee shop where he was unable to eat or drink anything, Nivaldo said that talking about his ordeal only seemed to make it worse. The voyage was ill fated from the beginning, he said. "The most difficult thing was the trip. It was four days long but we were in the water for three days." By the time the group left shore it was almost 2:30 in the morning of November 21. Under the shield of darkness on a moonless night, they hoped to evade detection from the Cuban Coast Guard. There were two five-year-olds in tow when they left: Arianne's beautiful, curly-haired daughter, Estefany, named after Princess Stephanie of Monaco, and Elián, Elisa's son. While Estefany cried and cowered fearfully from the huge, dark waves, Elián delighted in the adventure. He teased passengers who he said were eating too many of their crackers. Everyone giggled at his precocity; his mother glowed.

The mood on the boat darkened abruptly less than two hours after they took off, when the motor clacked and sputtered, then died. "We could still see land," recalled Nivaldo. Using oars, they paddled back to the nearest key off Cárdenas. There they hid out for fourteen hours until sunset, then paddled back to Cárdenas at 6:00 P.M.

Although it was clearly a poor omen, Nivaldo said no one was deterred from going except Arianne, who was having second thoughts about bringing Estefany, who was crying and fretting. Elisa had unwavering confidence in Rafa—after all, he had made the trip twice before, with even less of a boat than they had. And she could not bear to be parted from Elián.

While the men repaired the engine, Arianne walked her daughter back to her mother's home on Calle Vives and returned to the boat alone. It was a fateful, prescient decision that she is certain saved their lives. Had they struggled to save or calm her daughter as the others had done for one another, they too would have drowned.

Rafa repaired the boat by inserting "a piece of scrap metal in the engine from another part of the boat," according to Nivaldo. "They fixed the engine, it was fine, we left, everything was perfect." Having lost a full day, they finally motored off at 3:00 A.M. on November 22, a Monday. Arianne said she would never forget the date, because it happened to be her twenty-second birthday "and I spent it in the water." In lieu of life jackets, they took along three *gomas*—the large black inner tubes used on Russian-made trucks. The plan was to have seven, but Rafa decided that they could make do with three.

A few hours later, in the glare of daylight, they were spotted by two cruisers from Cuba's Guardia Frontera, who ordered them to return and threatened to use a water cannon on them. Nivaldo claimed that he seized Elián and held him high over his shoulders. "We have kids in here!" he called out, bluffing them. "There's five, maybe six children aboard." Arianne had no memory of the event; Nivaldo said that the guardsmen backed down but continued to trail them for another hour. Before turning back, they would radio the American Coast Guard and pass on the position of the boat and its direction. The U.S. Coast Guard confirmed that they had been alerted but never located the craft.

The group was relieved that they didn't encounter the U.S. Coast Guard, which, under current policy, would have immediately returned them to Cuba. They knew they had to make it to shore to qualify for residency under what is known as the "wet foot/dry foot" policy. A peculiar confection of U.S. policy that was created in 1994, it grants any Cuban who makes it to land the right to stay. Haitians, Dominicans, Mexicans, and everyone else get tossed back whence they came.

Notwithstanding its heavy human cargo, the boat zipped across the Florida Straits, making excellent time. In roughly nineteen hours they had come within thirty-five miles of U.S. shores—two thirds of their journey. To reach the U.S. in thirty hours or less was their goal. But suddenly the sky blackened and the ocean roiled furiously beneath them. They had steered directly into a storm, a nasty Northeaster. Bitter cold winds and relentless rain lashed at them. "It was a bad time, there was a cold front with very big waves," recalled Nivaldo. "A lot of water getting into the boat. Then the engine stopped and it wouldn't start. We were nervous and afraid."

The flailing winds jostled one fuel tank loose, spilling gasoline that burnt a hole in one of the inner tubes. And then, said Nivaldo, "a huge wave hit and flipped the boat over." All fourteen were thrown into the churning Atlantic. Through the night, they clung to the edges of the boat calling out to the few passing slaps, which didn't hear their cries. "The first day we were all together holding on to the boat," said Nivaldo. When the sun rose again, they expended their strength trying to flip the boat hack over—but the craft capsized and sank along with the damaged inner tube—leaving fourteen people at the mercy of only two tires in the pitch-dark Atlantic. What few possessions they had—clothes, food, blankets—and all their water had tumbled into the sea. Arianne could feel the spilled gasoline burning her back.

The group split into two—the men huddled on one inner tube, the women and Elián on the other, some clinging to the sides of the tires, others, the nonswimmers, tethered to them with rope. They had succeeded in tying the two tubes together, thus keeping the group together. But hunger and dehydration quickly took their toll. The first casualty was seventeen-year-old Jikary Munero, Rafa's younger brother. "Look, land, there's land, an island. I can see lights," he shouted to the others, then dove into the sea, swimming off to find it. Raft immediately dove in to rescue his brother. Soon after, the group heard calls of "¡*Ayúdame*! Help!" and Nelson Rodríguez swam to the aid of the brothers.

It was an unforgiving, starless stormy night, without moonlight, and no one could see what was happening. After fifteen minutes, when none of the three young men had returned, the group feared the worst. Elisa began to mumble over and over again: "I think they drowned. I think they drowned." Silently, their helpless families realized that Nelson, Jikary, and Rafa, the architect of the trip, had drowned. Worse was to come.

Lirka Guillermo, a pretty twenty-five-year-old medical student who lived across the street from the Rodríguez family, was the next casualty. She had planned to reunite with her boyfriend, who had made the voyage successfully a year earlier with Rafa. "I want black beans and rice," she cried aloud, then suddenly released the inner tube and swam off toward the other tire. Nelson's brother Juan Carlos, a thirty-five-year-old maintenance man who lived in Havana, tried to save her. Juan Carlos had left his family behind—his nine-year-old daughter and his wife, who was too ill to come following a failed kidney transplant. Nivaldo said that he tried to rescue Lirka in the dark sea but could barely see anything. He swam toward them, he said, but both she and Juan Carlos had gone under.

Fatigue soon brought down Rafael Munero, and his wife, María Elena, having seen her two sons and husband perish, no longer had the strength or will to hang on.

The following day, as sunlight broke through at dawn, Manolo Rodríguez, who had witnessed the drowning of his sons, disappeared from the inner tube. Next, Nelson's wife, Zenaida, who had a lifelong fear of the ocean and couldn't swim, slipped into the sea.

Mérida, Manolo's wife, having watched her entire family drown, barely clung to the tire with Nivaldo and Arianne. Delirious, she kept asking for her family. "Mérida kept trying to drown herself, sliding down into the water. She was saying, 'I want to die. I want to die,'" recalled Arianne. Nivaldo would push her back up and comfort her, telling her that they would be rescued. "Leave me alone I want to die," she mumbled like a chant. Nivaldo dozed off, and when he awoke, Mérida was no longer crying. She had slipped away. The coroner said she died of a heart attack and then drowned.

"People were drowning from fatigue," said Nivaldo, "until it was Arianne, me, Elián, and Elisa." Strangely, Elián seemed removed from the entire drama. He was gaily dressed in an orange jacket selected by his mother, who had heard that the bright color deflected sharks. Draped across the tire, he dozed much of the time. "He was just sleeping and when he was awake it was like an adventure for him. He wasn't panicked at all. And he world wake up and say, 'I'm hungry.'" Elisa comforted him but said nothing. "She couldn't say anything because there was no food." But she covered him in her jacket—protecting him from the grilling sun and nipping fish. Before the shipwreck, Elián seemed excited by the journey "He knew we were coming here because Rafa would say, 'Where are you going?' And Elián would say, *Me voy pa' La Yuma*—'I'm going to the U.S.'" (*La Yuma* is Cuban slang for America, adapted from the title of a 1957 Glenn Ford movie, *3:10 to Yuma*, which was based on an Elmore Leonard short story.)

Arianne found a bottle of water floating in the sea. She said she offered it to Elisa, telling her, "This is for Elián." And before they drowned, Rafa and the other men would throw their bodies over Elián, protecting him from the immense waves and keeping the salt spray out of his mouth.

By now Elisa's strength was ebbing. She had seen Rafa, the great passion of her life, die, and now she struggled to live only to protect her son. She had nothing to offer him when he cried for milk. "I want to die," she mumbled. "All I want is for my son to live. If there's one here who has to die, let it be me, not him."

The following morning, Nivaldo and Arianne awoke and found themselves bobbing alone in the immense Atlantic. Sometime during the night, the rope securing the two inner tubes together had torn apart. Nivaldo and Arianne said they had no idea what had happened to Elián and Elisa, but they knew one thing: Elisa could not swim. "I'm the morning we couldn't see them anymore," said Nivaldo. "I don't know what could have happened to her. She could have lost her strength because of the current or a shark ate her. Something big must have happened because her body never turned up."

Two more nights would pass and Arianne and Nivaldo would feel fish nipping and biting their legs and arms. They saw dolphins everywhere, which they prayed would keep the sharks at bay. On their third night in the water, Nivaldo became delirious, ranting, "We're going to die! We're going to die!" Arianne grabbed him fiercely and talked him down until he snapped out of it.

That night, they could finally see the glimmer of lights from the Florida shoreline. Exultant, they put all their energy into swimming but the current was against them and they eventually dozed oft on their inner tube. At daybreak, they could see that they were even closer. They swam and paddled exhaustedly—their arms and legs thrashing at the water until they made it to shore. Two early-morning fishermen, Juan Ruiz and Reinel Carmenate, in Key Biscayne's yacht harbor watched them, startled, then ran to help them. They had made it to land. They could stay. They were "dry footers."

Cárdenas, once a bustling Spanish colonial seaport, has a unique L-shaped geography: ninety miles east of Havana, ninety miles south of the tip of Key West, Florida. Notwithstanding a population of 100,000, it has a small-town feel, where people meet and greet one another with affection and embraces. Despite a polluting plume of black smoke from the Havana Club rum refinery, Cárdenas has certain charms not found in Havana. Locals do their errands in horse-drawn carriages for a peso a trip and street vendors on bicycles sell paper cones filled with peanuts for even less.

Sustained by Varadero, Cuba's most lucrative tourist resort, a half hour away, Cárdenas enjoys one of the highest standards of living on the island. But that hasn't lessened its appeal for *balseros*—rafters who favor its coastline with its ocean currents that glide cleanly toward Miami. Most everyone here has family "over there" in La Yuma. Thousands have chosen Cárdenas as their point of departure, where smugglers charge anywhere from $500 to $10,000 per person depending on the seaworthiness of the craft. It is estimated that only about half of those who attempt the crossing make it alive.

As the Elián hullabaloo hit critical mass, *balsero* departures dropped off dramatically, the result of a government crackdown. By February 2000, they had resumed, and more stories of death and dying at sea were whispered about. Everyone in Cárdenas, it seemed, knew someone who had perished on one crossing or another. All the blather about Elián only underscored the official silence about the thousands who have drowned. For Elián's shipmates there were no memorials, no services, no funerals. The only government action involved seizing the homes of those who left—to be quickly assigned to other Cuban families to fill the country's desperate need for housing.

The grief was still palpable at the Hotel Paradiso—Punta Arenas in Varadero in early February, where Elián's mother, Elisa, and Zenaida and Nelson Rodríguez had worked. While suntanned Canadian and German tourists buzzed about sipping tropical drinks, the staff seemed almost listless—stunned by the loss of three of their own. Unlike *habaneros*, who love to gossip, people in Cárdenas seem to avoid mean-spirited *chisme* (gossip), and lean toward understatement. For six months, street banners proclaiming the town's adoration for Elián were hung across a half dozen streets and the locals had grown weary of the perpetual Elián Show. One of Elián school chums told me that the "all Elián, all the time" activities in school were "very boring," adding, "We want Elián to come home so we can do something else."

Lisbeth García was Elisa Brotón's good friend. I found her on the fourth floor of the hotel cleaning a room. "We were always together," she said softly. "Elisa was my best friend and we worked together. Zenaida worked on the seventh floor and was the godmother of my five-year-old daughter." Lisbeth's eyes welled up with tears, which she wiped away on her white maid's uniform. Nelson, Zenaida's handsome and sweet-humored husband, worked in the maintenance department.

Lisbeth had been close with Elisa for more than ten years, since her marriage to Juan Miguel. She said that Juan Miguel was "a very good man, simple, *simpático*," adding with a smile, "though not necessarily an intellectual. But he's from a good family." Elisa, she said, was remarkably similar to Juan Miguel in that both were quiet, unassuming people with modest ambitions. Both had quit school in the tenth grade and had received their high school diplomas by attending night school. "She didn't love sports or dressing up, but she was exceptional," said Lisbeth. "She had a great passion for her son. All her heart was for her son." Though only thirty, Lisbeth looked very tired, her skin pale and strained by grief. We agreed to meet later when she wasn't working.

The next day I found her at her home in Cárdenas. Like most Cubans, Lisbeth lives with an extended family—her mother, daughter, some in-laws. Her home is typical of Cárdenas—something like a roomy New York City railroad flat of five rooms but with a front porch and a small, scraggly backyard. As in most Cuban homes, there is no hot water. Water for cooking or bathing has to be boiled.

Wearing cheap black patent leather shoes and loose plaid slacks with a black sweater, Lisbeth glanced glumly at her nails and chipped fingernail polish. She had given up on Cuban men, she said, and was resigned to raise her daughter alone just as her mother had raised her. "Divorce here is normal," she noted. So is going to Miami. "I have five paternal uncles in Miami." Many are less fortunate, she says. Before the Elián saga, she said, "people left every day." She paused and surveyed her ragged fingernails, then said quietly, "The sea is a cemetery of people."

Lisbeth learned the bad news the way Cubans learn everything—by *la bola en la calle*, street gossip. "A neighbor found out because she had seen Zenaida's daughter moving her stuff from their apartment. 'I have bad news to give you. The godmother of your daughter is gone,' she told me. I told her, 'That's a lie!' Then I changed clothes and went over to the daughter's house. I found her crying with all of Zenaida's things around the house. Zenaida had left her a note telling her that she was leaving and to come and get her things. They left Saturday and I found out on Monday. On Thursday, they found Elián. It was days of uncertainty, not knowing if they arrived or not. At the hotel, everyone knew about it, everyone was crying."

Juan Miguel found out through a mutual friend, she said, who went to his house and told him what had happened. "I did not want to go myself because I did not have the strength to tell him the news," she said. "On Monday night I went to Elisa's house to see if her mother, Raquel, knew. That's when she tells me that Elisa had sent her a letter saying that she had had problems with Munero and she was in Havana and that when she returned she would move back and live with her again. I told Raquel that Elisa had left with Nelson, Zenaida, with the parents and all. Then she started to cry because she still believed what Elisa wrote in her note."

Moments later, Juan Miguel raced up the stairs. Elisa had told him that she was taking Elián to Havana for the weekend and would return on Tuesday. Now, he said, everyone is saying that she has left the country. He had been to Elisa's small apartment and found it empty and locked and ran over to Rafa's parents' place and found the same thing. "I was on my way to your house," he told Lisbeth, his face flushed with emotion. "I want you to confirm the whole story to me." "Then I told him that it is all true," continued Lisbeth. "That Elisa left and took the boy. He started to cry—inconsolably—for both of them, he loved Elisa—she was the mother of his child, and because they were good friends who had known each other for twenty years."

Juan Miguel raced home and spoke with his mother, Mariela Quintana, a woman of uncommon fortitude, who worked for the Ministry of justice. Immediately she picked up the phone, then charged about town, pulling every string available to her. She would lobby her boss and his chief, who was one of the town's top politicos, Ricardo Chapelín, first secretary of the Communist Party for Cárdenas. But to no avail. No one knew anything other than that the group had left for La Yuma.

On Thursday, November 25, when Elián was discovered bobbing in the sea, an exultant Juan Miguel rushed about putting his papers in order: Elián's birth certificate, his wedding decree, and his divorce papers—knowing he would need them to claim his child. Soon he would be reunited with his son, he told friends.

Elisa and Juan Miguel had met at a friend's *quinceañera*, a fifteenth-birthday party celebration, and began dating when she was fourteen years old. The couple abandoned school to marry when she was sixteen. With both of them working in tourism, the newlyweds prospered enough for Juan Miguel to buy a 1956 Nash Rambler station wagon and to raise a family. For years they tried unsuccessfully to have children. Prior to Elián's birth, Elisa had miscarried seven times. In 1989, she lost a seven-month pregnancy, leaving the couple devastated. "She had everything prepared for the birth," said Lisbeth. The couple divorced in 1991 but continued seeing each other and redoubled their efforts to have a child, even seeking out obstetric care and counseling. In 1993, they finally had a child, Elián. His birth came at the same time that Elisa's father was battling terminal stomach cancer and leavened her sadness. "Elián was a child very much wanted by her and Juan Miguel," said Lisbeth. His name, in fact, was an elision of their two names with an accent over the fourth letter. Eliding names or creating fanciful confections of nomenclature is as popular in the provinces of Cuba as it is in the inner cities of the U.S. Elián was an exceptional child, "very alive and intelligent," who loved mango juice and the little cones of peanuts hawked by street vendors on bicycles.

Neither Elisa nor Juan Miguel was known to be interested in politics, nor did either have a rebellious streak. They both had been members of UJC—the Young Communist League—and both later joined the Party, assuming roles like their parents, who had always been active members. They participated in the local CDR (Committee for the Defense of the Revolution), the neighborhood watchdog group that monitored the community, and Elisa held a fairly important position in the local Communist Party. "She was second secretary of the nucleus of the Party in our department," explained Lisbeth, a "very responsible" position, and she attended meetings up until the time she left.

A few years after Elián's birth, the couple drifted apart. Juan Miguel's philandering, which had dogged their marriage from the beginning, was at the root of the breakup. Lisbeth García didn't mention it during my first interviews with her, but when I returned to Cárdenas some months later, she confirmed my suspicions. The marriage had two significant stresses: the frustration of having lost seven pregnancies before Elián's birth and the fact that Juan Miguel was what Cubans called a *mujeriego*—skirt-chaser. "Here in Cuba, the men are like that," Lisbeth said ruefully. "He was a little *salsero*. He tried to make it so Elisa would not find out because he was never going to leave her . . . but she was never sure he wasn't with another woman. Mariela [Juan Miguel's mother] always defended Elisa, not Juan Miguel. And despite all this, Raquel [Elisa's mother] adored him. She never wanted Elisa to have another husband."

But after years of coping with his infidelities, Elisa left for good. "She didn't trust him anymore," Lisbeth said with a shrug, adding that Juan Miguel was shattered when she finally left and he begged her to return. "Elisa was the love of his life."

At a Varadero nightclub in August 1997, Elisa met and fell headlong in love with Lázaro Munero, known to his family and intimates as Rafa, a high school dropout six years her junior. Bold, impulsive, and entrepreneurial, Rafa couldn't have been more different from Juan Miguel. "He was fun and liked to party," says Lisbeth. "We went out a lot. He liked discos. He enjoyed life. Rafa had lots of spirit, lots of ideas, he was quick-witted. He wouldn't think things through, though. He was very wild. He was called El Loco," and, at times, he could be "a spoiled brat." Two months later, he moved in with Elisa at her mother and stepfather's comfortable apartment above a pharmacy on Calle Coronet Verdugo.

Elisa, said Lisbeth, "was lost in love" for Rafa, "too much in love."

One thing was clear early on: the decision of the Miami relatives of Elián González to keep the five-year-old and not return him to his father was a gift from God for Fidel Castro. To the horror of his critics, Castro claimed the moral high ground. He had grasped immediately that no matter the outcome, the situation would be a win-win for him and a black eye for the Miami exiles.

Castro immersed himself in the Elián drama with the same obsessive zeal with which he had attended to the Cuban Missile Crisis. Virtually daily there was a *tribuna abierta*—open town meeting—or government-organized demonstrations on behalf of Elián, often rallying as many as 100,000 Cubans.

By the time I got to Havana in February, Elián Fatigue was a nationwide epidemic. On television, even cartoons and children's programming were preempted for Elián updates. A popular newscaster who dared to use a mildly sarcastic tone when providing the schedule of more Elián coverage vanished from the screen for several months. A noted intellectual greeted me, hollering aloud, "I hate Elián González," and even a high-level government official confided with a weary shrug, "¡*Ya basta!*"—it's enough already. Dissidents and intellectuals puzzled and groaned over why and how the Miami exile leadership picked such a loser of a cause to champion.

Once the Elián Show became the centerpiece of Castro's foreign policy, Cárdenas was treated to a quick makeover. The entire block on Cossio Street where Elián lived was completely repainted, as was his schoolhouse. Even a hole in his desk had been repaired. Although everyone was dismissive of the propaganda sweepstakes at work, no one believed the government was on the wrong side. Most cringed at the thought of being in Juan Miguel's shoes: having their child snatched by angry Miami relatives who wanted to get even with Fidel Castro. Neighbors howled about how Juan Miguel had even given up his bed for his Uncle Lázaro when he visited from Miami and slept in his car during his 1998 visit—only to be repaid with him stealing his son! "¡*Qué desgracia!*" they scolded.

In Cárdenas, Juan Miguel and his family were well known and well liked. Even Elisa's boyfriend, Rafa Munero, had maintained an amicable relationship with him. Vivian, a neighbor whose children played with Elián, said that Juan Miguel was an unusually dutiful dad. "He was always fretting about the boy. Always bringing him gifts, toys, taking him out for visits and spending the weekend with him."

On January 30, Elián's grandmothers, who had been dispatched to the States to plead their case for the return of their grandson, had completed "their triumphant tour" and were greeted at the airport as heroes of the revolution. They were installed in a swank Havana protocol house in El Laguito to be on call for government-organized events. Cubans were chagrined to hear the two grandmothers had been elevated to Che-hood and compared to Maríana Gragales, the iconized mother of Cuban revolutionary heroes Antonio and José Maceo.

On February 4, as I was chatting with some of Elián's classmates outside his house, a van pulled up. Out popped Juan Miguel, Elián's grandmothers, and their spouses. As I would later learn, they too were sick to death of the Elián Show and craved a little privacy in their own homes. A small crowd of neighbors gathered to greet them—it being their first day home since their whirlwind U.S. tour. Everyone headed inside Mariela and Juan González's home at 170 Cossio Street, which is directly next to Juan Miguel's house and had previously been the home of Juan's parents. I decided to tag along and get a look at the González family without any handlers around.

Raquel Rodríguez, Elisa's mother, is a small, thin woman with a face etched with grief and worry. Prone to tears, she seemed fragile. As there had been no funeral for her daughter, some friends had suggested that she place a large photograph of Elisa in her living room. "She asked me for my opinion," said a close friend. "I told her no. She has always been a woman with a nervous condition, taking little pills. I told her that if she did it, every time she would look toward that corner of the living room, she would remember."

Out back on the patio, an elderly neighbor bounced a baby in her arms, coaching it to chant, *"Que venga Elián . . ."*—"Let Elián come. Let Elián come"—which had become the national mantra.

The González men, described by one friend as being "like a family of state troopers," have all held low-level jobs in the Ministry of the Interior—which is basically spies and cops. Juanito—the father—is retired. Tony did police work at the dock, and Juan Miguel worked as a guide and cashier at Parque Retiro Josone, a twenty-five-acre nature resort in the center of Varadero, popular with tourists. All the men are chain smokers. They're uncomfortable with making small talk. The most amiable is Tony, who once applied for an American visa until he was talked out of leaving by his family. Tony cheerfully dissected his father's complex family tree for me: three brothers and two sisters live in Miami, while two sisters and his father stayed on in Cárdenas. One of the nine siblings, José Luis, had died in 1983.

Juan González, the patriarch, a slight, dark-haired man partial to *guyaberas*, the traditional short-sleeved tailored shirt of Cuba, was wary of chitchat. He declined to bash his brothers, Lázaro and Delfín, for keeping Elián in Miami, saying only, "Myself, I am convinced that they have been pressured to behave like this. Otherwise they would not do this to me." On another occasion, after the *New York Times* broke the story of his brother's troubled history with alcohol and repeated drunk driving arrests, he stressed that Manuel, who supported reuniting Elián with his father, is "the one who doesn't drink." He confirmed that "Delfín and Lázaro have always liked to drink. This has always been so." Asked if there was a family history of alcoholism, he seemed to take offense. "They are not alcoholics. They just like to drink."

A few blocks away on Calle Vives, I met the other estranged six-year-old, Estefany Herrera Horta, Arianne's daughter. Estefany, whose features have a dusky, exquisite beauty, is a child of mercurial moods. During my first visit, she charged around the house like a renegade train, pausing only to grasp at her grandmother as she flew by.

Estefany, who was hyperactive, was receiving psychiatric help. Her grandmother said that her condition was exacerbated by the loss of her mother. "She needs to be with her. I don't know if it's today or tomorrow but it is her only daughter," said Arianne's mother, Elsa Alfonso. "I miss my daughter, I love her. How must she feel about this one that is here. No matter how much I love her I am not her mother."

However, under American law, Arianne could not apply for her daughter's visa until one year after her arrival. There was another impediment at that time: Estefany's father, Victor Herrera. I caught up with Herrera, a drop-dead stunning man with bronzed skin and black hair, who works as a bartender at the Hotel Internacional in Varadero. "I am not worried about Estefany because she's not going anywhere," he said. "She has her grandmothers, her father, her friends, her school, and her neighbors. Maybe when she's fifteen or older—that would be okay."

Arianne claimed that Victor had been somewhat of an

absent dad until the celebrity of the shipwreck. "He was the richest man in Cárdenas but he didn't pay for anything," she fumed. "I can't say that he smokes or takes drugs, but saying that he takes care of the girl is a lie." Nivaldo chimed in, also claiming a paternal role: "I bought everything for her. When Arianne speaks with her, she always wants to talk with me. I took her out and would buy her ice cream."

But however belatedly, Victor had discovered the joys of fatherhood. Now he was visiting his daughter regularly, keenly involved in her affairs. Even Arianne's mother nodded in approval. Victor, who described himself as "a revolutionary" seemed nervous at our first visit. He reluctantly acknowledged that he had had several visits from government officials. Six months later, he was considerably more relaxed. He spoke of Estefany's vivid memories of her near-death boat trip. "She remembers everything that happened on the boat that night and everybody who was on it," he said while tending bar at the Internacional. "When she saw a photograph of Elián, she told me, 'Look Daddy, look Daddy, that's Elián.'" She said that she and Elián were playing together on the boat. And that one of the women, I think it was Lirka Guillermo, was eating a lot of cookies and Elián had said, 'Let's throw her in the water because she's eating too many cookies.' He was joking around. She remembered everybody and everything on the boat."

Several weeks later, in mid-February, I visited with Arianne and Nivaldo again. The two had moved out of her aunt's house into a cozy one-bedroom place of their own a few blocks away. They were doing better financially but were bickering with each other. Both were working at a Metro Ford dealership owned by a director of the Cuban American National Foundation; Arianne was doing clerical work, Nivaldo maintenance on the cars. Nivaldo, wearing a blue pin-striped Metro Ford dealership uniform with a matching blue cap, sat next to Arianne, sifting through photos of their families I had brought back from Cárdenas.

The fissures and ill will between the couple and the relatives of those who died had deepened. Nivaldo, said Munero family members, was only an acquaintance who learned that Rafa was leaving and insisted on coming. "Nivaldo would follow Rafa about—even sleeping outside his house for the last week begging to leave with them," said Dagoberto Munero. "Arianne had waited outside Bata's home the night before they left. Rafa told me that he had agreed to take them for $700."

Nivaldo protested that Rafa was a friend of his and the two shared a passion for music, discotheques, and motorcycle races. He insisted that they didn't pay for the trip, contradicting what he had told the Miami-Dade police on his first day. He added that when Rafa traveled to Jagüey to purchase the boat and motor, he went with him. Arianne even disputed Dagoberto's account, saying he did not have a fight with his brother but stayed at the shoreline and waved them off.

María Díaz, a cousin of the Rodríguez family who lives in Miami, recalled that after the disaster neither Arianne nor Nivaldo could identify the others when shown photos by the police. "She didn't know Lirka's name and would just say, 'The one in the flowered bathing suit.' It was clear they didn't know the others." Some of the relatives had darker suspicions. Why were the two outsiders the only ones to survive? Milagros García and her husband, Ricardo Sardinas, say that the Coast Guard also had suspicions and did a thorough investigation and autopsy of the recovered bodies. Their conclusion: a seriously overloaded boat but no evidence of foul play.

Still, Ricardo personally viewed the bodies to assure himself. He felt that Arianne and Nivaldo badgered Rafa into letting them come along—further overloading the boat. The relatives also said that the Coast Guard told them it was impossible for them to come ashore the way they did with currents going the other direction that day.

Border Patrol anti-smuggling agent Verne Eastwood said that he has seen many "staged landings" but there was no hard evidence that this was the case with Arianne and Nivaldo. He said that the two were interviewed separately for several hours after their arrival at Jackson Memorial Hospital. "They looked pretty good for what they had been through," said Eastwood. "They're pretty tough." He said that the two independently confirmed that they had paid $2,000 for their fare. The couple also told the Border Patrol that Rafa and his father, Rafael, were the co-captains of the trip but said that they were unfamiliar with most of the others on board. They identified Elián only by a photograph, not by name.

Sometimes Arianne's version would be at odds with Nivaldo's and sometimes with what they told investigators and with what they told reporters. On November 28, while still in the hospital, Arianne told reporters that they swam "against the current to get to a boat that rescued them." Later, the couple insisted that they had swum all the way to shore.

By May 2000, questions emerged as to whether the couple and their rescuers were entirely telling the truth. In a *Miami Herald* story, air-conditioning installer Reniel Carmenate, who had been out fishing with his friend, said that he had not found Arianne and Nivaldo on shore as he had previously stated. "I guess I'll have to tell you what really happened," he was quoted as saying. "The real story is that we found them several miles off Key Biscayne," possibly as much as seven miles from shore. Carmenate said he took Nivaldo and Arianne to shore at Crandon Park Marina before calling authorities so the couple would not be automatically returned to Cuba. Carmenate knew the drill: he had been a *balsero* only two years earlier. By his account, it was a staged landing.

A young businessman who leases boats near the dock at Crandon Park where the couple said they swam ashore said he did not believe their story. "Hundreds of Cuban rafters land here every month," he said. "They get to the sandbar out there and then the smugglers go out and get them and bring them ashore. Everyone knows but no one talks about it because [the local authorities] could shut us down if we complained about it. You cannot mess with the Cubans in Miami."

After being told Carmenate's story, Arianne still insisted that they had swum ashore, and Nivaldo refused to comment at all. "He is saying that so he can be famous," she protested. The conflicting stories only darkened the misgivings of the relatives of those who had perished in the shipwreck.

Whatever happened on that boat, Arianne and Nivaldo paid a far steeper price than they could ever have imagined. Within the year, strains in their own relationship were evident. Nivaldo, she confirmed, was "too possessive," and he seemed uncertain and nervous around her. Two years later, they had separated and Arianne started seeing someone else.

One evening, Arianne read me her night-school homework, a long essay she had written in English: "I want to speak about my life. I am not very happy because I don't feel complete. I am twenty-two years old. I am from Cuba, I am been [sic] in United States from three month [sic]. I live in Hialeah. I have a daughter that is five years old. She lives in Cuba and her name is Estefany. She is beautiful. I am very sad. I am not completed [sic] because I miss her and need her in my life. . . . I am going to the school. When I finish my school I am going to my house and sleep. I clean my house on Saturday. On Sunday I go out. My life is not what I want because I miss my daughter. She is not here with me. I am very sad."

In May, Arianne said she had made efforts to visit Estefany in Cárdenas, but she had been defeated by the bureaucratic struggle to obtain a visa and new passport and, of course, by the problem of raising the money. Despite the passage of more than two years, it is unlikely that Arianne will see her daughter any time soon. As students of exile politics well know, the most enduring legacy of the Cuban Revolution is the shattered family.

JOY GORDON

Cuba's Economy

MAKING SENSE OF CUBA'S economy is not easy. There's a joke I heard when I was in Havana recently: The CIA sends an agent down to live in Cuba and report back on the state of the economy. He returns six months later, babbling, and is carted off to an asylum. "I don't get it," he mutters over and over. "There's no gasoline, but the cars are still running. There's no food in the stores, but everyone cooks dinner every night. They have no money, they have nothing at all—but they drink rum and go dancing."

It's an economy of loaves and fishes, where things somehow come out of thin air, ingenuity, and sheer will. It's also an economy that is recovering from the

JOY GORDON
is a frequent contributor to The Atlantic Monthly *(where this piece originally appeared in 1997).*
She teaches political philosophy at California State University-Stanislaus, and is a former visiting professor at the University of Havana.

crisis triggered by the disintegration of the Soviet Union and the collapse of the socialist bloc. From 1989 to 1993 Cuba's gross domestic product declined, according to official estimates, by 35 percent. Imports dropped 75 percent, and the deficit reached 33 percent of GDP. Oil imports from Russia fell from 13 million tons in 1989 to less than 7 million tons in 1992. Cuba not only had to replace the oil and support it had received from the Soviet Union but also had to establish an entirely new set of trading partners, because 85 percent of its trade had been with the socialist bloc. Making matters worse was the U.S. economic embargo.

The Cubans prefer the term "economic blockade"—not unreasonably, since the United States does not simply decline to do business with Cuba but directly interferes in Cuba's trade relations with other countries.

The pettiness of the blockade is striking as one looks at the particulars of its enforcement over the past several years. A Swedish corporation, for example, has been prohibited from selling a sophisticated piece of medical equipment to Cuba because it contains a single filter patented under U.S. law. Dozens of other transactions between Cuba and foreign corporations—involving spare parts for X-ray machines from France, neurological diagnostic equipment from Japan, parts to clean dialysis machines from Argentina, Italian-made chemicals for water treatment, and many others—were likewise prevented by U.S. law.

But in spite of U.S. harassment and meddling, Cuba has found scores of new trading partners, and has embarked on joint ventures and foreign-investment projects with firms from Argentina, Australia, Brazil, Canada, France, Germany, Great Britain, Israel, Italy, Jamaica, Mexico, Russia, Spain, and other countries as well. These projects range from the construction of five-star hotels to enterprises in mining, oil exploration, telecommunications, and biotechnology. And many of the projects are not small. Investment projects include a $1.5 billion deal with a Mexican telecommunications company, a $500 million nickel-mining venture with a Canadian company, a $500 million mining deal with an Australian company, and a $500 million textile deal with a Mexican company. A Monte Carlo—based company built a new terminal in Havana harbor for cruise ships, which has already opened for business. At last count there were 240 joint ventures in Cuba, involving fifty-seven countries in forty areas of the economy. The foreign investment projects announced to date total some $5 billion.

For seven years Cuba has been actively investing in new modes of production, restructuring the economy, and establishing new trade relations around the globe. Now the investments may be starting to pay off. After five years of a sinking GDP, the economic decline came to a halt in 1994: Cuba showed a slight growth in GDP of 0.7 percent. The GDP grew by 2.5 percent in 1995. In the first half of 1996 (the most recent figures available at the time this magazine went to press) the GDP was growing at 9.6 percent, with continued annual growth projected.

At the level of daily life the economic recovery is dramatic. In 1989 the Malecón, a six-lane seaside highway, had more Chinese Flying Pigeon bicycles on it than cars. The occasional car would be a tourist taxi, or an aging Lada (an inexpensive Fiat manufactured in Russia), or a Chevrolet from the 1950s. Although Cuba's economic infrastructure and basic social institutions were holding (schools, hospitals, and factories were still operating), by 1992 and 1993 electrical blackouts occurred in residential areas for most of the day several days a week. Homes had water for only a few hours a day. Lack of fuel oil forced factories to cut back production. Buses were rare, unpredictable, and liable to break down.

Last summer, watching the traffic on the Malecón, I could barely believe I was in Havana. On the street in front of me were a bright-green new Suzuki Sidekick, a new Mercedes-Benz truck, a new Honda sedan, a new Toyota van—and a constant flow of Ladas and '57 Chevies. For those with dollars gasoline was plentiful. Down the road a bit was a new Fiat dealership. Half the models in the showroom cost about $12,000; the others, vans and small trucks, were going for $22,000 or $23,000. A few hundred yards away was a gleaming new hotel, its massive foyer all marble, with Mozart playing softly. A touch-screen computer gave information in several languages about services, restaurants, and shopping. The cheapest rooms were $150 a night, the executive suites $400. And it was obviously not just a tourist hotel: it had conference rooms and a business center with computer facilities, fax machines, photocopiers, laser printers, copies of Cuba's foreign-investment laws, and full-color directories of banks, hotels, restaurants, government offices—and anything else one might need if one were, say, thinking of initiating a joint venture somewhere on the island.

In Havana some of the new wealth is clearly starting to be felt in the population generally. On almost every block, it seems, is a freshly painted house. The discos are jammed every night with both Cubans and foreigners. A fast-food chain called El Rápido has sprung up, its patios full of brightly colored tables crowded with Cubans and foreigners eating hot dogs and pizza and drinking Cokes.

Even during the worst of the economic crisis Cuba managed to avoid starvation, or even widespread malnutrition. Indeed, one of the remarkable things about Cuba's response to the crisis is how the country could keep functioning after its economy was cut by a third. Basic indicators have held steady throughout the economic crisis: Cuba's infant-mortality rate in 1989 was about ten per thousand live births, and life expectancy was seventy-six years—comparable to the statistics for the United States and the other Western industrialized countries. The Cuban infant-mortality rate has even improved slightly since then—it's now about nine per thousand live births. The literacy rate is 98 percent, and no measurable homelessness exists. Cuba still has more doctors and teachers per capita than almost any other country in the world. In a population of 11 million, more than half a million Cubans hold university degrees.

Media accounts often mention "rationing" as evidence of how desperate Cuba's post-1990 situation is. In fact Cuba has had "rationing" since thirty-five years before the crisis began: every person, regardless of income, is entitled to a basic allotment of food and essentials—beans, rice, vegetables, fruit, eggs, meat, soap, cooking oil, cigarettes, gasoline, and so on. Shortly after the revolution every child up to age seven was guaranteed a liter of milk a day for twenty-five cents; in the 1980s children up to fourteen, along with the sick and the elderly, received this entitlement. In 1990 the guarantee of milk was reduced to include only children seven and under again. Also, through the 1980s parallel markets supplied a range of goods, from bread to wine to meat to canned food, that could be bought with pesos without restriction. As the economy sank, these goods went "on the book" (the *libreta*, or ration book) or disappeared altogether. Bread was rationed, meat rations shrank, canned goods were hard to find—until virtually all goods were available only through the rationing system, and even some of the guaranteed items didn't always appear as promised.

There was enough food to get by, but just barely. "We have enough," a friend of mine said in 1992. "There's food on the table every day; the kids are going to school. But you want something more once in a while. You want to buy a Coke, or a new dress. You want to sit in a café, or go dancing, or just buy a can of something for dinner instead of soaking the beans again and hoping that the cooking gas will come on before two in the morning."

As the economy plummeted, prostitution returned. With it came painful memories of the Batista era, when Cuba was a playground for wealthy foreigners, and money laundering, gambling, and prostitution were among the nation's most visible economic institutions. The official position in recent years was that this prostitution was different from that prostitution: that prostitution was what women did to buy food for their starving infants; this prostitution reflected a malaise born of boredom and frustration rather than economic desperation. Hundreds of thousands of tourists were now flooding the country each year, with their Nikes and Walkmans, jewelry and credit cards, while Cubans were increasingly standing in long lines to catch overcrowded buses to go to work at a factory or a university that might shut down partway through the day because of an electricity shortage. By mid-1994 the peso—which in principle was equivalent to a dollar—was trading on the black market at 120 to a dollar. It was clear that as long as the economic crisis continued, prostitution, petty theft, and black-market activities would grow.

Salaries in Cuba can range from 100 pesos a month to a few hundred. A factory worker might earn 120 pesos a month, a professor 350. Anyone who has completed a university education will automatically earn at least 195 pesos a month. A top surgeon might earn as much as 600. It has been common in the past few years to see in the U.S. press that "Cubans are now living on the equivalent of a dollar a month." But this misrepresents the nature of the economic situation. The Cuban economy is simply not structured on the model of dependent capitalism. Basic necessities, at consistent, easily affordable prices, are still bought in pesos, regardless of what the exchange rate is. Rent for Cubans is around 6 or 8 percent of their monthly salary, no matter how much they earn. All the food provided "on the book" would cost a family of four perhaps thirty or forty pesos a month. Education continues to be free, medical care is free, buses cost a few cents. The peso's loss of purchasing power did not mean that people lost their homes or couldn't afford to send their children to school. Rather, the economic crisis has meant that nothing except necessities could be bought with Cuban currency.

The Cuban government responded to the crisis in part by developing trade and investment and in part by introducing elements of a mixed economy. In September of 1993 the government announced that the state-run farms would be dismantled and replaced by worker-managed cooperatives. By the fall of 1994 Cuban fuel supplies had climbed back up, and the electricity shortages became brief and infrequent. The Cuban government also legalized the small business enterprises and farmers' markets. Food prices at these markets vary—some are affordable for everyone, some too expensive for anyone not running a private business in dollars. But the presence of the markets meant that the food shortages were over—and, perhaps as important, that the sense of shortage was over. The monotony of people's diets, the starkness, the sense of being limited to the goods "on the book," have by now given way to the far more tolerable project of just managing on a tight budget.

The economic changes in Cuba go to the very structure of the Cuban economy. Joint ventures have been permitted since 1982, but for many years the foreign partner could not hold more than a 49 percent share unless there were exceptional circumstances. In 1992 the Cuban constitution was modified to recognize a variety of new forms of property. New kinds of foreign investment, Cuban corporations, and joint ventures were legalized. Foreign corporations were given the right to repatriate profits freely. The law was modified again in September of 1995, to permit foreign investment with up to 100 percent foreign ownership. Foreign investors are guaranteed full protection of their assets and the right to remove profits in hard currency. And they may also acquire and develop real estate, although they may not buy or develop residential properties for Cuban nationals. Foreign investment is permitted in all sectors of the economy except health, education, and the armed services.

Cuba's development strategy in the face of its economic crisis contrasts sharply with the policies of other countries in Latin America and the Third World. Typically, foreign investors come to Third World countries because there are far fewer environmental restrictions and protections for labor than in First World countries. A textile factory in Haiti can pay its employees twelve cents an hour. A factory in Cairo can pour untreated pollution into the air with little or no concern for environmental laws. Cuba, however, is trying to attract investment without making these tradeoffs. It requires foreign nationals to include in their investment proposals provisions for waste disposal and land use consistent with sustainable development. "Look," a Cuban economist told me, "in the end it means there will be more interest in foreign investment rather than less. If you build a multi-million-dollar hotel on the beach at Varadero, you want to have assurances that there won't be any chance of leaky oil tankers a half mile down, from some company doing oil exploration. It's one of the advantages of a centralized economy. We can actually make a company's investment more secure than it would be in an unregulated economy."

Employers can fire unsatisfactory employees and hire new ones through a government agency, although a worker can challenge a dismissal as unfair or discriminatory. Foreign companies, like all Cuban enterprises, are prohibited from discriminating on the basis of race, sex, or ethnicity.

The restructuring has now started to pay off. Furthermore, the increase in GDP reflects growth that is distributed broadly throughout the economy. In 1995 nickel production increased about 65 percent, tobacco 52 percent, and tourism 20 percent. Exports increased 20 percent, and imports 21 percent. Fifty thousand new homes are under construction. Cuba's biotechnology industry competes in the world market, with more than 160 products developed by fifty-three research centers, ranging from genetically engineered crop seeds that are disease-resistant to a vaccine for hepatitis B. The level of Cuban tourism is now greater than it was at its height in pre-revolutionary Cuba. In 1994 Cuba had 617,000 tourists, putting it on a par with Aruba and the U.S. Virgin Islands. In 1995 the number of tourists was conservatively estimated at 750,000. Income from tourism grew from $165 million in 1989 to more than $850 million in 1994 and to $1 billion in 1995. From January to April of last year—the period in which the Cuban-American planes were shot down and the Helms-Burton bill was passed—Cuba had 375,000 tourists, an increase of 44 percent from the same period the year before.

To say that Cuba is now inviting free enterprise does not really describe the country's economic restructuring. For the most part there are two different kinds of profit-based enterprises in Cuba: very large and very small. Foreign investors account for the very large, individual Cubans for the very small. Cubans obtain a license, for which they pay a fee based on the income anticipated for that type of business. A family might turn its living room into a small restaurant; someone with a car might start hiring it out as a taxi; a woman might make traditional Cuban pastries and sell them in her front yard. Thus there is now a substantial legal "informal sector."

The informal sector in Third World economies typically involves a high degree of economic insecurity. A highway intersection or a city sidewalk will be crowded with "entrepreneurs" hawking their wares—parrots, mangoes, hubcaps, hood ornaments, U.S. dollars, computer parts, pistachios. On a bad day the entrepreneur may return home with no earnings at all, and his or her family will literally go hungry the next day. In Cuba, since everyone is already guaranteed that an extensive set of basic needs will be met, the income from the new private enterprises goes almost entirely for consumer goods. In the living room of a woman who serves dinner for four dollars is a Sony stereo system with enormous speakers, a new color television, and a VCR. A taxi driver is wearing a new leather jacket. Children playing at a home where pastries are sold in the yard are wearing new Nikes. Thus, ironically, for many Cubans private enterprise feels much the way ideologues of capitalism describe it: with economic freedom, they say, you are your own person, you earn what you earn, and you spend it as you like. Yet this is possible in Cuba only because and insofar as it has remained socialist.

During the 1980s the external debt of Third World countries increased enormously. In the face of their inability to meet debt-service requirements, and under pressure from the International Monetary Fund and the World Bank, many instituted "structural adjustment" programs, selling off any state enterprises that were profitable and reducing expenditures on food subsidies and health care for populations that were already living very marginally. The resulting profits and savings have generally gone not into social investment or job creation but into what Latin Americans call *la deuda impagable*—"the unpayable debt." After the collapse of the Soviet bloc, Cuba's future did not look bright. If it followed the road of dependent capitalism, it could expect to end up like Brazil or Guatemala, with pockets of extreme wealth alongside widespread poverty, starvation, unemployment, and violence—in short, Cuba could expect to return to the way it was before the revolution. Instead Cuba has in seven years restructured its entire economy. But it has done so while maintaining its commitments to many socialist principles, including the belief that all members of society are entitled to food, housing, education, and medical care.

Cuba's economic transformation has profound implications for the United States, particularly the U.S. business community. It is a country of 11 million people with middle-class tastes and a middle-class lifestyle, hungry for TVs,

VCRs, Cuisinarts, and boom boxes. It has a healthy, stable, highly educated workforce, useful to those seeking to establish complex manufacturing enterprises. Finally, it is now showing solid annual economic growth, and has already started investing again in its infrastructure. As the Cuban economy grows, companies from everywhere in the world—except the United States—will be selling consumer products, running resorts, and investing in agriculture, tourism, mining, and manufacturing. U.S. firms should not expect that much of the economic pie will be left for them five years from now—or even two.

The U.S. embargo has cost Cuba a lot, but it has neither crippled the Cuban economy nor undermined Castro's leadership. And the embargo not only has failed to persuade the international community that Cuba should be "punished" but in fact has isolated us within the world community. The Torricelli bill of 1992 and the Helms-Burton bill of last year are widely considered to violate international law, in that they claim jurisdiction over-and the right to impose penalties on—foreign companies that choose to do business with Cuba. Because of the Torricelli bill the United States has been condemned by ever larger margins by the United Nations General Assembly each year since 1992 for interfering in Cuba's trade with other nations. The most recent vote, last November, was a scathing 138 to 3.

The Helms-Burton bill, which President Clinton signed into law last March, has alienated U.S. trading partners and allies further. The bill permits U.S. lawsuits against foreign companies if they make use of any property in Cuba that was confiscated from anyone who is now a U.S. citizen. If a Cuban plantation owner emigrated to the United States in 1959, and thirty-five years later a Spanish company built a hotel on the old plantation site, the migrator, if a U.S. citizen, can sue the Spanish company in a U.S. court for "trafficking in confiscated property." Thus the U.S. court is exercising jurisdiction over actions of a foreign company that took place in a foreign land, for the benefit of someone who was at the time of his loss a foreign citizen. Furthermore, the bill denies U.S. entry visas to executives of foreign companies (and their spouses and children) if their employers do business in Cuba involving properties that were owned by U.S. nationals prior to the revolution. The State Department has already denied visas to Canadian and Mexican business executives along with their families.

Helms-Burton in principle could force corporations from Argentina, Brazil, Canada, Great Britain, Italy, Mexico, Spain, and other countries simply to abandon their hotels, mines, and other investments in Cuba or to pay millions in damages to the prior owners from the 1950s.

Consequently the State Department predicted that the Helms-Burton legislation would have a "chilling effect" on Cuban commerce. But so far it has not. There have been few confirmed cases of companies pulling out, and there is every indication that the economic recovery continues to be solid. Last July, Cuba's vice president announced that the nation's GDP for the first six months of the year grew by 9.6 percent. Even after the devastation done to the crops by Hurricane Lili in October, the GDP for 1996 is expected to show growth of at least 5 percent. Furthermore, Cuba has put in place new laws that will make foreign investment even more attractive. Last June, Cuba enhanced foreign companies' incentives to trade with the island when the National Assembly passed a law reducing tariffs on imported goods. A few weeks later the National Assembly passed another law, establishing free-trade zones and industrial parks, where businesses will receive huge tax breaks.

In recent years the United States has invoked international law to justify both the Persian Gulf War and the invasion of Panama. However, because of Helms-Burton now we are being widely condemned for violating international law and major trade accords such as GATT and NAFTA.

Last July, President Clinton tried to stave off the fury of U.S. allies and trading partners by suspending the implementation of the most controversial provisions of Helms-Burton for six months, although they are still valid law. Not surprisingly, our European trading partners have continued to show "unadulterated, undiluted anger," in the words of Stuart Eizenstat, of the Commerce Department. Last fall the European Union brought an action against the United States before the World Trade Organization. This was followed by retaliatory legislation from all fifteen EU states, prohibiting European countries from obeying the Helms-Burton provisions and permitting them to countersue American companies in European courts to recover any financial penalties imposed by U.S. courts. Canada and Mexico passed retaliatory legislation as well.

In the meantime, U.S. business is losing out: it is conservatively estimated that if the Cuban embargo were lifted today, the United States could export goods worth $1–$2 billion annually to the island. American goods have been making their way to Cuban consumers by a variety of routes for years—U.S. companies sell goods to a non-U.S. distributor, who sells them to Cuba, or the goods are sometimes just smuggled in. Coca-Cola, California wines, Mr. Clean, Gerber baby food, Sylvania light bulbs, Quaker Oats—all can be found in Cuba. U.S. companies are clearly eager to set up shop in Cuba. In 1990 representatives of more than 400 U.S. businesses visited Cuba; in 1995, 1,300 businesses visited. General Motors, Sears Roebuck, Avis, Hyatt, ITT Sheraton, Bank of Boston, Gillette, and Radisson Hotels are among the U.S. companies that have sent CEOs and representatives to Havana to look into future business opportunities. Dozens of U.S. firms have already signed letters of intent to do business if the embargo is lifted.

Up to this point both Congress and Clinton have been more interested in condemning Castro than in abiding by international law. But the furious protests from our major trading partners lead one to wonder how long Congress and the administration can hold out. In this new game of chicken that we are playing with Cuba, the smart money in the international business community may well be on Cuba.

CHRISTOPHER HITCHENS

Havana Can Wait

I N LA BODEGUITA DEL MEDIO, a drink shop on Calle Empedrado, in the Cathedral quarter of Old Havana, where Ernest Hemingway used to absorb his *mojito* thirst quencher before moving on to his daiquiri at the nearby Floridita restaurant, there is an inscription in the visitors' book. *"Viva Cuba Libre!"* it reads. *"Chile espera."* The words Cuba Libre also connote a cocktail—a fang-crumbling and nauseating blend of rum and Coke—but one can be reasonably certain that the author of the scrawl was not toasting his hosts in that way, because the signature of Salvador Allende follows, with the date of June 28, 1961. At that time, Allende was a fairly obscure Chilean physician with a rising reputation in opposition politics. Six and a half

CHRISTOPHER HITCHENS is Professor of Liberal Studies at the New School in New York City, as well as a columnist for Vanity Fair (where this piece originally appeared in 2001) and The Nation. His books include Letters to a Young Contrarian, and The Trial of Henry Kissinger.

years later, he dispatched personal emissaries to the Chile-Bolivia border to help rescue the tattered rabble who had survived Ernesto Che Guevara's suicide mission to the Andes. Three years after that he was elected president of Chile and, as his first act, broke the embargo against Cuba by restoring relations and inviting Fidel Castro for a state visit. In September 1973, Allende was murdered in the presidential palace in Santiago, on the orders of the same General Pinochet he had promoted to be his army chief.

As I downed my own melancholy *mojito*—these days a rather standardized and automatic concoction of weak rum and limp leaves of mint—I could hear the street musicians outside, offering routine versions of that still-beautiful ballad to Che: "Hasta Siempre Comandante" (Forever Commander). In London, General Pinochet, now eighty-four, was about to undergo medical tests to determine his fitness to stand trial for crimes against humanity. In Chile, Ricardo Lagos, sixty-one—an old associate of Allende's—stood a fighting chance of winning the presidency in a runoff. And in Old Havana—this was the turn and cusp of 1999—they were marking the centenary of Hemingway's birth on one hand and hawking T-shirts of Guevara to the same tourists with the other hand. I veered nostalgically between the ironies of history and the importance of being either Ernesto.

As if to confirm his mooring in a time warp, Fidel Castro, seventy-three, had declared that January 1, 2000, was not the beginning of a new millennium. Determined as ever to remain at an angle to the rest of the world, he announced that the true year would be 2001. This eccentric if mathematically correct gesture had a surreal feeling on an island where official figures and statistics mean almost nothing, and where the revolution climaxed on New Year's Eve 1958. I was staying in the faded palace of the Hotel Nacional, that harborfront resort where Graham Greene's hapless British pseudo-agent Wormold survived a poisoning plot in *Our Man in Havana*, and where mob summits occurred before Mob rule flamed out, as in the best-remembered moments of *The Godfather Part II*.

The placards in the lobby summoned me to celebrate not the closing of a thousand-year epoch but the opening of Year 41 of La Revolución. Forty-one: the unarguable onset of middle age.

Cuba. The very name—short, pungent, yet romantic—has ineffaceable associations. Cuba—the place where the United States received a foretaste of Vietnam in its humiliation at the Bay of Pigs. Cuba—where the missiles of October gave the world its longest and steadiest look at the nuclear furnace when that hellish door swung briefly open in 1962. Cuba—home base to the gangsters who clustered around J.F.K. and may even have killed him. Cuba—whose exiled fanatics were caught in the Watergate building. Cuba—whose troops inflicted the salutary military defeat on the South African forces in Angola. Cuba—an island, like Ireland, which refuses to accept its real size and weight in the world, and whose writers and poets and musicians populate our imagination. Can such a place undergo a graceful menopause, like a veteran of some Buena Vista reunion?

Middle age can be vigorous and affirmative—oh, that I would see forty-one again—but Cuba today exists in a state, and as a state, of suspended animation. The leadership emphasizes this in ways of which it may not even be aware. REVOLUTIONARIES FOREVER YOUNG proclaims a billboard of Castro's long-ago guerrilla associates, their bushiness and trimness making a bold contrast to the Maximum Leader's paunch and thinning fur. (People call him "Fidel," but I find I can't, since I don't know the guy.) Even the endless hysterical rallies outside the U.S. Interests Section on the Havana waterfront, for the return of six-year-old Elián González from Miami, contain a forlorn attempt to reanimate a lost and rebellious childhood. For a better clue to the true position of affairs, look up the statement made by the kid's divorced father. Naturally, I can provide for him here in Cuba, the man said. Don't I work in the tourist-services industry?

At first look, the word *espera* in Allende's message seems to mean "hopes," as in *esperanza*. But it actually means—Spanish being such an ironic language—"waits." To wait is to hope, of course, and in some ways to hope is to wait. But, at present, Cuba just waits. And while it waits, it sells itself to pass the time. What it waits for and what it hopes for may both be radically different from what it gets.

In the seaside town of Cojimar, the setting for *The Old Man and the Sea*, the aging and practiced charmers at La Terraza can spot a gringo scribbler from several furlongs away. Out come the folkloric appurtenances: the photos of Hemingway with Castro; the giant fish gaping at the lens; the sepia shots of Anselmo Hernandez—"The Old Man" or

"Old Santiago" himself—who died in Miami. Then there's the ancient captain to be visited a few blocks away: Gregorio Fuentes, who kept Ernest's boat in the water and who on the day I met him was approaching his one hundred and third birthday. In another week, he would have lived in three centuries. Amazingly raddled and wattled, he nonetheless executed a very strong handshake and immediately lit and puffed upon the truncheon-size Cohiba that the photographer and I had brought as an anniversary tribute. Things were, he opined, in general, in the hands of God. (I always love the wisdom of ancient mariners and peasants.) Round the corner dwells Raúl Corrales, the dapper and silvered veteran who photographed The Revolution—always somehow capitalized in ordinary speech—and who is a full member of the system's cultural elite. He, too, was willing to receive guests and to submit to reverent curiosity. Then it was back to the bar and to a series of delicious but costly pledges to international friendship. I've done this routine before, yet this time was slightly different in that everyone, at every stage, hit me up for money. (I slightly exempt Captain Fuentes, whose son put the squeeze on me on his behalf, but then, at age one hundred and two one is entitled to say, like Castro himself, *"Yo no soy marinero, soy capitán,"* and let others do the soliciting.)

"This is a country," says one of my oldest comrades on the island, "where everybody is on the take." Old people sell lavatory paper, square by square, at the doors of public bathrooms. Avid vendors of everything jostle outside the hotels. Ungifted street musicians remove their fingers from their instruments as soon as they see a hand drift toward a pocket. Girls—and boys—strike up conversations, only to reveal that they don't just like you for your mind or even—this is especially hurtful—for your body. It seems a long, long time since Guevara was in charge of the national bank, signing the currency notes with a contemptuously scrawled "Che," or since there was serious public discussion of the abolition of money. (This Utopian accomplishment has been at least partially realized, since the Cuban peso note would now be refused even by those whose job in life it is to sell lavatory paper by the sheet.)

They are waiting, all of them. In the sweet little town of Viñales, in the rural province of Pinar del Río, a beautiful girl persuades me that her restaurant is the best. "The finest pork in Cuba." She insists on showing me the grill, where whole pigs lie marinating. She presses a porcine sample on me, full of crackle and taste. It's delectable, which is just as well, since there's nothing else on the menu save the black bean–white rice combo known as Moros y Cristianos (Moors and Christians). At this point I detect, from the silver Star of David round her neck, that she is neither Moorish nor Christian but Sephardic. "Oh, yes," she responds brightly. "My family was from Jerusalem and we expect an Israeli tour party today." And her job is to sell fresh hot pig from dawn to dusk. Easy to tell what she's waiting for. She's waiting for Miami—not for her to visit it, but for it to visit her.

In the town's main square, there's a little sociopolitical set piece, like those you can still see in some parts of Italy and

Greece and eastern Germany. On one side the Communist Party office, with faded red flags and curling posters. On the other, a church, with garish icons and a wooden shelf of tracts. Between them, a sort of armed truce, and in the square, young couples and old people taking the air and making the *paseo* (promenade). Across the road stands a bookstore, next to the workers' club. It is laden with flyblown Bulgarian and East German editions of a decade ago, diluted with a few cheap versions of children's classics and—on the topmost display—some furtive works on sexual hygiene. I handle a dusty copy of *History Will Absolve Me*, the bravura speech that Fidel Castro made from the dock before being imprisoned in the dreaded Isle of Pines penal colony in 1953. In the second paragraph he says: "He who is speaking abhors, with all his being, childish conceit, and neither by his temperament nor by his present frame of mind is he inclined toward oratory or toward any kind of sensationalism."

The speech goes on for eighty-one pages: arguably the shortest and best one he ever gave. For over four decades now, this great *solipsista* has monopolized the microphone for rhetorical marathons of several hours. I decide I must have the pamphlet. It costs an exorbitant amount in dollars, exacted from me by a wispy old lady who wears a heavy crucifix. She has a waiting attitude, also.

I first came to Pinar del Río province in 1968, wondering if the news about the Cuban Revolution could really be true. And some of it was. It was true, for example, that official racism had been abolished. (In the grisly old days, even the dictator Batista was refused membership in certain clubs on the grounds that his hide was insufficiently pink.) It was also true that illiteracy had been almost eradicated, and that no Cuban with any illness had to live in fear. Moreover, much of the rest of Latin America was sweltering under uniformed despotisms like that of Somoza, and these juntas enjoyed the most cynical indulgence in Washington. Salvador Allende was not the only intellectual or idealist to see Havana as a beacon. There were aspects of the society I didn't like—the boring emphasis on sports and on military virtues, for instance, and the inculcation of compulsory enthusiasm reminded me of a boarding school. Even worse, the Castro leadership that year decided to endorse the Soviet invasion of Czechoslovakia, and thus to betray its own stand against superpower bullying.

Bad enough. But now look. The only leader in Latin America who always wears a military uniform, and who steadfastly and on principle refuses elections, is Fidel Castro. Cuban citizens are forbidden by law to use hotels reserved for the rich and may not even enter many stores and pharmacies which trade only in dollars. After forty years, there are few senior black faces in the supposed "leadership." Many doctors have been trained, but they are paid less than the hotel doormen or policemen in the segregated tourist districts. The regime publishes a daily newspaper which all the literates can read, yet I cannot improve on the description of it given by the late Argentinean editor and dissident Jacobo Timerman, who described his morning encounter with that same paper as "a degradation of the act of reading." (One old man in Hemingway's Cojimar came close when he told me that "if you listen to the radio you don't need the newspaper.") No intellectual or idealist voyages to Cuba anymore in search of debate or passion or enlightenment: the best book ever written on the expunging of mental life on the island was, paradoxically if you like, written by the Chilean writer Jorge Edwards, who was Allende's first accredited ambassador to Cuba. (The book is called *Persona Non Grata*, because not even his status as an envoy from Allende's socialist Chile prevented Edwards from being unceremoniously chucked out for his friendship with independent-minded intellectuals.)

"Seventh-rate citizens in our own country." So I was told by Miriam Leiva, one of the small but increasing number of open, declared oppositionists. Until a few years ago, she and her economist husband worked in the Cuban foreign service, and were last stationed in the embassy in Belgrade. ("Easy to see that Milosevic was turning into a Fascist," she remarks calmly of the man who is defended in the official Cuban press almost every day.) Fired for the expression of deviant views, the couple hang on in a tiny windowless apartment in the Playa district of Havana, surviving by a bit of translating here, a bit of writing there—and by waiting.

"If Karl Marx were a Cuban, he would be in jail or in Miami," says Dr. Oscar Espinosa, Leiva's fifty-two-year-old husband. "From each according to his abilities—to each according to his need.' That's the old slogan. But the average salary here is $11 a month, and only the army and the bureaucracy get what they need." Slowly emerging behind the Fidelist flourishes and slogans is a system not unlike in

China, where capitalism and profiteering are permitted but democracy and free expression are not. You might call that the worst of both worlds. "We are told to have faith," he comments sardonically. "And in our language the word for faith is *fe*. So now we say that faith is literally f.e.—*familia exterior*, or 'family outside.' Only those with relatives in Florida can beat the system." The good doctor goes on to point out that this, too, leaves black Cubans at the bottom of the heap, because they are the least likely to have cousins in Miami. They get to cut the cane and roll the cigars, which remain Cuba's chief products, just as in Batista's day.

On the following afternoon, Leiva takes me to meet Elizardo Sanchez, the public face of Cuban dissent. Now fifty-five he lives in a moderate-size family villa, overrun with guests and relatives for New Year's Day. Chicken wire protects the porch and the windows from stone-throwing and spitting mobs, who trucked to his door by the regime as volunteers until a short while ago. (Since Sanchez began to receive international human-rights prizes, and also calls from visiting statesmen, the gallant spontaneity of the crowd appears to have declined somewhat.) Here is a man who knows how to play a waiting game. Like most of the native and domestic dissidents—and in colossal contrast to the Miami exile leadership—he is a veteran social democrat with a background in the pre-Castro Communist Party. His ideological mainspring broke, as did that of so many, with the crushing of Alexander Dubcek's Prague experiment in 1968. After he signed a protest against Cuban endorsement of that atrocity, he lost his job as a professor of philosophy, went in and out of jail, and was subjected to various slanders and indignities. Now he collects lists of political prisoners, monitors the press, and lives in the few inches of protection that are afforded by friendship with a handful of correspondents and diplomats. He dryly hands me a card, and I notice only later that his telephone number has the words *"si funciona"* [if it's working] printed after it in parentheses.

"There are no death squads in Cuba, and no political murders," he says. "But we do have a closed society, and we do have a political oligarchy which exploits the workers. There's no free press, no free trade unions, no Red Cross inspection, no right to leave the country or to leave it and return." Side by side on his crammed bookshelves are the memoirs of Gorbachev and a long history of the eclipse of Franco in Spain. Which model, I ask him, does he think is more likely? "Well, the regime is in its terminal and moribund stage. It cannot last. The only question is how it will change. The *grupo duro* [hard-liners] in Miami denounce me for saying this, but I believe that Fidel Castro should lead the transition. If he does not, we could see social breakdown, violence, uncontrolled emigration, revenge. . . ."

In spite of the squalid and cramped and frustrated lives that most of them are forced to lead—it's amazing to see the sheer abject slumminess of the streets in the very center of Havana—the Cuban people are so welcoming and so decent that it's hard to picture them turning nasty. Yet I was warned time and again that there exists a large underground reservoir of acidity and resentment—against the system of informers, against the tourist apartheid, against the shortages and bully- ing, and against the endless, dreary, nonuplifting speeches. Last year, the U.S. Interests Section interviewed candidates in a lottery for 16,000 travel documents. Known colloquially as El Bombo, or the raffle, this offer was printed in the Cuban press. More than 500,000 applications were immediately received. Given that applicants had to be between the ages of eighteen and fifty-five, given that an application to leave is not always considered a friendly act by the regime, given that only one application per family is considered, and given that the total population is 11 million, this was something like a proposal for a mass evacuation of the island. Of those howling at official "Return Elián" rallies outside the US. Interests Section, many must have been expressing a repressed desire to join him.

On an earlier visit to Cuba during the Gorbachev era— and, boy, how Castro despised Gorbachev—I happened to be reading Ralph Ellison's *Invisible Man*. I underlined a striking sentence where, recalling a potent college president under whom he had studied, Ellison wrote, "Whether we liked him or not, he was never out of our minds. That was a secret of leadership." It all keeps coming back to Fidel Castro, who is now, with a mixture of defiance and compla- cency, preparing to celebrate the departure of the ninth American president since he took power. The part he plays, in the imagination of his subjects and of his foes, is almost totemic. But he, too, is a mere mortal mammal, and he, too, must be waiting for something, even if it's only the end. "I can propose a title for your article," says Elizardo Sanchez.

"Why not call it 'Chronicle of a Transition Foretold'?" Gabriel García Márquez, who has somewhat prostituted himself for Castro, believes in historical irony as much as historical inevitability. On either grounds, I think I'd still prefer to title it "The Autumn of the Patriarch," because if autumn comes, can The Fall be far behind?

WALTER RUSSELL MEAD

The Cuba Embargo

I N 1962, JOHN F. KENNEDY declared a total economic embargo against Cuba with the goal of making living conditions intolerable for ordinary Cubans so that they would rise up and overthrow Fidel Castro. For twenty-seven years after that, the Soviet Union subsidized the Cuban state, and Kennedy's embargo did not achieve its strategic objective. We can call 1962 to 1989 Embargo I. Embargo I failed. After the Soviet Union fell, proponents of the policy thought, Ah, now is the hour of the embargo. We can call 1989 to the present Embargo II. And admittedly, in the early 1990s things on the island looked bleak, as Castro's economy fell into a deep depression. But for reasons we'll get to in a moment, that has changed. We can now

WALTER RUSSELL MEAD *is Senior Fellow for U.S. Foreign Policy at the Council on Foreign Relations. His work has appeared in the* Los Angeles Times, Worth *magazine,* Foreign Affairs, *the* New York Times, *and* Esquire *(where this piece originally appeared in 2001.*

say definitively that Embargo II has failed. It is time to do something else.

1994 was the embargo's best year and the last, best chance for it to work. In 1994, Havana was a city that broke your heart: Some of the finest architecture in the Americas was falling into the sea. The drive along Havana's world-famous seawall took you past one beautiful facade after another that was being eaten by salt; mansions were crumbling to dust before your eyes. With more old houses being washed away in the rains than new ones being built, Cubans used to say that you could calculate the date when all of Havana would disappear.

Cathedral Square in downtown Havana was unpainted and in decay; there were old women begging for food, arms as thin as broomsticks. Hungry street kids hung around, begging for pennies and scraps. A mysterious epidemic of blindness, apparently linked to malnutrition, struck the country in 1993. That same year, the Cuban peso collapsed against the dollar, falling as low as 120 to 1; at that rate, most Cuban salaries were worth less than two dollars per month. Prices in the state-controlled stores remained low enough that, technically, you could buy enough beans and rice to live for a month; the trouble was that there weren't any beans or rice in the state stores. The following year saw riots break out in Havana, and tens of thousands of Cubans fled Castro's collapsing economy on rafts and boats.

On a visit that year, over cognac and steaks (the upper class the world over always seems to have a way of remaining insulated from economic catastrophe), distraught Cuban economists explained the situation to me. Without its key markets and deprived of its low-priced oil, Cuba's inefficient economy had fallen into a deep depression. In four years, the GDP had fallen by 35 percent—a bigger drop than the U.S. suffered during the Great Depression.

The country was on the verge of total collapse.

You don't hear this anymore. I went back this year to see how things had changed, and what I saw certainly wasn't good news for America's Cuba policy. Havana is turning into a huge reconstruction and renovation site. One street after another in the Old City has been systematically restored; there are jazz bands at hopping cafés in plazas I first saw as crumbling, empty ruins. Homeowners all over the city are sprucing up their houses, repainting, adding new rooms.

In 1994, there was only one hotel where the phones worked reliably; now there are world-class hotels all over the city where you can watch CNN and phone out whenever you want. The service, which used to be casual and sloppy—a mix of Soviet charm and Caribbean efficiency—is excellent.

And the embargo clearly has more holes than a sieve. You can get a Coca-Cola anytime you want in Cuba, and hotels offer dishes like "Shrimp in Jim Beam" on their menus. The Cuban government broadcasts pirated Hollywood movies (vetted for political content, of course) on television; things you and I can see only on HBO and pay-per-view they get free down there.

Several factors drive Cuba's recovery. First, there is the money from Cuban Americans. Most Cuban Americans think the embargo is essential in the abstract but not a policy they want applied to their own families. Since the summer of 1993, when Castro shrewdly made it legal for ordinary Cubans to own and use dollars, Cuban Americans have sent hundreds of millions every year to relatives and others on the island. And since roughly one out of every twelve people born in Cuba now lives in the United States, that's a lot of money to a lot of families.

Result: Because of Miami, Castro nets more money from his enemies than from most of his state-run economy.

Second, there's tourism. Americans aren't allowed to travel to Cuba, but that doesn't stop us. Cuban immigration officials don't stamp U.S. passports, and there are quick and easy flights to Cuba from popular Caribbean resorts like Cancún and Montego Bay. According to Cuban estimates, a quarter of a million Americans are expected to visit Cuba this year; add that to almost two million Europeans, Mexicans, Canadians, and others, and you see why hotels—and Fidel's treasury—stay full.

Third—and this matters more than you might think—the Soviet collapse drove Castro to do something that for him was totally new: He made some good economic decisions. Cuban state enterprises set up to earn hard currency by serving tourists and producing goods for world markets (sugar, tobacco, nickel) have gotten leaner and better managed. I've watched Cuban bureaucrats make PowerPoint slide presentations for foreign investors; these guys are much slicker than they used to be.

For the average Cuban, life is still very hard. The necessities are usually available in farmers' markets, but state salaries are less than fifteen dollars per month, and that doesn't go far in the free-market economy. Cubans still spend much of their time finding creative solutions to shortages and other problems. And they are sick and tired of deprivation. But they no longer fear sliding into a bottomless pit.

In the old days, I'd sit in a café or a bar and young Cubans I talked to would worry about how the country would survive. Now they complain that the only good jobs are in the tourist business. Why should I study hard at the university to be an engineer, one woman told me her college-age son keeps asking, when I am going to have to work as a bartender or a tour guide anyway?

A good question, and it's a problem for the government, but not being able to get the job you want is a very different problem from not knowing if you can live at all.

And this is roughly where Cuba is today.

The worst is over, and they know it.

None of this, of course, has had any effect on U.S. policy toward Cuba. President George Bush literally owes his election to the roughly 120,000 Cuban Americans in Florida who voted for Bill Clinton in 1996 but voted Republican last year to punish the Democrats for returning Elián González to Cuba. Given that First Brother Jeb Bush faces reelection in Florida in 2003, the Bush administration looks more likely to tighten the embargo than to end it.

Miami—meaning the most powerful elements of the organized political leadership of the Cuban American exile community—still supports the embargo, and when it comes to Cuba policy, Miami still rules.

That's too bad, because the single biggest beneficiary of the U. S. embargo against Cuba, the one person who truly wants and needs it to last for a thousand years, is Fidel Castro—a man whose one constant strategic goal from 1959 to the present day has been to build a Cuba independent of the United States culturally, politically, socially, and, above all, economically. If he could, he would row the island out into the Atlantic.

The Cuban national nightmare, the thing that keeps good revolutionaries awake at night in cold sweats, is the example of Puerto Rico—a Spanish Caribbean island whose independence and culture has been largely swallowed up by the giant to the north. There is an acute Cuban fear that American investment, American tourism, American cultural influence, and an American political system (fueled, of course, by good old American campaign contributions) will someday swamp Cuban society and turn it into a cross between Cancún and Las Vegas.

Therefore Castro has almost always had two goals in foreign policy. While he doesn't want the United States to become so angry that we actually invade the island, he wants the embargo to remain, and he wants everybody—in Cuba and around the world—to think that the embargo is America's fault.

Beyond that, his major strategic goal is to build up a new Cuban elite who will continue the revolution when he leaves the scene. The embargo keeps the Cuban Americans in Florida while doing nothing to stop the new Cuban establishment from learning management techniques from Europe, Canada, and Latin America.

While we remained calcified in our Cuba-Cold-War posture, the revolution went to business school. Fidel's younger allies and protégés are much better equipped to manage the island's economy in the post-Castro era than they were five years ago. Give them another five years of this and Cuban Americans will have permanently reduced their future influence in Cuba.

So if the embargo works so well for Castro, why does Miami support it so fanatically? Why are Cuban Americans so firmly determined on a course of action that strengthens Castro and cuts them off from the role they hope to play in shaping a post-Castro Cuba?

The first reason is that Miami politics is exile politics. Exiles everywhere always make the same mistakes: They consistently underrate the solidity of the regime they fled and exaggerate their own future role. Exile society is a hothouse of gossip, intrigue, and breathless rumors about imminent splits in the leadership, the imminent death of Castro, or some other miraculous development that will bring the whole ugly government down. Miami overestimates its importance and the importance of the embargo to life in Cuba; after forty years of exile and thirty-nine years of embargo, they still think that success could be just around the corner.

Second, even if the embargo doesn't overthrow Castro, Miami hopes it will work after Castro leaves power. By keeping Cuba poor, isolated, and technologically backward, the embargo, the thinking goes, will ensure that a post-Castro Cuba will desperately need the capital and the know-how of the exile community.

The last and deepest reason is sheer anger and bitterness. Fidel Castro destroyed the world the exiles knew and loved; his oppressive regime and confiscatory economic policies made it both economically and socially impossible for them to stay in their homeland; over the decades, he has showered them with infamy and filth and done his best to offend every patriotic, religious, and personal sensibility they have. Miami is furious, and Castro knows how to twist the knife to keep the wounds always fresh. Castro wants Miami so tormented by fury and pain that it can't think straight—and it works every time.

Besides assisting Castro in his prime goal of building a Cuba that is free of American influence, the embargo allows him to blame Miami exiles for Cuba's economic problems.

It also helps make him an international star. Castro needs international celebrity the way a fire needs oxygen. Thanks to U.S. policy and its misguided backers in Miami, he gets it. In an age when most Third World leaders couldn't get media coverage if they doused themselves with gasoline and set themselves on fire outside their houses of parliament, Fidel Castro can mesmerize the international press corps with old war stories, as I witnessed last spring at a Havana conference commemorating the fortieth anniversary of the Bay of Pigs. One of the single biggest sources of support for Castro at home is Cuban national pride at the way he has put the country—a resource-poor, economically impoverished island roughly the size of Virginia—at the center of world politics.

The dirty secret of Cuba policy for the last generation has been that whatever his failings as an economist or as a democrat, Castro is an infinitely smarter politician than his exiled and defeated enemies in Miami. Time after time, he plays them like a violin. He can provoke them into paroxysms of gibbering rage, he can lock them into self-destructive political options, he can even turn their greatest strength—their ability to monopolize the American political debate over Cuba policy—into a pillar propping up his regime.

During the last few years, I've had a chance to watch the evolution of U.S. policy toward Cuba up close. As staff director of an independent Council on Foreign Relations task force on U.S.-Cuba relations, I've met with senior officials, policy makers, and economic and political leaders in both countries. Gradually but decisively, American policy makers and business leaders are taking another look at America's Cuba policy, and as a result the end of the embargo is, I think, closer than ever.

The American corporate sector, originally outraged and horrified by Fidel Castro's nationalization of U.S. properties in Cuba during the early years of the revolution, calmed down as time went by and it became increasingly clear that Castro's example was not spreading through Latin America. Cuba might be communist, but Mexico, Argentina, and Brazil still want U.S. investment. Cuba is a relatively small country, and after forty years of communist misrule and embargo, it has a tiny economy; its GDP is less than the net product of South Dakota. The loss of the Cuban market was a sacrifice American business was willing to bear, and while tourism and airline companies might like the idea of getting back on the island, there are, after all, plenty of other islands in the Caribbean.

What jolted American business out of its indifference to Cuba policy was a law Miami succeeded in putting through the Congress as part of its plan to intensify the embargo after the collapse of the Soviet Union. The Helms-Burton Act was basically an attempt to internationalize the U.S. embargo. Other countries had refused to support the U.S. boycott of Cuba with embargoes of their own. But under one of the law's provisions, foreign companies can be sued for damages in U.S. courts by anyone who alleges that the foreign company is "trafficking in" (that is to say, using) property that was confiscated from the complainant by the Castro government. In other words, a French company that purchases property from the Cuban government—a transaction that is legal under both Cuban and French law—can be sued in American courts.

Although American presidents have, up to now, used their authority under the law to suspend such suits, Helms-Burton infuriated both the European Union and our NAFTA partners. Led by (surprise) France, international reaction has been swift and sharp—and full enforcement of Helms-Burton would lead to major trade and economic sanctions against a wide range of U.S. multinationals.

Helms-Burton presents another thorny problem for American business. Under its legal theory, American companies could become entangled in lawsuits all over the world. Egypt, for example, could pass a law allowing lawsuits by Palestinians alleging that U.S. corporations were using "confiscated" Palestinian property in Israel.

Add to this that the collapse of global farm prices has

made American farmers hungry for new markets, and Miami and Havana are having to deal with a new—and often strongly Republican—set of players who want change in U.S. policy toward Cuba.

At the same time, foreign-policy makers and strategic thinkers are changing their assessment of U.S. interests with respect to Cuba. During the cold war, these thinkers looked at Cuba from the perspective of the U.S.-Soviet rivalry. The U.S. wanted to isolate Cuba in the Western Hemisphere as part of its broader policy of containing communism, and even if the embargo didn't bring Castro down, it forced the Soviet Union to pay his bills—billions of dollars the Soviets couldn't use for other purposes.

With the collapse of the Soviet Union, most U.S. policy makers thought that communism in Cuba would collapse, as it did in Czechoslovakia and Poland. Now the realization that Cuban communism has survived is slowly percolating through the U.S. establishment, and a new sense of the national interest is beginning to emerge. In this new picture, a strong Cuban government is an asset to American strategic interests; a strong government can control immigration and assist American efforts to stop the flow of drugs across the Caribbean. The great danger for the U.S. today is not that post-Castro Cuba will stay communist and strong; it is that Cuba after Fidel will be divided, unstable, and weak. In a worst-case scenario, civil war could break out, with Cuban Americans fighting with and supplying arms to one side as hundreds of thousands of Cubans attempt to flee to the United States.

Ensuring stability in post-Castro Cuba while a gradual turn to democracy and free markets takes place is probably the best the U.S. can hope for. By isolating Cuba from American influence and by increasing its economic difficulties, the embargo only increases the chance for a rough landing in Cuba.

It appears that the private views of leading Bush administration officials, including the vice president and the secretary of state, favor an end to the embargo with Cuba—just as they favor normal trade relations with China and other communist countries around the world.

How this will work out in policy terms is anybody's guess, but my own proposal is for a Cuba Relations Act that repeals all existing U.S.-Cuba laws and redefines our relations with Cuba:

1. The embargo and the travel ban need to end, now.

2. The United States needs to restore normal diplomatic relations as soon as possible; we have a lot of things to talk about.

3. While the U. S. should maintain its opposition to Cuban participation in the Organization of American States (one of the great achievements of the last twenty years in this hemisphere has been the consensus that all the countries in the Americas should be democracies), Cuban membership in organizations like the World Bank and the International Monetary Fund should be encouraged, not blocked.

4. Guantánamo, a U.S. naval base in eastern Cuba that the American military no longer needs, should be returned to Cuba.

The Miami considerations of this new Cuba Relations Act will annoy some people who think that Cuban Americans already have a much sweeter deal than most immigrant groups. This is, to a large extent, true, but again, Cuban Americans, especially the earlier arrivals, are not classic immigrants; they are exiles. They are the only significant group of Americans who aren't legally allowed to visit their relatives abroad more than once a year or who break the law when they send more than $1,200 a year to their elderly grandmothers. Unlike Dominican or Mexican Americans, they can't retire to Cuba in their old age to live on Social Security and be cared for by their families. Mexicans and Canadians who live in the U. S. can claim their relatives back home as dependents under U. S. tax laws if those relatives meet standard IRS rules; Cuban Americans cannot.

A Cuba Relations Act should end all these disabilities, and it should do more. The Cuban exiles who stormed the Bay of Pigs did so because they had assurances that Washington would back them up with air cover and other support. We lied and left them stranded on the beach. Some were killed; virtually all the survivors faced captivity in Cuba.

The Cuba Relations Act should provide for a presidential commission to fully investigate and make recommendations, as appropriate, for a formal presidential apology, for compensation, for recognition of individual acts of heroism, and, as justified, for pensions and health care for survivors and their families.

Additionally, the Cuba Relations Act should establish a U. S. government commission to review and document the claims of Cuban Americans for property confiscated without compensation and should offer to purchase newly certified claims in a way that provides the most compensation most quickly to those who need it most, especially the many elderly and low-income Cuban Americans who didn't make a fortune in the United States and may never have recovered from the losses they sustained when they were forced to flee. However, even wealthy Cuban Americans who can substantiate their claims should receive a fair settlement offer.

Ultimately, the U. S. government would seek reimbursement from Cuba for the value of these claims; diplomats have many time-tested ways of settling these disputes.

A Cuba Relations Act along these lines won't please everybody. It might not please anybody. Miami will object to the provisions concerning renewed relations with Cuba, and passionate embargo opponents won't like all the chocolates and flowers it sends to Miami.

But this is life in the big city. If the United States is serious about regaining control of its Cuba policy from Fidel Castro, this is the approach we must take. Miami and Havana are important to the future of Cuba and the region. After forty long years, Washington needs to have a sensible policy for both.

BEN CORBETT

A Post-Castro Cuba

O NE SWELTERING DAY ON MY WAY to Old Havana I dropped by Armando's for a bottle of mango juice to tell him that I was leaving soon for the United States. During our conversation, he invited me back for supper. The typical supper at Armando's was soup two nights in a row. The next night it would be eggs over rice with a cabbage-and-cucumber salad, followed by chicken the

next evening, and then three days of leftovers. All of this with the traditional black beans and rice and a variety of fried plantain. But this night was special; he'd received his sardine ration.

Cubans eat late, usually around 8:00 P.M., and I stopped back early to catch the news. Armando's television set is one of

BEN CORBETT
is a freelance journalist
who has spent the past
years researching and
writing almost exlusively
on Cuban culture, politics,
and economics. This piece
was excerpted from
his 2002 book This Is
Cuba: An Outlaw
Culture Survives.
He lives in Colorado.

those that you have to play with for fifteen minutes while tapping and jiggling it around to get it working. Once he does finally get it fired up in the morning, he simply leaves it on all day to save himself the hassle. On this night, the news was a twenty-minute recap of an interview with Castro's younger brother, Raúl, now seventy-one years old, along with several decorated generals of the Revolutionary Armed Forces. It was a casual interview. Raúl leaning back on a sofa with a warm, self-assured glimmer in his eyes, the crook of one knee folded over the other, dozens of medals dripping from his uniform. The interview centered mostly around Cuba's current military strength, but the climax came when the interviewer asked Raúl, "What do you have to say about the future of Cuba?" It was a loaded question. She was really asking, "What will happen when Fidel dies?"

Raúl paused a moment for reflection, knowing exactly what the interviewer was getting at, and after taking a breath, in that deep-throated warble, said, "I'm no prophet, but I do know this. *La lucha* will continue."

The living room was silent as we leaned into the television to absorb Raúl's words. It was as if everyone really wanted to hear something different for a change, but there it was, the same old disappointing message: "*La lucha* will continue." In a way, Raúl was only half sincere. There was the subtle hint of a chuckle when he uttered the words, no matter how serious he tried to appear. It was as if he, too, knew that it was a farce, but what else could he say? Raúl is like that. If Fidel is the father of the revolution and the people are his children, Raúl is the mysterious uncle over in the periphery, chuckling with the wisdom of old age. I asked Armando what he thought of Raúl's statement.

"*La lucha, la lucha*, everything is *la lucha*," he said. "They won't be happy until they have us all living in caves. The people are tired."

After our sardine dinner, we spent the evening playing Cuba's board game, *Deuda Eterna*, "eternal debt." This game is Cuba's version of Monopoly. It was designed in the mid-1970s by orders of the comandante because he wanted the people to understand the principles of imperialism and why Cuba would have no part of it. There are very few complete sets of *Deuda Eterna* left in Cuba, but Armando and Carmen took very good care of theirs. All the pieces are still there, even the game's instruction booklet.

The object of *Deuda Eterna* is simple. The players start out with nothing. They must borrow money from the International Monetary Fund (IMF) to launch certain industries. There are the lesser agricultural industries such as banana and sugar, which sit at Balsam Avenue, leading around the board to the energy industries, oil and utilities, which sit at Boardwalk. On the center of the board is a map of the Americas. The players are in the Third World, and the IMF is the United States. Whoever gets out of debt, which is next to impossible, wins the game. They must pay taxes and loan interest, and each player gets three small plastic bars of gold, to be forfeited upon passing Go. The IMF banker is a separate entity and doesn't actually play; instead, he sits like a monarch, overseeing the game. On this night, Armando's daughter designated herself the banker, and before we started, she explained the rules. It had been a few years since she'd played, so she flipped through the rulebook to brush up.

"Oh yeah," she said, reading a passage. "Players may make secret deals with the banker."

"Secret deals?" I asked. "How do these work?"

Everyone around the table burst out laughing. "Hah, Benjamin. The yanqui capitalist! Only he would ask this question!"

"What I think is even funnier," I said, "is the idea of a Cuban running the IMF."

The game was a lot of fun, but there were certain ironies about the entire evening. First, we watched Raúl Castro promising more of *la lucha* on a television that barely works, just before eating a $2 sardine dinner, which in Cuba is almost like a sacred holiday, followed by a game of *Deuda Eterna*. Because of Castro's refusal to play the real-life game of eternal debt, the Cuban people must continue to live in an impoverished society that barely functions. And Raúl Castro was only promising more of it.

"They won't be happy until they have us living in caves," Armando had said earlier. "The people are tired."

As it did many times in many living rooms, the conversation drifted toward a post-Castro Cuba. Would more sectors of the domestic economy be privatized? Who would become Castro's successor? What did the people want?

The mystery of Castro's successor has become one of the world's biggest guessing games, and Castro likes to keep it that way. As written into the Cuban constitution, Raúl Castro is lawfully slated as Cuba's next president. But this is unlikely. Raúl lacks the support and respect of the people. His street nickname is "The Frog." Castro's is *El Caballo*, "The Horse," and many Cubans joke that Raúl is the filly. Clearly, Raúl is not presidential material. As a career military leader, he doesn't have the economic savvy necessary to administrate Cuba in the new revolutionary themes, and both he, Fidel, the ministers, and the people know this. Although Raúl is the first vice president of the Council of State, a total of five vice presidents have the authority to succeed Castro.

The second name that many have been throwing around as Cuba's next president is Ricardo Alarcón, who was once the minister of Foreign Affairs, making him a prime candidate as Fidel's successor. However, in 1993, he was demoted to the slot of president of the rubber-stamp People's National Assembly, a relatively powerless position reserved for once-important leaders whose names outlive their significance to the cause when the revolutionary themes change.

Now that the government and the economy have somewhat stabilized and the island is under control, the survival of the Cuban Revolution has transformed into absolute economic terms. The next Cuban president must necessarily be an economic guru, someone who will make the right decisions and who will concentrate on transforming Cuba into a Caribbean empire while continuing to build a global support network with other nations. At this time, there are only two minds in Cuba with these abilities. One is thirty-seven-year-old Felipe Pérez Roque, the current minister of Foreign Affairs, and the other is fifty-year-old Carlos Lage Dávila, the first secretary of the Council of Ministers. They are the only leaders now being groomed to succeed Castro. Unless the revolutionary themes change again, barring war, one or the other will likely become Cuba's next president. Raúl Castro's sole function will be to maintain military order during the transition of power. He will also oversee the provisional government and seize control should things go haywire.

As a candidate for the next presidency, Felipe Pérez Roque is important because, as foreign minister, he has all the necessary contacts with the outside world. He is the bridge builder, the diplomat, the man responsible for maintaining Cuba's umbilical cord with the international community. This is the highest position in Cuba today. Pérez Roque is even more powerful than Castro himself, who has essentially become a mere figurehead. Carlos Lage, on the other hand, is essentially the mastermind behind Cuba's economy. He is a brilliant economist, a young, modern thinker, and by making good decisions, he is largely responsible for the island's relative wealth and economic success since the Special Period. Pérez Roque and Lage hold the most imperative positions in the Cuban leadership. Over the past several years, both have been given more and more air time on Cuban television as they have risen in revolutionary importance. When Castro collapsed during a speech in the summer of 2001, it was Pérez Roque who immediately took the microphone to quell the confusion, an illustration of his importance.

Which of these two the Cuban people want as their next president is a toss-up. While Pérez Roque sometimes seems the more likely successor, the feeling in the street is that Carlos Lage is the people's candidate. He's charming and likeable, more mild-mannered, less like Castro. The Cuban people feel that he'll be more responsive to their needs and will strike a good balance between Cuba's economic strength in the international community while focusing on the domestic welfare, which has been left in neglect by Castro. Pérez Roque, although young and talented, is geared a little more into the path of international *"amistad,"* which has been Castro's principal domain for the past forty-three years. Pérez Roque's experience on the domestic front is inferior to that of Carlos Lage. However, both are economic geniuses, both are presidential material, and as a team, both are and will continue to be the island's most powerful leaders no matter who takes the title of president. Raúl Castro's task has been and will be to oversee the government from the periphery and make sure that the system functions properly; if it deviates from the program, he will seize military control and forestall coups.

When I asked Armando about the possibility of Ricardo Alarcón's succeeding Castro, he shot me a cross look and said—like others I had posed the question to—"Nah. Alarcón is just another Castro. The people don't want it. I'm almost certain it will be Carlos Lage. The people like him. He's more amicable. More understanding."

"What about Pérez Roque?" I asked,

"It's possible," said Armando, "but he, too, is like Castro, and he's too young. He hasn't yet earned the respect of the older people. Both the old and young people respect

Carlos Lage. He's young enough to understand what the young people want, and old enough to know what the older people want."

Besides the question of Castro's successor, many have been asking the question: Will Cuba become capitalist after Castro? Really, Cuba already is capitalist, both in the peso and dollar economies. Cuba is not communist. Revolutionaries call it a "market socialism administered by communists." However, because of the degree of exploitation people have undergone since 1991, the Cuban government has become capitalist in the classical sense, which is the greatest irony of all. It has turned into what it purports to stand against, and it must continue to be capitalist so that it can continue to stand against capitalism. This is the gist.

If Cuba reverts back to the old-track socialism, which might be possible when the regime finds the economic footing, this new capitalism will be short-lived. For now, the ends justify the means. Clearly though, the people want Cuba to become a fully operating market economy. The proper question is: After Castro, will there be less control?

Cuba can move from its current state of survival into a wealthy empire only if the people are permitted to compete freely in the domestic and international markets. This is what the world demands, and the government will necessarily have to bend. Cuba must provide creative outlets to people with innovative ideas while educating the masses not just in basic English but also in how to participate in the global market economy. There are thousands of talented young Cubans who, with support, could be earning the island a taxable mint. The government must facilitate more tax incentives for average Cubans, not just the foreign corporations, so that Cubans themselves can acquire the ability to develop their ideas and eventually run their own island in a full dollar economy. Currently, Cubans live in a peso mentality, which means they are operating at only a fraction of their potential. Until the entire population thinks in dollars and rejects its enforced dependency on the welfare state, the economy will continue to suffer. After all, Cuba belongs to Cubans, but on the current track, the island is once again becoming the property of foreign investors. The people are in the same old rut of serving foreign enterprises. Cuba cannot withstand another ten years of the current stagnation, and everyone knows this. Reforms are needed, and Castro is only standing in the way of progress. The longer reforms are postponed, the more desperate Cuba grows, and the more sweeping the changes are likely to be after Castro.

On a morning when I was staying with the Ibáñezes, Castro was giving a televised speech: "Up in the United States, the imperialists always talk about this 'post-Castro Cuba,'" he said. "The revolutionaries will start talking about a post-Castro, post-communist Cuba when they start talking about a post-capitalist, post-Bush United States."

"Listen to that crazy talk!" Martina exclaimed, twirling her finger around her ear. "He has obviously lost his mind."

"A post-capitalist United States!" huffed Rolando, punctuating his wife's thoughts. "Listen to him. It's unrealistic. It's deranged."

Today, Castro is irrelevant. He's only holding up the

show. He refuses to follow through with the reforms he himself designed and instead eliminates them every chance he gets. He still complains about how the world cheated Cuba when it switched from the gold standard to the stock exchange. He lives in the past and cannot seem to move forward. This is not the destiny the Cuban people envision for themselves. There is only one place for Castro to go, and that is to the grave.

Castro knows this, as do half of Cuba's administrators who are under fifty years old. They are young, and they know that if Cuba is to survive, it must join the competitive global economy. The only way this can occur is to break free from the stagnant and slow implosion of a social experiment that is long overdue for change. They, too, are waiting for Castro to die, and deep down he understands this. The ultimate truth for Fidel Castro is very sad. In the depths of his mind he realizes he has lost his people. He realizes that his mission has become a matter of preserving his place as the first successful liberator in what amounts to a forty-year pit stop in Cuba's ongoing search for *Cubanidad*.

Today Cuba is colonized by outdated and meaningless war symbols. The people are ready to move past the war and get on with the independence part of the equation. The conclusion Armando and I arrived at was this: The Castros, indeed, all the old-school communists and their identities are linked directly to *la lucha*. They know of no other way to exist. As revolutionary veterans, to end *la lucha* would be to take away the meaning of their 1959 victory, and in doing so their own significance. The problem is that these men have retained the power and have transferred the significance of the revolutionary war to an "economic war" against the United States. They embody their entire cause against another nation and its policies. Their importance today lies in being soldiers against the U.S. embargo. When a couple divorces, how healthy is it to spend the next forty years hating the ex-spouse and playing the victim? Against any odds, the divorcée must eventually take responsibility and move forward, even in the face of aggression. It is time for Castro to do this and face up to the waning support of his people rather than foster the role of victim merely to remain in power.

Until now, the embargo has been as important to Fidel as to the Miami exile. Both camps profit from it, and both maintain it. For the exile, the Florida version of *Cubanidad* has been built in a private war waged with Castro. Because the Cuban American identity is for the most part emblematic of this struggle, the embargo is a means to sustain a symbolic lock on Castro, who in turn uses the same embargo to sustain a lock on his own people and, in turn, his power. Today, the economic war boils down to a war between Castro and Miami, and the battle is being fought on a field of newsprint. Every time Castro gets a toehold into some economic growth and power, Miami launches a new smear campaign, and Castro reacts. This happened in 1977 with the "Castro Connection," which eventually died in 1999, just days before Elián González washed up in the Florida Straits and became the new crux of the battle. Both Castro and his enemies in *la fundación* are running out of Eliáns, and the media war is losing strength because the rest of the world is wising up to the game.

As Castro approaches his death, it is imperative that he get the embargo lifted so that he can say to his people, "It was I, Fidel Castro, who gave the Cuban people their victory. We have won." He needs to go down in history as the liberator. Across the gulf, Miami's principal goal is to keep the embargo intact until Castro dies, cheating him of this victory. As trivial as it may seem, this is the bottom line, this is what *la lucha* has devolved into.

As Fidel's hour approaches, his desperation to get the embargo lifted grows. In October 2000, the U.S. Congress voted to allow direct food and medicine sales to Cuba, using third-country banks to finance the transactions. In reaction, Castro proclaimed Cuba wouldn't buy "a single grain" of U.S. agricultural products unless it was a two-way trade, meaning, "You give us your tourists, we'll buy your food." Cuba imports most of its food products from Europe, paying 10 to 20 percent more for shipping than it would if it imported the same products from U.S. markets. On the surface, Castro's refusal to buy from the United States seemed to be a revolutionary principle. In reality, he merely wanted to wiggle a carrot before the noses of U.S. agriculture firms then as now drooling over the estimated $2 to $5 billion a year market that Cuba represents. A two-way trade ultimatum would force the agricultural lobbies to get the travel ban lifted, which would appease the communists and enable the new Cuban market to be tapped. If the travel ban were lifted, Cuba's tourist income would likely double overnight, thus empowering the regime and adding to Castro's prestige for the books; at the same time, it would pave the way for a full lifting of the embargo. No doubt the idea frightens the European suppliers and shippers, who currently profit considerably from trade with Cuba.

July 2001 was a pivotal month for the warming of the embargo. On July 15, the new law to sell food and medicine to Cuba was ironed out, and the list of now-saleable commodities was enormous. Not only grain, poultry, and beef were permitted, but also items manufactured from them, including such products as canned ravioli, and even beer. The U.S. agricultural corporations, the manufacturers, the shippers, everyone was excited. A week before the list was released, George W. Bush, under pressure from the old-school exile, gave new orders to reinforce the travel ban on Cuba and increase the fine for illegal travel to Cuba from its former $1,500 to $7,000. Yet a week later, Bush waived a provision in the Helms-Burton bill that gives foreign enterprises who suffered losses from the 1961 nationalizations the right to sue Cuba in U.S. courts for damages. If signed, the provision would essentially lock the embargo into law until these damages are paid. Bill Clinton regularly waived this provision for six-month periods during his tenure. Bush's doing so marked his own tone toward the outlawed island. Waiving this provision is a means of keeping the door open with Cuba, no matter what Bush was saying on television. Although the Senate shot it down, a week later (coincidentally, a day before Castro's national revolutionary holiday), the House of Representatives, under pressure from the agriculture lobbies, voted by a large margin to stop enforcing the travel ban.

The travel ban is what Castro needs lifted most urgently. Castro knew he was getting close, especially in November 2001, when Hurricane Michelle devastated the Matánzas province east of Havana, and the U.S. government immediately offered humanitarian aid to the island. Instead of accepting the aid, Castro offered to buy a one-time $30 million shipment of U.S. food products to help alleviate Cuba from the hurricane's impact. The catch? Castro offered cash. He could easily have taken his money to England or France for the foodstuffs. Instead, he wanted to scrape another crumb off the plate and let the U.S. agriculture sector drool a little more, thus turning up even more pressure on Congress and Bush to lift the travel ban; this would inevitably have led to the embargo's lifting, which would result in "The Victory" timed perfectly to precede Castro's death. Since the 1970s, this is how the dialogue with Washington has functioned, up and down, up and down. The actions taken on each side are weighed more in tone, not in impact, and the tone since Clinton opened the door on January 5, 1999, was to begin taking steps toward lifting the age-old embargo.

In 2000, after tourism had grown at an annual rate of 19 percent, 1.8 million tourists visited Cuba. Forecasts for future years were looking hopeful; however, in 2001, only 1.8 million tourists came again. It then became apparent to the regime that, despite the world economic recession, perhaps the numbers were tapering off. There are only so many Buena Vista Social Club fans in the world, and although the trend of the world media is now more liberal, many tourists, because of the high cost of Cuba's tourism and its many deficiencies, aren't returning. Because of the tapering numbers, it is now imperative that the regime take steps to get the U.S. travel ban lifted so that it can tap the forbidden, lucrative, nearby U.S. tourist market. Castro is desperate. When the U.S., military began shipping al-Qaida prisoners to Guantánamo in the winter of 2001, not only did Castro button his lip, but he even went so far as to offer any assistance Cuba could offer in containing the prisoners. Cuba's recent invitation to former president Jimmy Carter and his May 2002 visit to Cuba was also geared toward getting the travel ban lifted. Why Carter? Because Carter had lifted the travel ban once so perhaps he could pull some strings to get it lifted again. Even if Carter had taken bad reports back to the United States, it was still good press for Cuba. It showed other Americans that Cuba is a safe country to travel to, not a dangerous pariah state with all the old Cold War stigmas that still resonate in the minds of most Americans.

When six barges full of corn and other U.S. agricultural products left from Louisiana for Havana in December 2001, it was the first U.S. shipment of food sold directly to Cuba in thirty-eight years. It wasn't publicized on the island, and most Cubans don't understand the implications of Castro's master plan. Few knew that the shipment was powder in Castro's economic cannon and that it would help him realize his much-needed victory. In October 2000, when the U.S. Congress voted to allow food and medicine sales, there was little news of the law's passing in Cuba. When I talked to friends about what it meant to them, they were severe and pessimistic. "So what. Even if Castro buys the food and medicine, we'll never see any of it. It will all be sold to the tourists for dollars." The people are equally skeptical about rumors of the embargo's being lifted. For years upon years they've believed the rumors, only to have their hopes dashed once again. But one thing is certain; after forty-two years of waging a war against the embargo, most Cubans expect sweeping miracles when it is indeed lifted. They believe their world will turn upside-down. And to provide the illusion that it isn't just the end of another small battle, like that of Elián González, but the true end of the war, the victory will have to be carefully orchestrated. Perhaps rations will have to be doubled, rum given away in the streets, and, of course, a national holiday declared, *El Día de la Victoria*, the Day of the Victory, when over four decades of Cuban suffering will be remembered in perpetuity. It is Castro's private war. One he is determined to win, even if it means standing against the desires of the people while the generations are tilled under the revolutionary plow.

One day I was walking through the Colón cemetery in Vedado with a twenty-five-year-old artist friend. Colón is a classic Latin American cemetery, and apparently there are a million graves there, equal to half the population of Havana. The *flamboyán* trees and bougainvillea, when in full bloom, lend a certain vibrancy to the texture of the place with their small explosions of orange, red, and purple flowers. From the dead and the past springs new life, new seasons, change. The lovely old architecture has been poorly maintained. The lids on many of the crypts are caving in, and gold and jewelry has been cleaned out by grave robbers. Here and there around some of the tombs loose bones are scattered. "The *brujas* steal the bones," my friend said, "for their religion."

The Colón cemetery is so big that it takes a day to see it all. Cuba's celebrities are buried here. Some of the graves are those of dissident students shot in cold blood by the police between the 1920s and 1950s. Many are revolutionaries from centuries past. Some even belong to U.S. citizens who loved Cuba so much they made it their home. However, most of the graves belong to Cubans from the wealthier classes, whose families, generation after generation, are buried in the family tombs. At the back of the cemetery is a shady little park with benches, where we sat down to rest. This part of the cemetery is called the Tomb for the Martyrs of the revolution.

"This is where all Cubans should be buried," I said. "Everyone who died since Castro is a martyr for the Revolution. All the hunger and the suffering. All Cubans are martyrs. However, the park is too small to contain so many Cubans. Why is it so important for Castro to win this war?"

Castro has always wanted to be the new Simón Bolívar," said the artist. "He's wanted to liberate all of Latin America from neocolonialism. But," he added, holding out his hand, squaring off a sliver of fingernail with his thumb. "This is how much Castro is compared to a man like Bolívar. He's nothing to Bolívar. And besides, Bolívar never did liberate Cuba."

"This was Martí's mission," I said. "To accomplish in Cuba what Bolivar couldn't achieve. Martí failed, and now Castro thinks he's Martí reborn."

"He thinks he's better than Martí!" said the artist.

There's a word that's said a lot in Latin America, *ojalá*. You hear it every day in Cuba. *Ojalá*. Loosely translated, it means "I hope so," or "I wish," or "With any luck," and in Cuba it always punctuates a thought with a severe gravity. If someone says to a Cuban, "Soon your lover will come and marry you and you'll be living in America, England, Italy," or, "Soon the United States will lift the *bloqueo*," the response will always be "¡*Ojalá*!" When Cubans say *ojalá*, it holds a meaning that is different from, say, the Mexican, Argentinean, or Venezuelan *ojalá*. In Cuba, more pessimism is implied, and a cross look goes along with the word. When the word *ojalá* is uttered in Cuba, it really means, "Yeah, tell me another one." Because the Cuban hopes have been dashed so many times, over and over, pessimism is inherent in the collective consciousness. It's as if everything the Cubans believed in during the last four decades failed them and so now they refuse to invest seriously in anything hopeful in case it turns out to be another disappointment. All Castro's promises which have vaporized over time. All the false promises of marriage foreigners have made to Cubans never to return. All the hopeful signs of the embargo's being lifted. Every time Cubans want to believe in something, it fails, so they think the worst, and if it turns out a little better than expected, then and only then is there cause for celebration. It's difficult to imagine living like this, in a world so shaky that you can't bank on anything but what is sitting on the plate in this very moment; a world in which the future is so unpredictable and unpromising that there's no way to plan, or seriously consider dreams and goals. As if this kind of human need, this future, except in the flimsy rhetoric, seemed to have been etched out of the culture as a whole. No one believes in anything anymore.

"Well, the future is looking good for Cuba," I said to the artist, as we passed a bottle of water under the trees at the Tomb of the Martyrs.

"How can you say this?" he said. "The future. The future. That's all everybody talks about is the future. Fuck the future. I want a now. I want my life to be more than just struggling. Castro will never let us proceed."

"Well look," I said. "He's seventy-five years old. He's going to die soon."

My friend looked at me square in the eye and said "¡*Ojalá!*"

It was the first time I'd ever heard a Cuban, in Cuba, say that he "hoped" Castro would die, and it took me by surprise. But the shocking thing was that when my friend uttered *ojalá*, it didn't have that Cuban pessimism implied in the word. He sincerely meant it.

"And let it happen soon," he added. "We are ready for change."

When Castro fainted during a speech on June 23, 2001, the Miami exile plotted and cheered. My friends on the island had various responses to the collapse. Some believed that the guards ushered a semiconscious Fidel off the stage, only to bring out his double from a nearby ambulance, refreshed and invigorated. Some felt the collapse was merely a staged test to measure Cuba's national reaction. But when Castro fainted, it did not become mob rule. There were no parades of anti-Castroists storming through the streets. It was a humble mixture of mostly sadness mixed with pockets of joy. Cubans themselves aren't quite ready to turn the page. While change is sought, there is also a resistance to it. When Castro turned seventy-five in August 2001, coincidentally close to the date of his fainting spell, Cubans began churning the scenarios in their minds. Most have always felt that he has an illness that is kept secret. Some say Parkinson's, others swear it's cancer. Every Cuban has his pet disease he's sure the comandante is suffering from. Some believe that Castro's inner circle is slowly poisoning him to get him out of the way. But in the street you'll hear a single phrase. Some say it with pride, others disgust: "Forget about it. Fidel will live forever."

Politically, Castro is already dead. Physically, he is dying. What he is dying from is a mystery; but his failing health is obvious. One week he'll seem dapper, animated, and sharp when he gives a speech. A week later, he's pale, gaunt, forgetful, and two or three assistants have to remind him every few minutes why he's even there. And to date, the military has refused to unseat him, which is evidence that he doesn't have long to live. They will not disgrace him and cheat him of *La Victoria* in his final hour, even though his mind is slipping.

Today Fidel Castro lives alone and fights a war that ended many years ago. The machinery that he built, the *Cubanidad* that he first offered and later imposed on the Cuban culture, is passing him by as he fights to the last breath for *La Victoria*.

Will there be a post-Castro Cuba? Never. His legacy

will outlive him for decades, even centuries. In many ways, today's Cuba is not much different from the way it was before Castro. There are the rich and poor. There is inequality. There is corruption, exploitation, racism. And although Castro's vision may seem like a failure to a growing number of Cubans, the comandante brought one lasting legacy to the culture. Before Castro, people were slaughtered indiscriminately. Political assassinations occurred daily in the power vacuum. Life was cheap. Peasants were abused. Soldiers shot and killed humans as if they were rodents. The dinner conversation revolved around which politicians should be assassinated. The violence before Castro indicates there was a desperate need for Cuba to free itself from its neocolonial chains. The in-fighting and the ego, the splintered political movements, the rights and lefts and radicals prevented the people as a whole from focusing their energies. One leader was needed in Cuba, and Castro became that leader. And when he came, he said "Stop! Let's see what we have here. Let's find the best part of the Cuban character and let it shine. Let us focus our pride."

Because of this belief, human life is now very precious to all Cubans.

Over the past four decades, the island has enjoyed enough peace and stability that the culture has been able to focus on slowly defining itself. The price of freedom is sacrifice, and Cuba has spent the past forty-three years paying its dues. No matter how hopeless it sometimes seems—the current hunger for change, the current desperation—the will to survive, to live, to endure, and even to resist, prevails. These

INSIDE CUBA

are the ingredients of focused human determination. Today, Castro only stands in the way of the people. They are now prepared to define Cuba's destiny. And in this preparedness, perhaps Castro achieved the greatest victory of all.

Acknowledgments

We gratefully acknowledge all those who gave permission for written material to appear in this book. We have made every effort to trace and contact copyright holders. If an error or omission is brought to our notice we will be pleased to remedy the situation in future editions of this book. For further information, please contact the publisher.

Excerpt from *Cuba Confidential: Love and Vengeance in Miami and Havana* by Ann Louise Bardach. Copyright © 2002 by Ann Louise Bardach. Used by permission of Random House, Inc.

Excerpt from *Blessed By Thunder: Memoir of a Cuban Girlhood* by Flor Fernandez Barrios. Copyright © 1999 by Flor Fernandez Barrios. Reprinted by permission of Seal Press, a division of Avalon Publishing Group, Inc.

Introduction by Andrei Codrescu. Copyright © 2003 by Andrei Codrescu. Printed with kind permission of the author.

"Picking the Flowers of the Revolution" by Andrei Codrescu. Copyright © 1998 by Andrei Codrescu. Reprinted by permission of The New York Times Company. Originally appeared in the *New York Times Magazine*, February 1, 1998.

Excerpt from *This is Cuba: An Outlaw Culture Survives* by Ben Corbett. Copyright © 2002 by Westview Press, Inc. Reprinted by permission of Westview Press, a member of Perseus Books, LLC.

"Cacharros" from *Cars of Cuba* by Cristina Garcia. Copyright © 1995 by Cristina Garcia. Reprinted by permission of Ellen Levine Literary Agency/Trident Media Group.

Excerpt from *Havana Dreams: A Story of Cuba* by Wendy Gimbel. Copyright © 1998 by Wendy Gimbel. Used by permission of Alfred A. Knopf, a division of Random House, Inc.